Framing Faust

Framing Faust

Twentieth-Century Cultural Struggles

Inez Hedges

Southern Illinois University Press
Carbondale

Library of Congress Cataloging-in-Publication Data
Hedges, Inez, 1947–
Framing Faust : twentieth-century cultural struggles / Inez Hedges.
    p. cm.
Includes bibliographical references and index.
1. Faust, d. ca. 1540—Legends—History and criticism. 2. Faust, d.
ca. 1540—Legends—Influence. 3. Civilization, Modern—German
influences. 4. Faust, d. ca. 1540—In motion pictures. I. Title.
PT937.H44 2005
809'.93351—dc22
ISBN-13 978-0-8093-2671-6 (cloth : alk. paper)
ISBN-10 0-8093-2671-X (cloth : alk. paper)   2005015420
ISBN-13 978-0-8093-2903-8 (pbk : alk. paper)
ISBN-10 0-8093-2903-4 (pbk : alk. paper)

For Victor and Diana

Je n'avais pas compris que le mythe est avant tout une réalité, et une nécessité de l'esprit, qu'il est le chemin de la conscience, son tapis roulant.

[I hadn't understood that myth is above all a reality, a necessity of the mind and spirit, that it is the pathway of consciousness, its conveyor belt.]

—Louis Aragon, *Le Paysan de Paris*, 1926

Contents

Figures

Preface

S ome years ago, the idea that "master narratives" were harmful to authentic cultural understanding gained currency in academic and intellectual circles. Even the word *humanism* became suspect, and "humanist values" were said to cloak agendas of cultural domination, whether based on geopolitics or gender. Much of this questioning of Western traditions has been valuable, indeed essential, to our developing awareness of the claims of diversity and globalism in its positive aspects. At the same time, I wonder whether that interrogation might be located within Western tradition itself and even within its so-called master narratives. In line with this thought, I have tried to break the rebel Faust out of the constraining way in which he is held up to promote traditional "humanist values." This circumstance limits my work at the same time that it focuses and enriches it. Limits it, because my particular emphasis does not encompass the entire landscape of the Faustian—indeed, this would be a task for many volumes and for an entirely different approach than the one I have adopted. Enriches it, because in focusing on the ways in which the Faustian rebel has surfaced in some of the most important cultural crises of the twentieth century, I have been able to explore the Faustian myth in its various political, aesthetic, and social contexts.

My approach is interdisciplinary and comparative. The Faustian myth is one of the great gifts of Germanic culture to the world and has fueled the creative imagination of major artists, writers, filmmakers, and musicians. But it does not belong to one nation or single academic discipline. I hope that my book will inspire more study, especially of some of the neglected works that I take up in these pages.

Despite the ubiquity of the Faust myth, the literary works that have wrestled with it most creatively are often not available in English or are out of print, while some of the films are only available in archives. This is true of the works by Hélène Cixous, Frank Wedekind, Léon Blum, Volker Braun, Else Lasker-Schüler, Hanns Eisler, and Michel Butor, to name just a few. I have had to summarize the outlines of their work and to provide my own translations of important passages so as not to leave the reader too much in the dark. One of my hopes is that these plays, essays, and novels will be resuscitated and will find new audiences. As for the films: John Farrow's *Alias Nick Beal* can be viewed only in the UCLA film archive, while Stan Brakhage's four Faust films are rarely screened, even in archival retrospectives of Brakhage's work (they are, however, available from Canyon Cinema). Early silent films by Méliès, L'Herbier, and Edison have to be viewed at archives in the United States and Europe and are not currently available to the public.

In the process of preparing this work, I have received the help of many wonderful people. Foremost among these is Madeline Matz, research specialist in the Motion Picture, Broadcasting and Recorded Sound Division of the Library of Congress. Without her patient assistance and invaluable research skills, this book would never have been completed. Linda Dittmar and Jost Hermand provided invaluable criticism and encouragement in the early stages of my writing, while Wolfgang Fritz Haug and Frigga Haug created a friendly and supportive community thorough InkriT (the Institute for Critical Theory) in Berlin. The staff at several film archives have also been of great assistance: Paolo Cherchi Usai, curator for film at the George Eastman House, Mary Corliss of the Museum of Modern Arts Stills Archive, as well as the staff of the British Film Institute, the UCLA Film Archive, and the Services des Archives du Film du Centre National de Cinématographie at Bois d'Arcy outside of Paris. Doris Schartel helped me obtain permissions for several film stills, and Walter Ross-O'Connor, circulation supervisor at the Widener Library of Harvard University, gave me his unstinting help through many years of research.

My work was initially supported by a faculty research grant and sabbatical leave at Northeastern University. Portions of chapters were presented at conferences organized by the American Comparative Literature Association in 2000 and 2002 and by the International Conference on Avant-Garde Cinema at the University of Edinburgh in 2004. I wish to thank the journal *Socialism and Democracy* for permission to reprint my 1999 essay, "Faust and Utopia: Socialist Visions," which constitutes a portion of chapter 3. My essay, "Stan Brakhage's Testament: The Four Faust Films," which constitutes a portion of chapter 5, will also appear in *Avant-Garde/Neo-Avant-Garde*.

I wish especially to thank Volker Braun for permission to reprint his poem "Property," and Karen Ruoff Kramer for her excellent translation, done in close collaboration with the author. Stan Brakhage wrote to me, before his untimely death in March of 2004, that he was glad that his Faust films meant so much to me. My great regret is that he will not see the book he said he looked forward to reading.

A special thanks goes to my editor, Karl Kageff, who steered my book through many shoals and brought it finally to a safe harbor, to managing editor Carol Burns, copyeditor John Wilson, and design and production manager Barb Martin. Any imperfections are, of course, my own.

Finally I wish to thank Victor Wallis who has seen the project through from first to last and has provided invaluable advice at every stage.

I hope that this book will be judged to have responded in some way to the urging of Terry Eagleton in January of 2004 that we, as cultural critics, begin to heed the "fundamental questions of truth and love in order to meet the urgencies of our global situation." Many of the incarnations of Faust discussed in these pages present him or her as a constructive rebel from whom we can take inspiration.

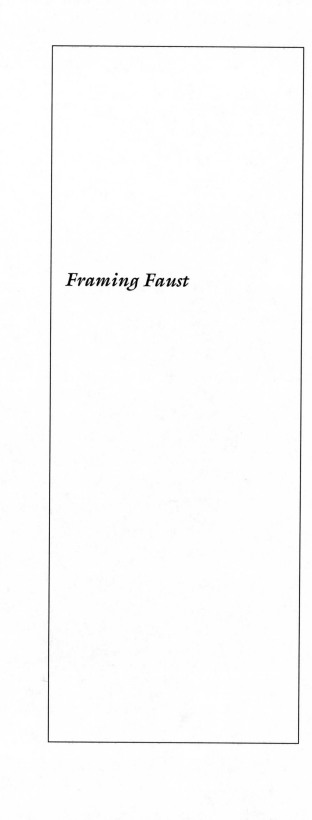

Framing Faust

Introduction: Inventions of Faust

In the sixteenth century, it fell to German culture to contribute one of the seminal modern figures with which Western civilization has come to be defined: the figure of Faust. He has few peers: Spain gave us Don Quixote and Don Juan; England, Hamlet.

Hamlet, Don Juan, Don Quixote, and Faust have become "types" in our culture. We talk of Hamlet's indecision, Don Juan's obsession with amorous adventures, Don Quixote's enthusiasm for hopeless causes (efforts that are now termed "quixotic"). With Faust, we mean someone who consciously, and usually irrevocably, betrays his (and later, her) sense of what is right in order to gain some desired advantage, and who thereby loses what is most precious and valuable about human life. The "Faustian bargain" necessarily involves two characters: the tempted, to be sure, but also the tempter. Mephistopheles is Faust's equal and counterpart, and the struggle between them is the very stuff of drama. In the first literary dramatization of the Faust story by Christopher Marlowe, *The Tragical History of Doctor Faustus* of 1594, Mephistopheles emerges as a fascinating character in his own right. Thus, Faust is unique in being opposed by a single, formidable opponent.

We associate Hamlet with Shakespeare's play of 1603 and Don Quixote with Cervantes's novel of 1605; but no one author can lay claim to Faust in this manner. Since the publication of a chapbook of Faust tales, the *Historia von D. Johann Fausten* in Frankfurt by Johann Spies in 1587, the story has been retold dozens of times by writers as distinguished as Marlowe, Gotthold Ephraim Lessing, Johann Wolfgang Goethe, Heinrich Heine, George Sand, Frank Wedekind, Mikhail Bulgakov, Paul Valéry, Thomas Mann, and, more recently, Volker Braun and Hélène Cixous; it has been illustrated, most notably by Eugène Delacroix, Salvador Dalí, and Max Beckmann; it has provided the theme for over eighty films from the silent era to the present, by directors including Georges Méliès, Friedrich Wilhelm Murnau, István

Szabó, and avant-garde filmmaker Stan Brakhage; and it has inspired major musical compositions, including operas by Hector Berlioz, Charles Gounod, Arrigo Boito, Ferruccio Busoni, and Alfred Schnittke. In his various transformations, Faust has become a revolutionary, a socialist, and even a feminist hero(ine)—the object of prolific creative energy. Perhaps only the Don Juan legend, since its first appearance in a play by Tirso de Molina in 1613, has had as many incarnations.

In the face of such diversity, we need to think of the many different paths that the Faust material has taken over five centuries not as the transformation of a single theme but as the history of its representations. As Paul de Man reminds us, regarding Faust, "The story is not a point of departure, a sort of mold that the author pours matter into: it is, on the contrary, the end result of poetic invention, the final sign that refers back to a prism of multiple inventions that criticism cannot break down by the sole observation of the final product."[1]

In considering Faust, it is important to go back to the elementary qualities that later underwent such multifarious and rich developments. A useful place to begin might be with André Jolles's landmark 1930 study, *Einfache Formen* (Elemental Forms).[2] Jolles usefully distinguishes between different types of cultural narratives such as legends, sagas, myths, fairy tales, and even riddles and witticisms. This is of precious value to understanding the function of the Faust story, which intertwines two important "elemental forms": legend and myth.

Faust as Legend

Jolles plays with two possible Latin roots of *legend*: *legenda*, "that which is to be read," and *leggere*, "to collect." The lives of the Catholic saints are legends, exemplary life stories presented for edification. The historical Georg Faust is said to have lived around 1480–1540, when he frequented the university towns of Wittenberg, Erfurt, and Ingolstadt. There he practiced medicine, astrology, and alchemy.[3] The humanist Ulrich von Hütten and the Protestant reformers Martin Luther and Philipp Melanchthon mention him in their writings.[4] Faust seems to have been something of a charlatan and bon vivant, whose violent death around 1540 spawned rumors that he had made a pact with the devil. In the decades after his death, the stories became ever more colorful as all sorts of previously existing tales of necromancy became attached to his legend. In one of these stories, Faust is even able to conjure up Helen of Troy, with whom he bears a son. By the time Johann Spies published his *Historia*, the basic outline was set: "The unmistakable characteristics of Faust are his scholarly hubris, the pride and thirst for power of the intellectual whose unchristian behavior is expressed not only in his pact with the devil, but also in his connection with Helen of classical antiquity who functions as Hell's emissary."[5] These tales became the basis for the puppet shows of Faust's adventures and damnation, which is how Marlowe and Goethe eventually came into contact with the story.

As legend, the Faust story departs from retellings of the lives of the saints in two important respects. First, as Jolles notes, Faust is a negative role model, a warning rather than an example presented for emulation.[6] Second, his context is not Catholic but Protestant; he represents the dissident Protestant belief in individual responsibility for salvation or damnation, determined not by adherence to the church and its practices but by personal acts.[7] As an antisaint, the Faust of the chapbooks performs magic rather than miracles. These can be motivated by his desire to avenge perceived slights, as in the case of the disrespectful farmer whose four wagon wheels are spirited off to the four city gates (fig. 1); by his desire to show off, as when he entertains the Count of Anhalt in a magical castle on the mountain of Rohmbühl and then burns it down; by his gluttony (Spies's *Historia* contains many enumerations of fowl, meat, and wine); or by a comic delight in tricks, as when he conjures up Alexander the Great and his spouse for Emperor Carl V, eats a hay wagon, travels on a magic coat to attend a wedding, transposes the heads of four rival magicians, and so on. At the end of the *Historia*, Faust's disciples are said to be incredulous that he has sold his soul for such idle things as "*Schelmerey, Fürwitz, und Zauberey*" (knavery, knowledge, and sorcery). The Spies edition ends on an assuredly moral tone: on the morning after the fateful, shrieking night, Faust's brains and blood streak the walls against which the devil smashed him, and his broken body is discovered on the dung heap, "head and limbs still twitching."[8]

Still, Faust is not just a negative role model. Klaus Berghahn has made the point that the historical moment of the legend's appearance links it to the uncertainty about traditional values during the Reformation. Perhaps for this reason, there is a hint that his descent into hell is no worse than an exciting visit to the underworld of classical mythology, a motif that harks back to Homer's *Iliad*. The devil reasons with him that Faust judges hell without having experienced it and doesn't really know what to expect.[9]

Dante's elaborate circles do not apply here—in fact, the geography of hell as laid out in the *Historia* seems remarkably Roman: Tartarus and the rivers Styx and Acheron are all part of it. Both Marlowe and Goethe explored the idea of Faust's marriage with Helen of Troy, while George Sand made it the center of her 1838 play, *Les Sept cordes de la lyre* (The Seven Strings of the Lyre).

As legend, the Faust story expresses the questioning of institutional authority characteristic of the Reformation and the resurgence of classicism that came about during the Renaissance. Although it ends on the note of a "moral lesson," its overall tone is that of an exuberant retelling of Faust's supernatural experiences and magical tricks. Admiration, as well as condemnation, surrounds this popular, antiestablishment figure.

Faust as Myth

Jolles writes that "where the world is created unto man out of question and answer we have the form called 'myth.'" Myths answer cosmological questions; to paraphrase the title of Gauguin's great triptych, they address the questions of who we are, where we came from, and why we are here. Jolles writes that in its elemental form, myth functions as the answer to a fundamental question about the "profound nature of all the elements of the universe observed at once in their unchanging state and their multiplicity."[10] He gives as an example the separation of night from day, of the sun from the moon, in the biblical creation myth. That myth, he argues, is an answer to humanity's interrogations: "What is the meaning of the luminaries of the day and night? What is the meaning for us of time and the divisions of time? Who placed them there? What was it like before they came to light up the sky, before the separation of day and night, before the division of time?"[11]

Faust has a mythical dimension as well. In the sixteenth century, scientific observation of nature came into conflict with the church. Copernicus (1473–1543) and Galileo (1564–1642), with their revolutionary cosmologies, were famous examples. Henri Birven describes Faust as a "Protestant of science."[12] Even though the "science" of the Spies text is resolutely medieval (for instance, in the *Historia*, the sun is still said to revolve around the earth), what's important is that Faust goes to see for himself. As Berghahn aptly says, "he became the symbol of all those who no longer wanted to be led along by the church, whose meager consolation—*sola fide*—was an offense to reason. That is what made Faust so daring and modern."[13]

As myth, the Faust story posits the new place of humanity in a world whose very foundations were being shaken by scientific discovery. Faust thirsts after knowledge above all else, because he believes it will unlock the key to the universe. His first attempt to make a pact with the devil fails, because he demands that the devil "withhold no information which [Faust] in his studies might require" and that he "respond nothing untruthful to any of his *interrogationes*."[14] The devil refuses, saying that he is not allowed to answer questions about the fate of humans after death, or about the rule and sovereignty of hell. Faust signs the pact anyway, settling for much less. Goethe will go back to the original demand and have Faust ask for even more.[15] He agrees to meet his end if Mephistopheles can ever make him content:

> Should I ever take ease upon a bed of leisure,
> May that same moment mark my end!
> . . . .
> If the swift moment I entreat:
> Tarry a while! You are so fair!
> Then I will gladly perish there!
>
> (1692–93, 1700–1703)

Faust demands to know all that humankind can experience. This contributes to the greatness of Goethe's Faust figure: in his mythic quest, he pushes against human limitations:

> And what to all of mankind is apportioned
> I mean to savor in my own self's core,
> Grasp with my mind both highest and most low,
> Weigh down my spirit with their weal and woe,
> And thus my selfhood to their own distend,
> And be, as they are, shattered in the end.
>
> (1770–75)

Of course, with Goethe and later with the many elaborations of the Faust material, we are no longer dealing in most cases with myth in its elemental form. Instead, the original question-answer principle is used by analogy and derivation to create a plausible story. Jolles explains that this kind of mythic explanation for real-world circumstances arises when there seems to be no rational explanation for them; in other words, when the questioner arrives at the limits of the known. Jolles calls these secondary myths "myths by analogy" or "relative myths."[16]

Faust as Dissident

Myth and legend leave a third aspect of the Faust story untapped, however. Faust, described in the *Historia* as the son of a peasant, came upon the cultural scene soon after the failed Peasant War of 1525. In this conflict, the exploited peasant class, led most brilliantly by Thomas Münzer, had joined hands with the urban artisans in an attempt to combat the cruel and unjust system of levies and taxes that forced them to live in misery. Sixteenth-century Germany was ruled by tyrannical local princes, city patricians, and princes of the church who all had the right to impose taxes and rents at will on the underclasses. For instance, the peasants had to pay, among other things, tithes, ground rents, war taxes, death taxes, land taxes, imperial taxes (to the emperor), and church taxes (to the pope). Unlike Luther, who advocated peaceful and gradual reforms, Münzer was a revolutionary who took literally the egalitarian philosophy of the New Testament, which Luther had made available to the people by translating it into German. On March 17, 1525, Münzer captured the city of Mühlhausen, but his troops were soon surrounded and defeated. He was decapitated in May of the same year.

Berghahn argues that Faust became a folk hero because he embodied the spirit of rebellion against the ruling classes that was brutally put down in 1525.[17] He touches here on yet another aspect of the Faust material: the figure of Faust as dissident. It is not just Goethe's Mephistopheles that represents the "spirit which eternally denies" (*der Geist der stets verneint,* 1338); part of this spirit is Faust's as well, in the sense that he refuses to accept things as they are.

In the twentieth century, the Faust figure was often portrayed as a dissident, as someone who embodies opposition. Paul de Man, who makes the case for a dialectical mode of approach, describes Goethe's Faust as one whose "path is strewn with those parts of himself that he had to abandon in the process of his own becoming."[18] Mephistopheles is the active agent, Faust's indispensable "other," at once provider and spoiler. Some Fausts, such as those that appear in feminist or avant-garde writings, oppose institutional or normative cultural limits on human thought and action. In other contexts (state socialism, Fascism), Faust's story became the battleground for the conflicting interests of those who sought to legitimize their ideology by laying claim to a validating cultural legacy.

Faust as a Constitutive Myth in Western Culture

In Western culture, the story of Faust has played the role of a constitutive myth, one that prescribes, as well as describes, a particular kind of experience and a way of relating to the world. As Jürgen Kühnel explains, modern myths are always evolving: "Changed situations and new experiences demand new answers and concepts, so myths are always challenged anew to perform their task, and mythic storytelling must be adjusted to different conditions. The historicity of myth lies in the history of its productive reception."[19]

In the twentieth century, the Faust myth performed a number of different functions—it played a role in the construction of identity, in the examination of the relation of the individual to society, and in the representation of the rebel and the dissident. These multiple transformations show that the Faust myth still has the power to shape our reality rather than just to explain it. It is inextricable from our cultural past and perhaps even from the direction our future history may take.

In Western culture, the Faust myth enjoys a kind of hegemony: it serves both as a form of shorthand for describing, with a dose of criticism thrown in, a certain modus operandi or modus vivendi and also for legitimating actions or behaviors that society officially condemns, by making them appear normal.

The cultural studies movement in Britain has explored the notion of hegemony in the light of work by Roland Barthes, Antonio Gramsci, and Michel Foucault. Barthes's work on modern myth—first published as *Mythologies* in 1957—opened up the definition of myth to all sorts of cultural formations, from the face of Greta Garbo to the Citroën car and the role that plastic plays in contemporary society. In Barthes's formulation, myth should be understood as an utterance (*parole*) whose signification is historically determined.[20] The work of myth is to gloss over historical contingency—to hide the fact that our cultural signposts are fabricated rather than natural. Barthes compares myth to metaphor: new ones are continually being created, and familiar ones become almost invisible as they are incorporated into normal communicative exchange. Myth allows societies to reflect on themselves as they respond to constantly changing pressures. Barthes writes about the way that myth can be used to legitimize social behavior that might otherwise be judged as objectionable: "Myth does not deny things, on the contrary, its function is to talk about them; simply, it purifies them, it makes them innocent, it gives them a natural and eternal justification, it gives them a clarity which is not that of an explanation but that of a statement of fact."[21]

The Gramscian notion of hegemony as a constantly renegotiated enforcing of dominance by ruling elites provides an additional element in the cultural studies model of social functioning:

> Gramsci's theory of hegemony holds that cultural domination, or more accurately, cultural leadership is not achieved by force or coercion, but is secured through the consent of those it will ultimately subordinate. The subordinated groups consent because they are convinced that this will serve their interests; they accept as "common sense" the view of the world offered them by the dominant group. . . . The achievement of hegemony is sustained only through the continual winning of consent.[22]

Foucault writes about the violence that either implicitly or tacitly underlines this "consent." Rather than Barthes's language model of social interaction, Foucault proposes the model of war: "The history which bears and determines us has the form of a war rather than that of a language: relations of power, not relations of meaning."[23] In this formulation, myth can be seen as a battleground on which opposing ideologies fight for power—in essence, as the site of dialectical struggle. Nazi ideology tried to arrogate the personality of Goethe for itself in part because its proponents wished to found their legitimacy on the notion that they represented the destiny of the German "*Volk*." As a consequence, they had to represent themselves as the true heirs to the best in the German cultural tradition.

To say that the Faust myth has become culturally hegemonic in the West is not to claim that every major cultural artifact exhibits some facet of it; rather, it is to claim that it is part of our cultural assumptions, our idea of how the world works. The proliferation of Faustian motifs in twentieth-century literature, film, music, and art of the West means that we have somehow consented to see ourselves in Faustian terms. One consequence is that those who aim to disrupt the status quo—feminists and avant-garde artists—produce narratives that attempt to displace the traditional representations of the Faustian and their claim of legitimacy.

Faust has also served as a rallying point for the politics of those who are out of power. The Cold War spawned a series of reflections on powerlessness that reached for Faustian models: in the United States, film noir explored the raw milieu of the petty-crime world and urban gangsterism as an allegory of capitalist Darwinism and anticommunist paranoia; in the Soviet Union, Mikhail Bulgakov's Mephistopheles in *The Master and Margarita* is able to confound the bureaucrats because he understands them so well; it takes the self-sacrifice of Margarita to break bureaucracy's hold on the Faustian artist.

Utopian socialists, from the Soviet Union to the German Democratic Republic, have drawn on Faust's vision, in part 2 of Goethe's opus, of a "free people" upon "acres free" (11580). Anatoli Lunacharski's hero in *Faust and the City* presents the people with a machine that will liberate them from toil—here technology still figures in an emancipatory role. In his *Nouvelles conversations avec Eckermann*, Léon Blum, the future French prime minister during the period of the Popular Front, explores some of the difficulties that arise from Faust's alliance with Mephistopheles in the name of progress. The pact with power ultimately threatens the success of the meliorative enterprise. It is in these representations that Foucault's point about struggle seems particularly pertinent, for these works are not just about how social issues are framed in discourse; they are also about how the array of political forces can quash the most idealistic of Faustian impulses. In the social and political struggle against German Fascism, Faust appears to lose his pact with the devil; the descent into madness of the Faustian figure in Thomas Mann's *Doctor Faustus* stands as a warning.

The transgressive force of dream logic, which in the twentieth century was explored with such fanfare by surrealism, shows the potent link between discourse and power. Hélène Cixous's narrator in *Révolutions pour plus d'un Faust* follows a trail of linguistic associations to range through the Western cultural legacy with a "fool" or "madman" as Virgilian guide, looking for whatever might be turned to a revolutionary purpose. Stan Brakhage's four Faust films target the preconscious with aural and visual compositions that seek to undermine even our traditional ways of seeing and making meaning. Brakhage aims to destabilize the way that information is channeled to the perceiver; if successful, his project would make us skeptical about any form of communication that relies on our learned conventions to convey its ideological messages.

The wide diffusion of the Faust myth in contemporary films, in journalism, and in forms of popular culture (from comic books like the *Spawn* series to computer games) points to its hegemonic status. It is almost as though the "Faustian bargain" has become part of our commonsense understanding of how success, power, and celebrity function. This assimilationist trend exists side-by-side with reworkings of the Faust material that have lost none of their critical edge.

The Faustian Dialectic

Over the past hundred years or so, the Faust story has been used repeatedly to express the complex tension between differences that cannot be reduced to absolute polarities. Like Goethe's Faust character, these modern figures are constantly learning and changing because of their cognitive development. As a result, the terms of their oppositional stance are also in continual flux. It is this dialectic, in the end, that accounts for the flexibility of the Faust story and its adaptability to contemporary social and ideological conditions—its continued relevance in a context where the "death of God," "the end of humanism," the subjectivity of observed phenomena, and the reconceptualization of gender (to mention some of the more salient benchmarks) have become so much part of our discourse.

There are two impulses that guide my discussion. On the one hand, I want to present a wide compendium of material to show that the Faust motif is prevalent throughout twentieth-century culture; on the other, I argue that these many instances of the Faustian are symptomatic of areas of important ideological contestation where some of the most essential concerns of the twentieth century are addressed.

Some chapters, such as those on the silent cinema, on feminist Fausts, and on the avant-garde, attempt to be fairly inclusive. Each of these chapters has its own logic, however. The presence of Faust in so many early films predisposed the development of film as narrative, an evolution that facilitated the growing role that the medium came to play in the public sphere. With feminism, the impulse is subversive, as the heroic Faust figure of Western humanism is turned inside out and subjected to ridicule or at least reexamination from a gendered perspective. In the case of the avant-garde, the Faustian quest for knowledge becomes displaced onto a quest for new aesthetic forms that will correspond more closely to twentieth-century constructions of identity and perception, as well as insights into the indeterminacy of what can be claimed as truth.

The three other chapters are more selective in their treatment. In them, I pursue a dialectical approach to cultural history and show how Faust became the subject of appropriation in the struggle against Nazism in the 1930s, the search for socialist utopias in the Soviet Union, France, and Germany, and the quest for legitimation on both sides of the Cold War conflict after 1945. In addressing these topics, my choices of primary texts as well as secondary sources reflect the particular trajectory of this book, which interrogates the usefulness of the Faust myth for our contemporary problems. The backward look at history is at the same time a forward look into our possible future, as I argue in my conclusion.

The various metamorphoses of the Faustian hero—in film, literature, music, and theater—offer a perspective on the history of ideas and the cultural landmarks of twentieth-century thought as well as a narrative of collective struggle, occasional failure, and dogged aspiration. For if Faust's pact is necessarily with the devil, the Faustian character often ends on the side of the angels once wisdom and experience have been acquired.

1 Faust and Early Film Spectatorship

I n the first transcription we have of the legend of Faust, the Spies *Historia* of 1587, he is a showman and entertainer as well as a quester after knowledge. In the early versions, which include Christopher Marlowe's *The Tragical History of Doctor Faustus*, Faust suffers damnation—but not until he has tasted every pleasure and indulged every irreverent thought. Perhaps the legend does conclude with a moral lesson (Faust's damnation), but Faust also embodies the spirit of rebellion against religious authority that culminated in the Reformation and the breakdown of the hegemony of the Roman Catholic Church. Even before Gotthold Ephraim Lessing, and most notably Goethe, decided to let Faust escape the terms of his pact, he was a figure of heroic rebellion. Faust simply has too much fun for the audience or reader to take his damnation seriously.

The illustrations that accompany the reimpression of several early Faust chapbooks by J. Scheible in 1846 in Stuttgart bear this out. From earliest times, the Faust legend lent itself to visual representation. The illustrations accompanying the Scheible edition (incidentally, the same edition consulted

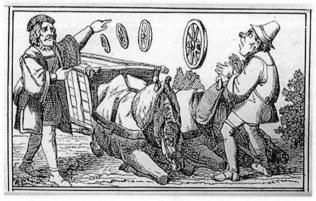

Fig. 1. Faust punishes a farmer by sending the wheels of his cart to the four gates of the town. J. Scheible's 1846 reprint of Widman's *Faust* (1599).

by Thomas Mann when he composed *Doctor Faustus*) testify to the visual appeal of the various magical tricks that came to be associated with the legend, from the story of the offending peasant whom Faust punished by sending the four wheels of his cart off to the four gates of the town (fig. 1), to Faust's placing antlers on the head of a nobleman. In another series, Faust is borne through the air by Mephistopheles, carouses at a tavern amid dancing jugs and bottles, and then travels in a fanciful dragonlike conveyance (fig. 2).

As visual spectacle, the Faust story was a natural for film. In the early film versions, however, the two antagonists of the legend suffer a curious reversal of fortune: Mephistopheles becomes the character with whom audiences are invited to identify. In almost every case, he personifies that use of diabolical magic that comes so naturally to the cinema and that in the chapbooks was an attribute of Faust himself.

Scholars of the silent film have argued for the role of the Passion genre and the boxing match in the birth of film narrative, since both required the stringing together of many tableaux into a story.[1] As the subject of over two dozen films in five different countries before 1913, it seems clear that the Faust material played a similar role. Like the story of the Passion, it was known to almost everyone. Goethe had added the love interest with Margarete (Gretchen), which had been further popularized in Gounod's opera. The Faust theme provided cinema with its most popular mythic romance and thereby with guaranteed audience appeal.

There were other reasons for the theme's popularity. Faust could be easily updated from Reformation rebel to twentieth-

Fig. 2. Faust travels through the air, diverts himself at a tavern, and travels in a fantasy conveyance. J. Scheible's 1846 reprint of Widman's *Faust* (1599).

century technological man. His alchemist's laboratory, represented in count-less artworks, becomes, in the film age, an industrial-era workshop with wheels and valves that evoke associations with the film apparatus itself (fig. 3). The tricks for which Faust was famous encouraged filmmakers to in-vent and exploit cinematic special effects.

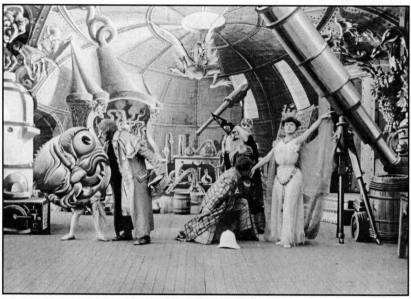

Fig. 3. The bearded Faust in his alchemist's laboratory (Georges Méliès as Satan, *left*). Georges Méliès, *Les Quatre cents farces du diable* (1906). BFI Stills, Posters and Designs.

The first silent films—especially those of Georges Méliès in France, which were made for working-class audiences—made fun of authority fig-ures, in the tradition of the chapbooks. But the increasing pressure on film producers and exhibitors to attract the more prosperous middle class had the effect of changing the function and emphasis of the Faust material. The very fact that Faust's tale was a story had an effect on the evolution of film narrative. In *The Magic Skin* (produced by Edison Studios in 1915) and the 1926 version of *Der Student von Prag*, the Faust story has a conservative func-tion and serves to legitimize film as commercialized bourgeois entertain-ment. At the same time, a director like F. W. Murnau could count on the spectator's familiarity with the story and create a visual spectacle that re-flects a personal vision—the beginnings of auteurist cinema.

France: From Subversive Intent to Bourgeois Entertainment

Noël Burch writes that France was the country where both the cinema and the moviegoing public were the most "popular," in the sense of "working class."[2] Although the date of the very first public exhibition of films to an audience is in some dispute, the date of December 28, 1895, when Louis and Auguste Lumière first projected their films to a live audience, has long been accepted as the birth date of the institution of cinema (as opposed to the technology of cinematography). Georges Méliès had the good fortune to be present. As a showman who already owned the Robert Houdin Theater, where he performed his magic acts, Méliès immediately recognized the audience potential for cinema. And while the Lumière brothers continued to film "real" events in the open air, Méliès built himself a couple of film studios and specialized in the creation of imaginary worlds and the telling of stories in what John Frazer has aptly called "artificially arranged scenes."[3]

In France, the first films were shown mainly at fairs where the audience was composed of urban working-class people. The Lumière brothers had shown their first films in the Grand Café in Paris, and for a few years afterward, films appealed to the public mainly because of the novelty of the moving image. But this novelty quickly wore out. By 1902, when Méliès produced his breakthrough film narrative *Voyage dans la lune* (*A Trip to the Moon*), film had been relegated to the fairground, where it figured alongside demonstrations of X-rays and bearded ladies; in the cities, films became a side attraction at the *café-concert* and in such venues as the Folies Bergère. Some department stores also tried to attract clients by showing films.[4] It didn't help that nitrate film had caught fire in the Bazar de la Charité in 1897 in Paris and resulted in the death of 125 people—this contributed to the fact that, initially, film was avoided by the bourgeoisie and relegated to the status of entertainment for the working class.[5] As an article appearing in *Ciné-Journal* put it, "To working-class people who have laboured all day long the cinematograph gives, for a few coins . . . the most unexpected kinds of illusions that they need."[6]

Méliès's *La Lanterne magique* (*The Magic Lantern, or the Bioscope in the Toy Shop*) of 1903 can stand as a metaphor for his particular type of illusionism. Two clowns, Pierrot and Pulcinella, enter a room full of props and assemble a large box, which they fit with a lens. Inside the box, they place a projection mechanism, which Pierrot lights with a large torch. This oversized magic lantern then projects the round, illuminated image typical of magic-lantern shows, except that these are moving images. The projected image undergoes a series of transformations—the two young lovers initially depicted turn into an elderly, squabbling married couple and then into images of Pierrot and Pulcinella, which move independently of their models.

With the first image projected by the lantern, Méliès has already initiated the theme of sexual desire as it relates to spectatorial fantasy—but now he goes one step further in his presentation of cinema as the "good machine." The clowns open up the box, and six dancing shepherdesses in long skirts emerge from inside; the lead dancer, in a short skirt, dances in the popular style Méliès enjoyed watching at the Moulin Rouge and does the splits on center stage.[7] When the box is closed up and then reopened, several ballet dancers in tutus emerge—but their classical steps are interrupted by the short-skirted dancer from the previous group, with her more popular style of dancing. The two clowns fight over her, and their beatings become so violent that the dancers run away as four soldiers appear.

From presenting the machine as an engine of eroticism, sexual fantasy, and popular entertainment (dance and slapstick), Méliès now moves to a more subversive plane. The two clowns take refuge in the projection box. When the soldiers open the box, they have disappeared, to be replaced by a long-necked, jack-in-the-box creature who easily evades their swords. Eventually the creature frightens them off. The ballet dancers return with the popular-style dancer, and they dance in a ring around the gratified clowns. Here, as in many other Méliès films, punitive authority has been overcome by comical and subversive figures, and classical art is replaced by popular forms of entertainment.

This short film represents the way that the apparatus of cinema itself functioned as one of the primary attractions in the early days of cinema, independently of what was actually projected. At the same time, it marks the transition between the exhibition of static magic-lantern images to moving images, with all the implied narrative possibilities opened up by movement in space and temporal development. In this sense, Méliès's image of the "jack-in-the-box" couldn't have been more apt.

With its roots in the puppet tradition, the story of Faust was a fitting one for the French public used to the spirit of the fair, the circus, the pantomime theater, and the music hall.[8] Between 1897 and 1904, Méliès filmed several versions of the story of Faust and Marguerite, using as his sources

Gounod and Goethe and the tale of Faust's descent into hell as dramatized by Berlioz (as in the French operas, *Margarete* becomes *Marguerite*).[9] In later films, he expanded on the theme of the pact with the devil or simply made movies showing various aspects of the devil's naughty tricks. Whereas at first he played the role of Faust, by 1903 he had switched to playing the role of Mephistopheles.[10]

In keeping with this spirit, Méliès emphasizes the tricks that Mephistopheles can pull off. Dancing girls, a staple of Méliès productions, are also particularly in evidence in the 1903 *Faust aux enfers* (*The Damnation of Faust*), where a batlike Mephistopheles raises his wings dramatically over his troupe (fig. 4). The combination of cinematic trickery with a story that was easy to follow allowed Méliès's Faust films to function as a bridge between what film scholars André Gaudreault and Tom Gunning have called the "cinema of attractions," in which filmed entertainments were strung along in the fashion of a revue, and narrative cinema.[11]

In the 1904 *Faust et Marguerite* (*Faust and Marguerite*), also distributed with the title *Damnation du Docteur Faust*, Mephistopheles, again played by Méliès, is clearly the hero of the piece. In this respect, it is quite different

Fig. 4. Mephistopheles (Georges Méliès) surrounded by his dancing troupe in hell (frame enlargement). Georges Méliès, *Faust aux enfers* (1903). Library of Congress Motion Picture, Broadcasting and Recorded Sound Division.

from Gounod's opera, on which the plot is based. Méliès's Mephistopheles is the upsetter of order and the rebel: in scene after scene, we find him exulting over his powers and dancing with mad glee at the consternation he has caused. In the first surviving tableau of this film, Faust appears as the bourgeois savant in a well-appointed medieval study. Mephistopheles conjures up an apparition of Marguerite at her spinning wheel. Faust is captivated by this vision, and Mephistopheles rejuvenates him so that he can win her. The duel between Marguerite's brother Valentin and Faust, as Marguerite watches helplessly from a balcony, is decided by Mephistopheles's pyrotechnics: fire spurts from Faust's sword even before the devil goes behind Valentin to give him the fatal stab in the back. At the cathedral, he frightens Marguerite by seeming to be a statue that comes alive (fig. 5). Finally, he finishes up the job of damning Faust by preventing a reconciliation between the two lovers in Marguerite's prison cell. As Marguerite falls unconscious, Mephistopheles wraps his cloak around Faust and disappears through the floor with him, headed for the nether regions.

Méliès exploited the theme of mischievous magic in many other films. *Un Homme de têtes* (*The Four Troublesome Heads*, 1898), in which Méliès removes his head and places it on the table four times and then leads the quartet of heads in song, could be based on the episode in the Spies *Historia*

Fig. 5. Mephistopheles (Georges Méliès) spies on Marguerite in the cathedral. Georges Méliès, *Faust et Marguerite* (1904). BFI Stills, Posters and Designs.

in which Faust punishes a nobleman by replacing his head with that of a stag. In *L'Alchimiste Parafaragamus ou la cornue infernale* (*The Mysterious Retort*, 1906), Méliès plays an alchemist who falls asleep in his laboratory and has strange dreams. First, a huge snake comes out of the furnace and transforms itself into a devil; then a giant spider with a human head appears in his retort. When he awakes, the retort explodes and kills the alchemist. In *Le Diable au couvent* (The Devil in a Convent, 1899), Méliès, as Satan, rises from the baptismal font of a church and assumes the garb of a priest. He then preaches heresy to some shocked nuns. As he transforms himself back into the devil, they flee. Satan kicks away the font and conjures up numerous infernal-looking gargoyles. Other devils jump out of the devil's cauldron, which has replaced the original font. The enormous head of a tiger appears, as more devils emerge from its mouth. The feral head is replaced by Satan astride a large frog. Finally, the nuns return, shaking their crosses at him, and he departs the scene.

Méliès reached the apogee of his craft in *Les Quatre cents farces du diable* (*The Merry Frolics of Satan*, 1906). Once again, the filmmaker plays the role of Mephistopheles, who offers the explorer Crackford a basket of magic pills that he can use to fulfill all his desires. In return, the devil (in his disguise as the alchemist Alcofrisbas) demands that Crackford sign a Faustian pact. This Crackford is ready to do, and he rushes home to try one of the pills in the family dining room. As soon as he throws the first one on the floor, six servants in powdered wigs appear. They quickly pack up his entire household, stowing the furniture into travelling trunks. Crackford, his wife, and four daughters climb into the trunks. No sooner are these lined up by the servants than they become train cars. Crackford's assistant, John, is in front, driving the locomotive, while the kitchen maid rides in the last car with her pots and pans.

Crackford's family is quickly lost when all but the first car fall into a ravine. Unperturbed, the adventurer pushes on with his faithful assistant. After a disastrous night at an inn where magic interrupts the travelers' attempts to have a meal, they get in a diligence pulled by Satan, who assumes the form of a skeletal steed (fig. 6). At the height of the marvelous adventures, Crackford's carriage lifts off into the air. The journey takes the voyagers across the heavens (recalling the account, in the Spies *Historia*, of Faust's astral voyage) until the magical diligence falls apart in the sky. Crackford and John are hurled earthward, although Crackford has had the foresight to bring his umbrella to ensure a soft landing. But a safe homecoming is not to be. The devil presents the signed pact and hauls Crackford down to hell through a trapdoor. In the final tableau, Crackford is being roasted on a spit while gleeful devils dance about him.[12]

Fig. 6. The explorer Crackford and his valet are drawn through the air by a skeletal steed. Georges Méliès, *Les Quatre cents farces du diable* (1906). BFI Stills, Posters and Designs.

The idea of making fun of the bourgeoisie is common to all these films: the victims are Crackford, the upper-class explorer, and the Faustian alchemists who seek to rise above the common lot by making deals with the devil. As Burch explains, the composition of the audience in France had a particular effect on the content of films, which tended to exploit the antagonism between the urban working class and its traditional enemies in France, the bourgeoisie and the peasants.[13] One of the reasons the working-class audience found Méliès's films so entertaining was because it could see its traditional class enemies ridiculed. The represssive and hierarchical power structure, represented by police, judges, lawyers, prison guards, soldiers, and representatives of the owning class (innkeepers, shop owners, and the like) is subverted by the sense of play and the comic reversal.[14] Paradoxically, Méliès the showman is also the forerunner of the commercial cinema, which maximizes its profits by aiming its productions to the taste and ideological orientation of its audience. As we will see, the cinema as an institution was ultimately unable to resist these pressures of commercialization and bourgeois assimilation.

As spectacle, Méliès's Faust films are among his most technically innovative. He returns with evident delight at least five times to the basic story itself between 1896 and 1904. To be sure, the story was a natural for the deployment of cinematic trickery (what later became "special effects"), and subsequent filmmakers have fully exploited the opportunities offered by the Faust material. Already in Méliès we can also observe the way narrative requirements lead to new techniques that will ultimately undermine his subversive intent.

In Méliès's films, the set functions like a theater backdrop. The camera never moves, and the story is told in static units as the action moves between fixed tableaux. As Suzanne Richard notes, the spectator's eye is typically guided toward the set without being made to imagine any offscreen space beyond it.[15] Yet the necessity to depict a linear narrative inspired Méliès to invent forms of cinematic continuity that transcended the static succession of fixed sets. In the 1903 Faust aux enfers, based on the opera by Berlioz, Mephistopheles gives Faust a tour of hell's caverns before precipitating him into the flames. This was the occasion for the creation of a narrative device that solved the problem of depicting the characters' progress through deep space: as Faust and Mephisto progress though hell, the decor is pulled away from the side and from the top, revealing "deeper" caverns behind. Temporal and spatial progression is convincingly represented within a single shot. Faust is treated to a spectacular sightseeing trip to the cavern of stalactites and stalagmites, the cavern of crystal stalactites, the "devil's hole," the ice cavern, and the cavern of the seven-headed hydra. The illusion of motion in Faust's final descent into hell is achieved by lifting the decor, a vertical tunnel inhabited by snakes and other creatures, past his stationary body. The film concludes with a devils' dance—the demons wear masks, while the women dancers have bat wings. Towering above them all, Mephistopheles (Méliès) deploys a more impressive set of black bat wings that assert his dominance (fig. 4).

Méliès's narrative sequencing of the Faust story, combined with the use of cinematic disappearing tricks and metamorphoses, remained dominant in French cinematic versions of the Faust legend.[16] Georges Fagot and M. Andreani's Faust (1910) is set in a bourgeois interior; its setting is calculated to coincide with films' increasing appeal to the middle class after the construction of movie palaces, which began in 1906. Despite its enhanced decor, the effects could have come from Méliès's old bag of tricks: Mephistopheles materializes out of a stream that runs next to the roadside altar where Marguerite is praying; later, he changes into a dog that throws Valentin off balance during the duel with Faust. Here again, the alert spectator can witness the use of new narrative techniques that move away from theatrical conventions: in the garden scene where Mephisto pairs off with Frau Marthe, he leads her offscreen left and reenters the frame from screen right. This early use of offscreen space in cinema has the effect of suggesting that the action is taking place within a larger diegetic (narrative) space and not just the stage set recorded by the camera.

By 1912, developments in the film industry and the evolution of film art both contributed to putting an end to Méliès's artisanal mode of production and distribution. Méliès's final contribution to the Faust theme in film was *Le Chevalier des neiges* (The Knight of the Snows), and it illustrates his failure to keep up with the innovations in film continuity that had been developed by that time. Here, an evil knight makes a pact with the devil so that he can kidnap a princess. With the help of magic, she is abducted in a cage drawn by a fire-breathing dragon. To save her, the hero (the "knight" of the title) employs "good magic," obtaining the help of an angel and a magic flower. The chevalier's rescue craft is as fantastic as the vehicle that abducted the princess—instead of a dragon, it has the angel at its helm. If the chase scene, by cutting between pursuer and pursued, employs the rudiments of parallel editing, the rescue scene experiments with continuity (already well established by this time) and comes close to a match on action (continuation of a character's movement across successive shots). During the rescue, the hero must get from outside the castle to the inner chambers. Méliès's mise-en-scène presents a series of tableaux in which the hero progresses through a tunnel. Screen direction is respected, although the transitions are not completely smooth. Méliès remains wedded to the rather static tableau-style presentation of his early style, despite the fact that film techniques had become considerably more evolved by 1912 (the landmark U.S. film *The Great Train Robbery*, by Edwin S. Porter, which employs a more dynamic and flexible editing style, dates from 1903). *Le Chevalier des neiges* ends with a damnation scene reminiscent of Méliès's early Faust films—after the rescue of the princess, the devil comes for the evil knight.

He presents the signed pact, and the villain is dragged down to hell through a trapdoor.

In France, Pathé productions had started out by imitating Méliès films but had then moved into longer formats. Charles Pathé, a businessman, also conceived of vertical integration: he not only produced and distributed films but also manufactured cameras, projectors, and eventually, celluloid film. In the beginning, Pathé sold copies of its films, as Méliès had done. In 1907, Pathé changed its distribution policies: it declared that films would be sent out only to five regional monopolies, who in turn would distribute them to the operators of fixed movie theaters. Pathé also reasoned that, as cinema moved away from music hall and fairground entertainment into its theatrical venue, it needed to become more artistic. In 1907, he founded the Société Cinématographique des Auteurs et Gens de Lettres, which was to assure the participation of well-known writers and actors in the film production process. French cinema evolved toward a new form, the art film, or *film d'art*.

Marcel L'Herbier's 1922 *Don Juan et Faust* is an example of the more artistically self-conscious films of the 1920s. L'Herbier filmed the scenes in Faust's study in cubist costume and decor, anticipating his more successful film *L'Inhumaine* of 1924. Here, a mad scientist (Faust) enlists the aid of his "diabolical" servant, Wagner, to abduct the woman whom Don Juan loves (Doña Ana, the daughter of the governor of Castille). He does so because he needs four tears from a virgin of noble birth for an alchemical operation (fig. 7). Wagner convinces Don Juan that Doña Ana has gone off with Faust voluntarily; Don Juan decides to console himself in the company of other women. Meanwhile, Wagner hands Doña Ana a dagger, and she kills Faust. She then goes in search of Don Juan but finds him at an orgy, where he has assembled all his past conquests. She is broken-hearted, especially after Don Juan fails to recognize her. Chased from his orgy by jealous husbands and lovers seeking revenge, Don Juan takes refuge at the tomb of Doña Ana's father. The *commendatore* later appears to him as he lies in bed; Don Juan falls down and repents and is later reconciled to Doña Ana when they both take orders at a convent.

One of the problems with *Don Juan et Faust* is that the two legends are not successfully integrated—the Faustian element is a minor subplot in the dominant Don Juan story. But L'Herbier's film marks a new departure in the stylish costumes, designed by Claude Autant Lara, and the large cast

Fig. 7. Faust (Philippe Hériat) and Wagner (Vanni Marcoux) try to obtain the tears of a virgin (Marcelle Pradot). Marcel L'Herbier, *Don Juan et Faust* (1922). Costumes by Claude Autant-Lara. BFI Stills, Posters and Designs.

he was able to employ. This was a film intended for a bourgeois audience (primed by the *film d'art*), and as such, mirrored the new respectability that French cinema enjoyed in the 1920s. Its conservative embrace of the aristocracy and of religious values distinguishes it sharply from Méliès's rebellious devil figures.

United States: Culture for the Masses

The differences in the treatment of the Faust material relate to the different composition of the film audiences from country to country. Noël Burch and Miriam Hansen have commented extensively on how American film from the beginning was part of a public space that was differently constructed from that of France. In the United States between 1896 and 1906, films were shown not only in working-class nickelodeons (so named because admission was a nickel) but also in more middle-class vaudeville theaters, where they were used to clear the audience between acts.[17] The American audience was a mass audience that, however, excluded the intellectual elite.[18] The vaudeville venue may account for the variety format of Edwin S. Porter's 1900 film *Faust and Marguerite*, which does not try to tell the Faust story but is content to explore the theme of trickery that is part of the thematic material. The one-minute film takes place in a well-appointed room in which two gentlemen play tricks on one another (for instance, one turns the other into a skeleton) in the course of their rivalry for a lady's heart. This short film seems inspired by Méliès: the idea of replacing one of the actors with a skeleton is one that Méliès used in the 1896 film *Escamotage d'une Dame chez Robert-Houdin* (*The Vanishing Lady*).

Judith Mayne recounts that in the United States, as in Europe, films began to develop into longer narrative form as exhibitors tried to appeal to a middle-class clientele. As women viewers became more numerous, producers began to film versions of novels that were familiar to middle-class female readers, in an effort to create an art form that was more "legitimate."[19] Hansen observes the relationship between film form and ideology: "The bid for cultural respectability (literary adaptations, casting of stage celebrities, gentrification of exhibition) coincided with the rise to hegemony of narrative film, with its debt to the 18th- and 19th-century novel, its claim to both realism and universality, its inscriptions of the close-up with connotations of intimacy, interiority, individuality."[20] She also notes that the emphasis on narrative had the effect of limiting the autonomy of the cinematic spectacle and integrating it into a homogenizing mass culture.[21]

Edison Studio's release of *The Magic Skin* in 1915, based on Honoré de Balzac's *La Peau de chagrin* (*The Wild Ass' Skin*) and written and directed by Richard Ridgely, shows the enhanced social status of film by that time. Balzac's hero is loosely based on Goethe's *Faust*, part 1: an impoverished young aristocrat named Ralph Valentin makes a "pact" by purchasing the skin of a wild ass from an antique dealer. The skin shrinks even as it grants his every wish. The young man accepts the pact even though he is warned that he will die once the skin has shrunk to nothing.

In order to make the narrative more easily comprehensible, the studio included even more Faustian elements in the story than did Balzac, who limited himself to remarking on the Mephistophelean aspect of the antique dealer. Valentin's tryst with Pauline, a virtuous middle-class girl, takes place in a garden setting that has overtones of the garden scenes in Goethe and in many of the early Faust films. Moreover, Valentin seduces and abandons Pauline (as Faust does Gretchen in Goethe's *Faust*), whereas Balzac's Paulette receives a rich inheritance and survives (unhappily, though, because she cannot rescue Valentin from his fate). In the garden scene of *The Magic Skin*, the devil/antique dealer looks on and rejoices, as in Méliès's early versions. This character also appears repeatedly in a ghostly superimposition, decked out with Mephistophelean horns, to taunt the hero. One of the greatest differences between the film and the novel is in the presentation of Flora. In Balzac, she is an independent woman who becomes the despair of her rich suitors because she sincerely wishes not to marry. In the film, Flora is represented as an evil and calculating temptress who is but another of the devil's incarnations—when Valentin dies, she exults, while a dissolve reveals her to be Mephistopheles in disguise.

The Edison Studio version already exhibits most of the characteristics of the "classical" model of film narration. The story is told by an omniscient camera-narrator, and the narrative centers on the psychology of the main characters, with clearly defined temporal and spatial coordinates. Continuity devices, such as the match on action, eyeline match (a shot of a character looking is followed by a shot of what the character sees), and shot-reverse-shot (back-and-forth over-the-shoulder shots during a conversation between characters), are employed in a seamless manner. There are few intertitles in this film, which relies mainly on the devices of film "language"—conventions that enable spectators to understand such things as temporal organization—to tell its story.

The Magic Skin concludes on a note of moral uplift when the entire story is shown, possibly, to be a dream. The hero awakens in the chair of the antique shop and pushes the skin away in horror. He flees when the antique dealer offers him the necklace intended for Flora and ends happily in the arms of Pauline. But then the film offers a second ending—the final shot shows the hero being dragged down to hell as the devil announces (in an intertitle), "Come: you belong to me."

The theme of *The Magic Skin*—the young man's desire for wealth and an opulent lifestyle—is related to the ideology of consumerism that films began to promote around this time. As Hansen remarks, "the creation of a spectator though classical strategies of narration was essential to the industry's efforts to build an ostensibly classless mass audience, to integrate the cinema with an emerging consumer culture."[22] At the same time, the film's use of continuity editing makes it a vehicle for pleasurable consumption by audiences and points the way toward what would become the commercially successful Hollywood classical style.

Germany: Film as Art

The first German film to be made around the Faust theme, the 1913 *Der Student von Prag* (The Student of Prague) is one of the earliest examples of the German *Autorenfilm*, or "author's film." Directed by the Dane Stellan Rye, the film was written by the novelist Hanns Heinz Ewers, and the title role acted by Paul Wegener, a prominent member of the theatrical troupe directed by Max Reinhardt. Taking their inspiration from the success of the French *film d'art*, German producers enlisted the collaboration of famous authors and actors after 1912.[23]

Film historian Anton Kaes has documented how the status of film was hotly debated in newspapers and literary journals. First seen as offering a "plebeian counter-culture" to the urban masses, film in Germany increasingly moved toward literary subject matter.[24] Kaes notes that "through its deft ability to adapt itself to the literature of the time, cinema was gradually able to overcome the stigma of its plebeian origins and to convince the bourgeoisie (which it needed to win over in order to broaden the base of its appeal) of its artistic potential."[25]

Rye's *Der Student von Prag* tells the story of Balduin, a poor student who strikes a bargain with the demonic Scapinelli. In exchange for wealth, Balduin has agreed to let Scapinelli take anything he likes from his modest abode. Scapinelli chooses Balduin's reflection, which steps from the mirror and follows his new master out of the room.

In several key scenes, the newly independent reflection comes back to haunt Balduin. This happens each time he is about to succeed in obtaining the favor of Countess Margit, the rich woman of his dreams. In their first tryst, in a Jewish cemetery, Balduin's double shows up as well. Margit, confused by the appearance of two identical suitors, rejects him.[26] Balduin's rival in love, Baron Waldis, challenges him to a duel after Lyduschka, a poor flower girl who loves Balduin, informs on him. After promising Margit's father that he won't harm the baron, Balduin comes late to the meeting place and finds that his double has already killed the man. When he tries to explain this to the countess, she notices that he has no mirror reflection. Balduin's double then appears, and she faints. Fleeing from his double, Balduin hails a coach, only to discover that the coachman is, once again, his double. Escaping again, he ends up in his old student digs. The double is already there, standing by the window. Balduin takes out a pistol while the double makes his way through the room to stand in front of the mirror. When

Balduin shoots, the mirror shatters. In the shards, Balduin is overjoyed to discover that he has regained his reflection. But his joy is short-lived—he is bleeding to death. By shooting his reflection, he has shot himself. Scapinelli sneaks into the room with the pact, which he tears up and sprinkles over Balduin's body. The final shot shows Balduin's double sitting pensively on his gravestone.

This film represents a quantum leap in the cinematic representation of the Faust material because of its realism. Film continuity techniques, such as the match on action, are used as a matter of course to denote temporal ellipsis and spatial transitions, even though the concept of consistent screen direction is not yet perfectly worked out. Most important, however, the cinematic techniques are no longer marked as "tricks" but are used instead to create an imaginary world that becomes believable. If Méliès and Fagot used an operatic form of presentation in which the tableaux succeeded one another while the spectator remained as objective observer, Rye retains a consistent focus on Balduin, who separates himself off from the other students in the very first scene. The narration never fails to emphasize the psychological effect of the events on Balduin himself by keeping him in the foreground and making him the focus of each scene. The high point in the film comes in a card game where those who are losing to Balduin leave the table and fade into the darkness. The last player to come forward is Balduin's double, who challenges him to a game in which the stake for one of them is death. In this scene, the lighting concentrates the viewer's attention on the horror that Balduin feels, as everything external to his confrontation with his double melts into the background. The film makes the idea of an independent double seem realistic, so that it seems logical that Balduin should eventually shoot it and believable that he should discover he has only shot and killed himself.

Rye's *Der Student von Prag* adds a psychological element to the representation of the Faust theme in cinema—a visual demonstration of Goethe's famous line in *Faust*: "Two souls, alas, are dwelling in my breast" (1112). Paul Wegener's mobile facial expressions, along with dramatic lighting touches by cinematographer Guido Seeber, add an element of expressionism to the film's overall realism.

André Bazin, writing on the metaphysical quality of the cinematic image, has said that cinema preserves the appearance of the body in time, with a greater realism than still photography can achieve: in cinema, for the first time, "the image of things is also that of their duration and something like the mummy of change."[27] It is quite significant, in this respect, that Balduin's separated mirror image does not evolve with him as he changes—it becomes an emblem of his soul, his true mortal self that he betrays. In this way, the film plays on the universal human anxiety about one's personal death and tries to show that anyone who seeks to flee from death will unfailingly encounter it in the end.

Stylistically, some of the film's mise-en-scène remains theatrical rather than filmic. In the opening scene, Balduin enters the frame from the left, to sit in the foreground, while the other students party at outdoor tables behind him. Scapinelli's carriage also enters from the left and occupies the middle ground. The students in the background then disperse, leaving the "stage" free for Scapinelli and Balduin, while Lyduschka watches in the background. The hunting scene also begins with a theatrical framing device, while the scenes in Balduin's room could easily take place on a stage. At the same time, the filmmakers use the resources of cinema to good advantage in the montage shots of the fox hunt; in all of them, the hounds and riders are framed with sharp changes in direction of movement and closeness to the camera so as to emphasize the dynamism of motion. These exterior shots bring a sense of realism to the screen, whereas in the pact scene itself, the film employs special effects to create magic. Scapinelli's gold coins flow endlessly from his small money bag—in fact, this is a composite shot made up of many different shots. And, of course, it is only in the cinema that a mirror image can take on its own identity and move about independently. Despite these forays into a more cinematic mode of narration, the theatrical mode of the story's presentation is acknowledged in the film's credit sequence, when the actors take bows before a theater curtain.

This commercially successful German film paved the way for advances in the German film industry during the war years when the dominance of French and American films was lifted, allowing indigenous production to get a footing. With Germany's isolation from the American and French markets during World War I, there was a demand for film entertainment in central Europe. German industrialists saw an opportunity to enter the lucrative entertainment market. In 1917, the Ufa (Universum-Film AG) was founded in Berlin, thus confirming the city's role as the center of the German film industry. With greater centralized control over German film production, the emphasis on film aesthetics increased, as Sabine Hake notes:

"The growing emphasis on film as the art of the masses required a more convincing balance between economic and artistic issues, with the industrial product now promoted as a work of art."[28] This was certainly true of Henrik Galeen's remake of *Der Student von Prag*, which was screened in one of Berlin's movie palaces, the Capitol am Zoo, which had been built in 1925. The construction of elegant movie "palaces" in the urban centers, which also played a role in the feminization of the film audience, had already begun before World War I and was accelerated after the war. In Berlin and other European cities, these luxurious settings for the showing of films were graced by regular live orchestras and sumptuous decors and had a significant impact on the way films were consumed. For Siegfried Kracauer, the legitimation of the film-viewing experience that was offered in these extravagant settings had reactionary overtones and reflected a rejection of cinema's potentially liberating role:

> The architectural setting tends to emphasize a dignity that used to inhabit the institutions of high culture. . . . The show itself aspires to the same exalted level, claiming to be a finely tuned organism, an aesthetic totality as only an artwork can be. . . . The cinema has acquired a standing independent of the theatrical stage, yet the leading movie theaters are once again longing to return to that stage. . . . Distraction—which is meaningful only as improvisation, as a reflection of the uncontrolled anarchy of our world—is festooned with drapery and forced back into a unity that no longer exists.[29]

Kracauer saw that film was in a position to entertain and thus to serve the need for distraction among the urban masses, while at the same time mirroring the *disorder* in society. This could prepare the way for what he called "the inevitable and radical change."[30] He argued that this galvanizing potential was thwarted by the movie palaces, where audiences were lulled into passivity by the reinscription of film's radical form into conventional modes of theatrical presentation.

Galeen's remake of *Der Student von Prag* is certainly devoid of any radical politics, although it does represent a considerable advance in film technique. The particular innovation of Galeen's film is to present all the scenes with a greater reliance on the specific resources of cinematic art. Where Rye framed his story with an insert of Alfred de Musset's poem on solitude, "La Nuit de décembre,"[31] the narration is now framed by two shots of Balduin's tombstone, which the intertitles translate: "Here lies Balduin / He fought with the devil and lost." The very first scene is shot with much more movement and depth—opening shots show streams of students converging on the tavern from different directions, intercut with shots of the tavern keeper and his family anticipating the students' arrival; the drinking scene includes details such as a bulldog lapping beer and Lyduschka flirting with the students. Balduin arrives from the back of the frame; as he moves through the crowd, the camera reframes him from the front, where he sits by himself. Scapinelli is first seen among the tavern guests glancing in Balduin's direction; after Balduin is serenaded by students with a popular song making light of "students who have run out of cash" (the words and music appear as an insert), Scapinelli approaches Balduin's table. Balduin tells him he is not interested in a loan: "A rich heiress gives me her fortune, then I'm your man."

The hunt scene is intercut with shots of Lyduschka singing and the student fencing contest (which Balduin wins) at the tavern. The hunt scene is one of the signature scenes of the Galeen version and one that marks it as distinctively expressionist. Standing in dark silhouette on a hillside against a gnarled and twisted tree, Scapinelli "directs" the hunt with his umbrella from on high. The huntsmen are seen as small figures running back and forth on the plain below, subject to the forces that Scapinelli has at hand. He appears to draw the helpless figures toward the inn, where the horses jump easily over the outdoor tables. But Margit, arriving last, has to fight her unruly horse, which refuses the jump. "There is your heiress," Scapinelli tells Balduin, who has come out of the tavern, fresh from his fencing victory. Balduin runs and catches the countess as she falls off her horse.

Scapinelli's supernatural powers are suggested in an expressionist play of light and shadow later in the film, when Balduin lures Margit outside on the terrace of his magnificent new dwelling and confesses his love for her. As the spying Lyduschka watches helplessly below, Scapinelli's huge shadow is thrown against the wall (fig. 8). The shadow of his clawlike fingers rises toward the lovers and seems to snatch Balduin's love note and send it wafting down to Lyduschka, who will present it to Baron Waldis and thus avenge herself for Balduin's indifference. Galeen's film also uses editing to enhance the eerie atmosphere surrounding Balduin's flight from his double—in the narrow streets of Prague, he meets the double at every turn (fig. 9). Fritz Lang, in his 1931 masterpiece *M*, would later explore the idea of the persecuted self—that flees, only to find itself followed by itself again—as the essence of the paranoid criminal personality.[32] The technique of Galeen's film has enough consistency in its basic cinematic syntax that violations are experienced by the spectator as disturbances in the natural order of things.

Fig. 8. The shadow of Scapinelli (Werner Kraus) looms below the two lovers. Henrik Galeen, *Der Student von Prag* (1926). BFI Stills, Posters and Designs.

Fig. 9. Balduin (Conrad Veidt) confronted by his double in the streets of Prague. Henrik Galeen, *Der Student von Prag* (1926). BFI Stills, Posters and Designs.

Although influenced by other literary sources such as E. T. A. Hoffmann's stories and the literary tradition of the double,[33] Galeen's *Der Student von Prag* is Faustian in spirit. As in the earlier version, Balduin's mirror double does not change when he changes but retains the dress and manners he had as a student. This signals that he does not change inwardly either—the mirror self remains dissatisfied, no matter how rich and successful Balduin becomes. As such, he represents the perpetually striving soul that cannot be satiated by anything Mephistopheles provides.

Galeen's Scapinelli is much more of a Mephistopheles than Rye's, although the idea that the devil fulfills the Faustian character's wishes, while at the same time frustrating his success, is present in both versions. In Galeen's version, however, the supernatural powers of Scapinelli are more in evidence. In his appearance also, with goatee and frock coat, he is more suggestive of the demonic trickster than is Rye's frumpy tempter. The amount of gold that showers from Scapinelli's small money bag is also reminiscent of Mephistophelean magic, which, in the folk legend as in Goethe, could transform dust into gold (fig. 10). This second version also has a "Walpurgisnacht" scene—the raucous celebration of evil spirits in Goethe's *Faust*, part 1—as Balduin parties with Lyduschka at the tavern after he has been rejected by the countess. The equivalent scene in Rye's 1913 version is a rather sedate affair, while Galeen's film uses rhythmic montage effectively to convey the increasing frenzy of the dancers. Several subjective shots convey Balduin's increasing drunkenness and loss of control—notably, a sawlike bow that a musician uses to play a bass and then seems to saw right into the protagonist's head.

In neither version is Balduin, the Faustian character of the film, a social rebel. As Thomas Elsaesser has pointed out, Balduin's way out of his lowly student status is to make a pact with the diabolical Scapinelli; later, he pursues only the rank and status that his sudden wealth affords him.[34] Yet the story that forms the basis for both films does criticize the role that money plays in love. A subplot of the story is the theme of unrequited love and loveless marriage: the poor Lyduschka loves Balduin, who wants only a rich heiress; and Countess Margit is being married off to Baron Waldis, even though she does not love him, in order to continue the family name and consolidate the family fortune. Balduin's "divided self" experiences the alienation that comes from the discovery that one's qualities (represented here by his excellence in fencing) do not count in the world unless accompanied by a personal fortune. To this extent, as Heide Schlüpmann notes, the

Fig. 10. Scapinelli (Werner Kraus) showers Balduin with gold and demands "something from his room" in return. Henrik Galeen, *Der Student von Prag* (1926). BFI Stills, Posters and Designs.

initial story of the film can be said to allegorize the loss of self-esteem experienced by the German middle class in 1913 as it was faced with a worsening of its economic status.[35]

Lyduschka, it should be noted, is also divided between love for Balduin and rage that her poverty makes her invisible to him. It is her small bouquet, a love offering, that Balduin goes to present to the countess, only to be embarrassed by the baron's lavish floral arrangement. Galeen makes much more of this scene than Rye—first Balduin stuffs the bouquet in his pocket so that the countess won't see it, and then he throws it out of his window onto the street, where the hapless Lyduschka finds it again.

Despite the role that Lyduschka and Margit play in the fortunes of Balduin, they remain minor characters in the story, foils for the protagonist's fate.[36] This will change in F. W. Murnau's films, which give greater development to the themes of home and hearth, eroticism and temptation, through his women characters. Some of the impulse behind this change in narrative emphasis might have had to do with changes in the gender composition of the film audience. In the days of the Weimar Republic, women

began to attend film screenings in large numbers. They were also avid readers of periodicals where film culture was actively discussed—Patrice Petro
notes that they made up the majority of readers of *Die Dame* and the communist *AIZ* (*Arbeiter-Illustrierte Zeitung*).[37]

The 1926 *Faust* by Murnau is the first major German film to deal overtly
with the Faust material. Predictably, the most common criticism of the film
was that Murnau had failed to produce a work worthy of his great literary
predecessor. As if in anticipation of this criticism, Murnau bases himself
principally on the folk legend of Faust—a strategy Thomas Mann would
also adopt some twenty years later in his novel *Doctor Faustus*. Made under the auspices of Ufa, the film premiered on October 14, 1926, at the
luxurious Berlin film theater, Ufa-Palast am Zoo, which since 1919 had
functioned as the flagship of Ufa productions. Klaus Kreimeier describes
the opening in *The Ufa Story* as a "neo-baroque event of the first order":
"The company's propaganda machine had worked overtime to keep the
filming of Germany's national poem by a master director very much in the
news. Now it promoted the premiere as a world-class event in which the
political and cultural *crème de la crème* of Germany's capital city were more
or less obliged to participate."[38]

Despite the grand style of the film's presentation to the public, Murnau's
film goes against the trend of film commercialization. He continually
arrests the narrative by emphasizing the visual, in part by multiple allusions to the history of European painting. Eric Rohmer, in his study
L'Organisation de l'espace dans le "Faust" de Murnau, already noted some specific "quotations" of paintings in the Murnau work: Rembrandt's etching
The Magus and Albrecht Dürer's *Saint Jerome* for the scenes of the old Faust
surrounded by the books and vials;[39] Vermeer's *Woman with a Pearl Necklace* for Margarete's trying on the necklace Mephistopheles places in her
drawer.[40] More important, he argues that Murnau's film complicates a photographic perspective that adheres to conventions of seventeenth-century
painterly realism by the addition of studio effects of lighting and foreshort-
ening.[41] The combination of these seemingly irreconcilable elements accounts for the tension and excitement of *Faust*, before which the spectator
is buffeted from one peak visual experience to another. In Rohmer's formulation, Murnau experiences motion as a painter: "It is rather in the representation of motion, rather than immobility, that he is able to achieve
pictorial beauty."[42]

Far from being a conservative move to elevate the cinema to the cultural status of the "great masters," Murnau's transposition of painting to the cinema extends the possibilities of the film medium by the innovative sculpting of light in motion, as, for example in the scene when Faust appears at Margarete's (Gretchen's) window (fig. 11). This is the moment of Gretchen's seduction. She presses herself against the wall, as if to escape; but the lighting on Faust's face and especially his outstretched hand establishes the limits of the space and traps her. There can be no movement back but only forward into the light. The lighting of this shot thus establishes a third dimension in which the space of the drama occurs in the middle ground. Faust's hand bursts out of its frame and seems already to enter another space. Murnau's framing invites the viewer's identification with Gretchen through his "frame-within-a-frame" device. Faust's hand gestures toward the space of the spectator, who, like Gretchen, is in the dark.

Much has been written on the spectator's identification with characters in the cinema, and it is no doubt too facile to suggest that every viewer will

Fig. 11. Faust (Gösta Ekman) penetrates into Gretchen's (Camilla Horn) chambers. F. W. Murnau, *Faust* (1926). Museum of Modern Art Film Stills Archive. *Rights*: Friedrich-Wilhelm-Murnau-Stiftung. *Distributor*: Transit Film GmbH.

react in the same way. The essential point here is the basic difference between theater and film, as noted by the French critic André Bazin: the presence of actors on the stage sets up a distance between the actor and the spectator that precludes any identification between them. In the cinema, that barrier is lifted since the actor is only a virtual presence. To this early insight, we can add theories of voyeurism (as developed by psychoanalytically oriented critics) and the recent work of Marxist theorists who argue that the choice of spectators' object of identification can also be influenced by their own "specific social and political positions."[43] Despite these caveats, considering the cues of the mise-en-scène, the use of point of view, and the considerable portion of screen time that Gretchen takes up in *Faust*, the invitation for the viewer's identification with her seems strongly marked.

If Murnau's mise-en-scène in the seduction scene suggests the influence of Caravaggio (a contemporary of the original Faust), other cinematographic effects call to mind the painter Kaspar David Friedrich—a contemporary of Goethe. In one scene, Faust, sitting on a cliff over a romantic landscape, starts up and utters the cry "*Heimat!*" (Motherland!). The scene is shot in soft

Fig. 12. Faust homesick for Germany. F. W. Murnau, *Faust* (1926). Museum of Modern Art Film Stills Archive. *Rights*: Friedrich-Wilhelm-Murnau-Stiftung. *Distributor*: Transit Film GmbH.

focus, evoking Friedrich's misty landscapes (fig. 12). The scene of Gretchen's flight through the snow, on the other hand, plays on quattrocento Madonna images (fig. 13).

Fig. 13. Gretchen as a suffering Madonna spurned by a townswoman. F. W. Murnau, *Faust* (1926). Museum of Modern Art Film Stills Archive. *Rights*: Friedrich-Wilhelm-Murnau-Stiftung. *Distributor*: Transit Film GmbH.

In addition, there are touches of German expressionism. These include some of the subjective "visions" seen by the characters, such as the shot of Gretchen imagining that she is rocking her baby in a snow cradle, or Faust's vision of the imploring hands of the townspeople when he is weighing his decision to sign the pact. When Gretchen cries out to Faust as he sits on the mountain, her mouth in close-up becomes a cavern, through which rushes a snow-bedecked landscape of mountains and pine trees (Murnau had already explored in the 1923 *Nosferatu* the idea that a loved one's cry for help can traverse great distances).

Other scenes hark back to the fantasies of Méliès. These include the flight of Faust and Mephistopheles over a landscape of medieval German towns and mountains (modeled after the sixteenth-century German painter Albrecht Altdorfer), accompanied by majestic, animated flying cranes and an artificial moon; the conjuring scene with its rings of fire; and the abduction of the Duchess of Parma with its use of stop-frame photography. *Faust* is obviously a studio film, and the construction of the sets does much to intensify the sense of claustrophobic space. The streets of Gretchen's little town are narrow and labyrinthine. Even the palace of the Duchess of Parma offers little in the way of spaciousness—as the airborne travelers leave the mountain peaks and waterfalls, they enter the Italian kingdom by skirting a dome; the camera then pans down along several balconies that appear at first as barriers to the vision of the dancing girls performing for the royal couple. Everywhere he goes, Faust seems enclosed: whether in his cavelike study, among the plague-stricken townspeople, in the canopy bed with the duchess, surrounded by mists on a mountaintop, or dallying with Gretchen in the garden. At the end, he must fight his way toward her through a crowd of soldiers.[44]

The conjuring scene also carries with it the sense of claustrophobia and entrapment. As in so many other scenes of *Faust*, the foreground, where the devil makes his first appearance, is dark. Faust's figure, in the middle ground, serves as the focus of lighting. As Faust flees, the cuts anticipate the place toward which he runs—in each case, toward the darkness in the foreground, where the devil already awaits him. With each cut, the frame becomes more and more crowded—in the last outdoor scene, the devil sits by a gnarled tree whose tortured branches frame the full moon. Finally, when the exhausted and terrified Faust reaches his study, the devil is already there as well.

The most brightly lit scene is the happy meeting of Gretchen and Faust in the garden and the prior shots of Gretchen surrounded by a ring of children. Yet even here, Murnau casts shadows from the flowering trees on Gretchen, so that she is never perceived in direct sunlight (fig. 14). In the preceding scene with her confidante Frau Marthe, the shadows of the window panes also cover her. This "foreshadowing" becomes literal as Gretchen lies in her prison cell entrapped by the shadows of the prison bars.

The lighting and framing of almost every shot of the film convey a sense of foreboding because Murnau chooses, for the most part, to keep the lower part of the frame dark. Often the foreground figures are mere silhouettes, with the light falling on figures in the center. This happens, for instance, in the first scene, which depicts street performers in the town. In this scene, a shadow play performed by two hands represents fighting animals. The perspective then shifts so that the shadow box nearly fills the right side of

Fig. 14. Shadows surrounding brightness: Gretchen in the garden. F. W. Murnau, *Faust* (1926). Museum of Modern Art Film Stills Archive. *Rights*: Friedrich-Wilhelm-Murnau-Stiftung. *Distributor*: Transit Film GmbH.

the screen image (Murnau prefigures the cinematic spectacle as light play here). One hand now models a bird attacking the other hand. Already the visual cues convey a sense of confinement. Not only does the screen-within-the-screen take up a growing proportion of the space but the "entertainment" uses two silhouetted hands in conflict with one another. Then a cut to a long shot of the whole town shows Mephistopheles towering above it, his black wings enveloping the houses, which appear crushed and diminished. The wings of the devil cast a shadow behind them, further constricting the space and suggesting that there is no way out—the entire world is a closed box. Smoky exhalations rise from the oppressed town. As we cut back to a collapsing acrobat, the image has darkened. The townspeople scatter in fear, and a fierce wind begins to blow—a visual translation of disaster.

In the figure of Gretchen, Murnau presents the image of ideal domesticity, which he also explored in several other films. In *City Girl* (1922), the story hinges on the initial rejection by the authoritarian father of the new wife from the city whom the son brings home to the farm. At the end of the film, she is finally accepted into the home. In *Nosferatu*, it is the wife who saves her husband and who finally sacrifices herself in order to rescue the world from the power of the vampire. Murnau frequently offers images extolling the virtues of "home": the wife waiting for her husband's return in *Nosferatu*; the waving fields of grain and the lyrical shots of the harvest in *City Girl*; the joyous homecoming of Gretchen's brother Valentin in *Faust*. The largely female gender of the Weimar film audience may account for Murnau's emphasis on the Gretchen melodrama in the plot and for the way in which he invites the audience's identification with her. Throughout, his *Faust* is notable for its feminine emphasis. In fact, he includes many scenes in which women play a role in the public space: the fair where the plague first breaks out, the village well where the girls scorn a pregnant companion, Gretchen's punishment at the village pillory, and the funeral at the church where Frau Marthe spurns Gretchen's advances.

Finally, we should stop to consider the figure of Mephistopheles, played by Emil Jannings. Not until István Szabó's 1981 *Mephisto* (based on the acting career of Gustaf Gründgens) would another Mephistopheles so dominate the scene. In the seduction scene between Faust and the Duchess of Parma, Murnau implicitly elevates the devil figure to the status of the director's alter ego. Mephistopheles hovers over the canopy bed where Faust consorts with the duchess and then cloaks the scene as though he were the stage director of a puppet play. Murnau's Mephistopheles owes much to Méliès's enactment of the same role, particularly in his gleeful participation in the seduction of Gretchen, where he acts simultaneously as the master puppeteer and observer (a role that enables Murnau to explore the technique of the point-of-view shot). Paradoxically, Murnau's distance from Goethe appears clearest in the Gretchen scenes, which are among the few inspired by *Faust*, part I: Mephistopheles has shed his ironic philosophical nihilism and appears simply as the force of evil, intent on spawning unhappiness and taking over the world.

The influence of Goethe is present in the prologue and epilogue, which deal with the wager between God and Lucifer. Just as Goethe's prologue sets up the Faust legend as a primordial dramatic conflict, so Murnau establishes the claim of cinema to be the ideal vehicle to express the conflict between the forces of light and darkness. Lucifer's dark, winged form, surmounted by a tiny horned head, covers the screen like a bird of prey. The archangel of light—the whitest image in the whole film—appears brightly behind him. This relation of the dark foreground with brightness centered in the middle ground repeats the pattern that runs consistently through the film. In the epilogue, the image is reversed—black Lucifer is obliged to retreat before the archangel's light. Murnau has effectively framed the Faustian story as one of the victory of light over darkness.[45] Here, the cinema finds one of its ideal subjects, and in touching upon it, discovers new possibilities.

Murnau's film enjoyed greater critical success outside the country than in Germany, where he was reproached for straying too far from Goethe's play.[46] Its worldwide box-office success was nevertheless limited, and it failed to earn back the initial investment. Then, a year after its release, it was branded as "immoral" by the Prussian Ministry of the Interior and temporarily barred from young audiences. The censorship board argued that *Faust* provided a bad example of someone who lives in an unrestrained sensual manner, both in his behavior with the Duchess of Parma and in his seduction of Gretchen.[47] The public outcry that greeted this attempt to censor *Faust* was in itself a measure of how the status of film had changed by 1926. The effect of the attempted censorship was to boost the film's popularity.[48] By the time the film opened in Berlin, however, Murnau himself had moved to Hollywood, anticipating by several years the exodus of German intellectuals and artists that accompanied the rise of Fascism.

Early Film Audiences

Early filmmakers had been attracted to the Faust story because it was universally understood in Europe and in the United States. Assuming the audience's familiarity with the material, Méliès could graft onto it his magic tricks and spoof the bourgeois class of his origins. Especially in his early films, Méliès as Mephistopheles delights in subverting the bourgeois order. As producers sought to woo the middle class into the movie theaters, however, the Faust material begins to play a more conservative role. In the French *film d'art*, literary precursors lend legitimacy to the Faust story and make it usable in cinema's bid for respectability. *Film d'art* in turn influences the productions of the German *Autorenfilm*, such as the 1913 version of *Der Student von Prag*. In the United States, there is a parallel move, exemplified by the Edison's Studio's *The Magic Skin*, toward longer narrative films designed to attract the bourgeois audience. Along with the longer form, film language moves toward a narrative style that privileges the pleasure of the viewing experience and that will become known as classical narration. Coming out of the complex social and artistic environment of Germany's Weimar

Republic, Murnau's *Faust* resists these trends and exemplifies, instead, an auteurist cinema inflected with elements of expressionism.

From the origins of cinema to the end of the silent era, the cinematic renditions of the Faust theme are symptomatic of the dialectical relationship between film form and the evolving film audience and economics of distribution and production. In the sound era, the explorations of Faustian narratives will find equal resonance in the entertainment-oriented Hollywood cinema, with its "seamless" and "invisible" editing, and in the more personal art cinema of Europe. If the Edison Studio version can be said to be a precursor of the Hollywood style, Murnau's *Faust* is an important founding work for the art film. Moreover, the earlier "cinema of attractions" or "spectacle cinema," as Tom Gunning calls it, was not simply absorbed by the development of narrative film—it resurfaces later in the avant-garde.[49] Gunning's description of early Méliès films as ones in which "the story simply provides a frame upon which to string a demonstration of the magical possibilities of cinema" is applicable to Jan Svankmajer's 1993 *Lekce Faust* (*Faust*).[50] The history of film style is thus inseparable from the Faust story, which, to return to the formulation of Paul de Man, is not a content "poured into" film form but rather works to constitute the shape of cinema history, both as artifact and as spectatorial event.

2　German Fascism and the Contested Terrain of Culture

Goethe made Faust into a cosmopolitan figure, a representative, as the Hungarian critic Georg Lukács writes, of the "destiny of mankind"; Thomas Mann, in his epic struggle with Nazism, brings him back to his German roots in the folktale. *Doctor Faustus*, written while Mann was in exile in California between 1943 and 1946, is the most sophisticated embodiment of the fight over German culture that took place during the first half of the twentieth century. Nazism's rise was not built on mere thuggery: its mythic aggrandizement and distortion of the German cultural past were calculated to enhance its appeal. The struggle for the hearts and minds of the German population included, in the early stages, racial interpretations of German fairy tales; academic writings in the fields of anthropology, history, linguistics, and philosophy that "proved" German superiority (with willful distortions, such as the idea that Germans, not modern Greeks, were the true descendants of classical Greece); and arguments about the "destiny" of Germany as world leader.[1] After Hitler assumed power, the cultural flank was expanded to include education (the rewriting of textbooks and the reorganization of university professorships to reflect the new racial theories), the arts (the creation of various ministerial branches, under the directorship of Joseph Goebbels, to oversee artistic activity), and the press (the forcing of dissident publications underground and the imposition of restrictions on all printed material). Moreover, Hitler's Reich did not stop at control and prohibition: it became actively involved in all aspects of the cultural sphere, including literature, theater, filmmaking, and art patronage and exhibition. One immediate effect was the exclusion of Jews from public participation in culture.

Those who had the foresight to emigrate included Jews and dissidents such as the physicist Albert Einstein; philosophers Herbert Marcuse and Theodor Adorno; filmmakers Fritz Lang and William Wyler; artists Max

Ernst and John Heartfield (who anglicized his name from the German *Herzfelde*); musicians Bruno Walter, Arnold Schönberg, and Kurt Weill; as well as literary figures Bertolt Brecht, Stefan Zweig, and Thomas Mann. After first fleeing to Switzerland in 1933, Mann came to the United States in 1938. In 1941, he went to California, where he joined a society of exiles that has been nicknamed "Weimar in Hollywood."[2]

"Taking Back" the German Legacy: Thomas Mann's *Doctor Faustus*

Doctor Faustus, the novel that Mann wrote in exile, is an apocalyptic work that recounts two disasters occurring in parallel fashion on different temporal planes. The narrator, classical philologist Serenus Zeitbloom, is living through the last years of the Reich in retirement, after having withdrawn from his teaching post in protest over Nazi policies. Rather than being a spokesman for Mann and the exile community, he embodies the contradictory position of those intellectuals who stayed in Germany during the war, full of misgivings and without wholehearted participation in the Reich's cultural affairs. As Germany's two war fronts gradually crumble, he cheers on Nazism's opponents, while at the same time grieving for the end of the Germany he knew and with which he identified. Mann has given us, in the person of Zeitbloom, a portrait of "Spenglerian man," convinced of Germany's greatness but appalled at the Fascist exploitation of national sentiment.[3] Too timid to assert himself against the rising intellectual tide of racism and nationalism in the intellectual salons, Zeitbloom is reduced to being the passive spectator of a cultural shift he registers with pessimism and consternation.

The second temporal plane is that of the biographical account he writes of his childhood friend, the composer Adrian Leverkühn. Here, too, is the story of a catastrophe: the artist, inhibited by his own coldness and lack of emotion, is drawn to extremes that ultimately provoke his downfall. His sexual intercourse with a diseased prostitute, arising from the uncontrollable eruption of powerfully repressed sexual instincts, at once liberates his powers of artistic creation and afflicts him with the incurable illness that seals his doom twenty-four years later. His fate convinces Leverkühn that he has made a pact with the devil. Zeitbloom is appalled to find, among his friend's posthumous papers, the transcript of a long conversation between the composer and a mysterious Mephistophelean figure (perhaps, Zeitbloom supposes, only the product of his friend's diseased imagination).

In the transcribed conversation, the devil voices the idea that disease and creativity are linked: "Creative disease, genius-bestowing disease, which takes all hurdles on horseback, springing in drunken boldness from rock to rock, is a thousand times dearer to life than plodding health."[4]

The transcript is dated twenty-four years before the composer's final public act—his confession of the "pact" in front of a group of assembled friends. At the end of the confession, Leverkühn proves himself unable to perform the musical work he has promised to present—his "Lamentation of Doctor Faustus." He has a stroke and lives out the last ten years of his life (until 1940) in a state of dementia. Three years later—in the midst of World War II—his horrified friend, still in a state of shock from his friend's catastrophic end, begins his retelling of Leverkühn's life.

Mann has often compared his method of literary composition to music. Such a comparison is particularly apt in this case, in which the two temporal strands develop independently, only to merge in the final chapters into a single theme of destruction. Leverkühn's demise is repeated as theme and variation on two allegorical levels. On the one hand, Mann's narrator offers detailed descriptions of the composer's two final musical works. The first is a choral work titled "Apocalypse," based on Dürer's woodcut illustrations, "Apocalipsis cum Figuris." In the second, the "Lamentation of Doctor Faustus," the composer sets to music the final chapter of Spies's *Historia*, which describes Faust's confession before an assembly of loyal friends and followers and moves on to the gruesome details of his violent death that same night. Yet Mann, through his narrator, moves to yet another allegorical level. Leverkühn, though apparently isolated from society, knows enough about what is going on in Germany to link his sense of personal destruction with that of German culture. He tells Zeitblom that he wants to "take back" the finale of Beethoven's Ninth Symphony—the "Ode to Joy."

Leverkühn's own sense of doom is amplified, especially at the beginning of chapters 21, 26, and 33, by the narrator's remarks about events in Germany during the time of his writing—the period from 1943, when the Allied air war and defeats along the Russian front began to turn the tide of the war against Germany, to its surrender in May 1945. To the composer's spirit of negation and canceling out of German culture, Zeitblom adds his own pessimistic view that the war has finished Germany: "Today, in the embrace of demons, a hand over one eye, the other staring into the horror, it plummets from despair to despair. When will it reach the bottom of the abyss?"[5]

The two temporal strands interweave as theme and variation on the apocalypse of German culture, as Mann explains in his accompanying work, *Die Entstehung des Doktor Faustus: Roman eines Romans* (*The Genesis of a Novel*). He describes the excitement that he feels in describing the outlines of the work to a visiting friend, and the aspects that the friend found particularly impressive: "the way the artist takes refuge from the difficulties of the cultural crisis by making a pact with the devil; the idea that, threatened by sterility, his proud spirit thirsts for the release of his inhibitions at any price; and then the parallel development of the popular intoxication of Fascism and his own pernicious euphoria which brings him ever closer to collapse."[6]

The Genesis of a Novel announces the presence of yet another voice in the parallel narrative strands. Mann's own time of writing *Doctor Faustus* coincides with that of his narrator, Serenus Zeitblom. Yet Mann is careful to distance himself from his narrator, who is seven years younger and still feeling his way between his attachment to his German heritage and his revulsion against what has been committed in its name. Above all, the narrator remains in Germany, in the state of mind later called "inner emigration," whereas Mann left Germany. Perhaps Mann may rather be compared with the hero, Adrian Leverkühn. Allegorically speaking, *Doctor Faustus* is the act of "taking back" the ending of Goethe's *Faust*, part 2, with its act of conciliation and forgiveness. The German Faust, Mann seems to say, is damned after all.

Mann's "taking back" of Faust's salvation should be seen as part of the struggle over the German cultural heritage between the Weimar spirit and Nazism. Just as the composer Leverkühn is said to reach back into the musical past for his forms (the "Lamentation of Doctor Faustus" is said to marshal "all the elements of music conceivable as bearers of expression . . . like an exercise of deliberate mastery over all the expressive characters ever precipitated in musical history"),[7] so Mann reaches back to the folk legend of Faust. And just as Zeitblom sees in German behavior the sign of the end of humanism as such, so Mann dramatizes the failure of Goethe's cosmopolitanism and tolerance. According to Mann, history has proven that German culture would develop instead along the path of barbarism.[8]

Through his narrator, Zeitblom, Mann is able to imagine himself back inside the Reich, as a somewhat distanced eyewitness who ends up having the last word on the cultural battles surrounding the German legacy. *Doctor Faustus*, published in Switzerland in 1946, is also Mann's claim of victory on that contested terrain. This is no small matter, given the importance of the space that Nazism awarded to cultural affairs. As the work of Germany's most celebrated author of the first half of the twentieth century, Mann's novel is an attempt to reclaim the German cultural past against Fascism.

Goethe in the Cultural Battlefield

The interest of the Nazi rulers in cultural affairs is an instructive example in the relationship between ideology and power. The fight over such issues as the legacy of Goethe and the folk wisdom of German fairy tales was understood by both sides to be crucial issues in consensus building. Moreover, the intellectual trends that abetted the rise of Fascist ideology started well before 1933. The first decade of the century already saw the publication of Goethe studies that fed into the rising tide of nationalism. As the writers of the groundbreaking article "Faust in a Brownshirt" note, "They instilled and legitimized a sense of duty for the German people—the will to realize a global plan—and the feeling of Germanic cultural, even racial, superiority. In other words, they laid the groundwork for later Goethe studies which stressed these nationalistic ideas even more."[9]

A key figure in the increasing influence of right-wing and anti-Semitic thinking was Houston Stewart Chamberlain. The son of a British admiral and the son-in-law of Richard Wagner, Chamberlain wrote several influential works, including a tome on Goethe, first published in Munich in 1912. His study focuses on Goethe as a "great personality" (*grosse Persönlichkeit*), a line of thinking that later fed into right-wing notions of the German as a heroic man of action. Chamberlain is clearest in his preface to the third edition of the work, which came out in 1921, after the defeat of World War I. Here, he accuses Jews of "robbing Germans of their identity" and states that "to be a hero is German."[10]

These tendencies reach their fullest expression in Georg Schott's study, *Goethes Faust in heutiger Schau* (Goethe's Faust in Contemporary Perspective), published in 1940. Schott repeatedly refers to the "Führer Faust," suggesting explicitly that Hitler is Germany's new Faustian striver. Like the commentators on both sides of the Faust debates, he focuses on the moment in *Faust*, part 2, when Faust looks out over the territory he has wrested from the sea and expresses his satisfaction. Faust's reclaiming of the sea will create new space for millions to live, not in total security, but actively free (*tätig-frei*):

He only earns both freedom and existence
Who must reconquer them each day.
And so, ringed all about by perils, here
Youth, manhood, age will spend their strenuous year.
Such teeming would I see upon this land,
On acres free among free people stand.

(11575–80)

Schott, writing at the beginning of the German military adventure, provides the exegesis:

> [This is] the idea that is dear to the Faustian Führer: to gain territory
> [*Raum*] for the "people without territory," in order to live "not se-
> curely, but free for action." Here, in compressed form, an illusory ideal
> is contrasted with a real one. "Security," in the sense of nonpartici-
> pation in the workings of the world, is the ideal of the philistine. It is
> not the task of the Faustian Führer to provide that. . . . With the grace
> of God, the Führer strives to obtain another ideal. For his people in
> need, he wants to create the possibility to live "free for action." To
> create work for a people which can work and wants to work and which
> is blocked from freedom of action by a real conspiracy of demonic
> forces: that, and that alone, is the goal of the Faustian Führer.[11]

In Schott's interpretation, Goethe is also used to bolster anti-Semitism.
Mephistopheles is a "slick Talmudic scholar" who resembles nothing so
much as the "Mephistophelean creatures, coffeehouse men of letters and
journalists, and satirical weeklies who make fun of the Führer." And he
warns of the danger that "Faustian man can quickly change into his Jew-
ish-Mephistophelean counterpart just as a wrongly treated photographic
positive can change into a negative."[12] Goethe's "two souls" concept is thus
modified to support the paranoid idea that no one can be trusted, since
anyone, even the most "Faustian" man, can suddenly become the site for
the eruption of the "Mephistophelean."

Alfred Rosenberg's *The Myth of the Twentieth Century*, which was first
published in 1930, presents another variation on the "two souls" theme.
Rosenberg explicates the passage from *Faust* that describes Faust's frustra-
tion with Philemon and Baucis, the old couple whose small home prevents
him from feeling a sense of total dominion over his lands. Nordic, Faustian
man, Rosenberg argues, wants to conquer in the abstract: his action-oriented

need for control is "Luciferan." Against this "Luciferan" quality, Rosenberg sets what he calls the "Satanic" character of Jews, who, he argues, seek control only for material gain: "It is not mere greed for riches and high living that is shown here but the urge of the master 'who feels bliss in commanding.'"[13] Rosenberg, who later became the author of the racial laws under Hitler—and who was one of ten Nazi leaders executed at Nuremberg— channels Chamberlain's concept of the "great personality" into the mainstream of Nazi ideology: "The German Reich, if it is to continue to exist after the revolution of 1933, will be the work of a league of men conscious of their goal. . . . All the forces which formed our soul had their origins in great personalities. . . . Goethe . . . represented our essence in *Faust*."[14]

Yet another commentator, Johannes Bertram, looked to Goethe for confirmation of the Nazi rhetoric about "German blood," recalling that Mephistopheles, at the moment of Faust's signing of the pact, says that "blood is a very special juice" (1740).

> Here a fact is presented that is at present still unclear to most people: the relationship between the blood substance and the nature of human will, of the innermost drive toward perfection. . . . It would be hard to overestimate the great importance of this way of considering blood for the modern theory of race, which is still too much overshadowed by materiality, and of recognizing the relationship between the individual soul and the racial soul. We see that back then Goethe touched upon things whose value and importance are fully understood only today.[15]

As Thomas Zabka has shown, these readings all adhere to a common logic: "A passage is completely liberated from its context, and above all freed from the speaking persona, and made into the mosaic piece of one's own ideology, with apparent legitimization by Goethe."[16]

Schott's and Rosenberg's imperialist and racist visions were by no means uncontested in Germany during the Nazi era; there were other figures who voiced their protest and who tried to prevent the appropriation of Goethe's work into the Nazi mythology. Wilhelm Böhm's 1933 work, *Faust der Nichtfaustische* (Faust the non-Faustian) presents the idea that "Faust's element is not so much to strive, as to err."[17] In fact, Böhm compares Faust to Don Quixote, hardly a comparison that would provide grist for the Fascist mill. Echoing these sentiments in 1941, Ernst Beutler, director of Frankfurt's

Goethe Museum, argues that Goethe presents Faust as a failure, like his other doomed freedom-fighters, Egmont and Götz von Berlichingen. Faust's sacrifice of the old couple Philemon and Baucis to accomplish his aims is Goethe's warning to the German people not to be bent on conquest.[18]

These writers may be compared with Mann's narrator Zeitblom, dissidents who remained in Germany and tried to argue against the rising tide of Fascist cultural ideology. Like Zeitblom, they were destined to fail. Mann's narrator describes how he remained too polite when archconservative views centering on ideas of the "*Volk*" and the "new barbarism" were expressed in public salons:

> A man of tender sensitivities finds disruption unpleasant; he finds it unpleasant to break in on a well-constructed train of thought with his own logical or historical objections culled from memory, and even in the anti-intellectual he will honor and respect the intellect. Today we can see clearly enough that it was a mistake of our civilization to have been all too generous in exercising such forbearance and respect—since on the opposing side we were indeed dealing with naked insolence and the most determined intolerance.[19]

The Struggle over German Identity: Retellings of Popular Fairy Tales

In the struggle over the German cultural legacy, the Faust story took its place alongside other popular legends, notably the German fairy tale. Here, the terrain was contested by some of the same cultural pundits. Schott's study, *Weissagung und Erfüllung im Deutschen Volksmärchen* (Prediction and Fulfillment in the German Fairy Tale), published in 1936, was an important voice for Nazi ideology. His discursive strategy is first to retell the story, following the original version of the Grimm brothers, and then to give an interpretation that appeals to ideals of German racial purity and German soil. In his reworking of the tale of Cinderella, the motherless girl who is no longer "at home" in her own house stands for the corruption of the German spirit by foreign influence, particularly after the defeat in World War I. Schott's interpretations of fairy tales were first published in 1924. The preface by Heinrich Gruber to the second edition of 1936 explains that the World War I defeat was "the time of Germany's greatest shame."[20] He further allegorizes the tale by equating Cinderella's deceased mother with the German motherland. At her mother's grave, Cinderella finds helpers who aid her in overcoming all the trials set before her and dress her for the ball. She triumphs, just as Germany's glory will one day be restored; and the usurping stepsisters are duly punished by having their eyes plucked out.[21]

Schott's concept of the "alien" is most clearly spelled out in his take on the fairy tale of the brave tailor. The little tailor who conquers giants and wins the hand of the princess by using his wits rather than his strength is, for Schott, the epitome of the Jew: "The problem is not just that the Jew occupies all the places of leadership in our economic life and in our state, but that he has insinuated himself into the hearts and cells of our people [Volk]."[22] In this concluding essay to his volume, Schott calls upon the German people to root out the hidden evil that, he says, is attacking the spiritual life of the nation.

Schott's work on the fairy tale was consistent with state policy after 1933, a fact that helps to explain why his book was republished in 1936. As Nazi Party official Alfred Eyd announced in 1935, "The German folktale shall become a most valuable means for us in the racial and political education of the young."[23]

In the essay that concludes the collection, Schott calls upon Goethe as an authority when he is making his points, mining Goethe's writings for ideas that are consistent with Nazism. During the "Easter walk" scene, Faust stops to converse with some farmers under a linden tree (949–1010). Schott argues that these peasants represent the Volk: "These are the forces that preserve the people [Volk] and the state, the ground from which new life continually springs."[24]

Goethe is also marshaled for the argument that women's place is in the home. After quoting Luther ("Women rule the house and distribute what the man brings in and earns honorably") and a letter from Goethe's mother to her son about the womanly virtues of remaining contentedly at home, Schott warns, "German Volk, awaken! Learn to understand the alien territory into which you are being led, when people falsify the ideal of the 'Eternal-Feminine.'"[25] Here, Schott has enlisted the much-discussed last lines of the second part of Faust—"Das Ewig-Weibliche / zieht uns hinan" (Woman Eternal / Draw us on high, 12110–11)—into the service of Fascist theories of women's domestic role.

In the cultural wars, both sides of the political spectrum recognized the way in which well-known folk legends and fairy tales could be used to quickly convey political messages. Schott's take on the Grimm brothers' tale of the cat who lived with a mouse is interesting in the context of counter-interpretations offered by anti-Fascist forces. A cat and a mouse cohabit and have saved up a pot of fat for the winter. But the cat keeps sneaking out of the house to plunder the provisions until the pot is licked clean. When confronted by the angry mouse, the cat eats her up too. Schott's explication illustrates his racist premise: "There are limits set by life itself. They consist of blood and race. If they are violated, revenge comes sooner or later. And blame is not to be sought at the end, but at the outset: it comes from the cohabitation which carried within it from the beginning the seed of that which is against nature."[26]

This same tale figures in an anti-Fascist photomontage of John Heartfield, which he published in the *Volks-Illustrierte* in Prague in 1938 (fig. 15). Here, the cat raises its paw in a Fascist salute and asserts the triumph of might over right. Heartfield's work points to the way that Nazism justified the use of force by appealing to such concepts as the Aryan/Nordic man of action and his "natural" drive to dominate. It is this strand of thinking, along with the incessant criticism of Jews as an alien and competing race, whose members allegedly succeed by trickery rather than honest work, that most clearly articulates the shift to the right in German intellectual circles that culminates in Nazism.

Fig. 15. John Heartfield's "Illustration for Grimm's fairy tale about the cat and the mouse" (1938). Courtesy of Akademie der Künste, Berlin.

Faust was only one of many popular German folk legends that Heartfield used in his works because they were readily identifiable.[27] Heartfield's photomontage works are assemblages of preexisting photographs that tend toward an overall visual coherence. After 1929, many of these appeared on the cover of the communist workers' paper *AIZ*. At the height of its circulation in 1931, *AIZ* was putting out half a million copies per issue. Its success may be measured by the fact that the Nazis began publishing an imitation magazine, the *ABZ* (*Arbeiter in Bild und Zeit*) in an effort to wean readers away from the Communist Party. The Nazi magazine employed a *photomonteur* to copy Heartfield's style. Topics were apolitical, concentrating on sports, homemaking, and health. *ABZ* floundered in 1933 after producing nineteen issues.

One of the most conceptually brilliant, as well as most aesthetically balanced, works is "The Thousand-year-Reich" of 1934 (fig. 16), which shows how the artist continued to use material from popular folk legend in order to drive home his political point. Heartfield prepared this photomontage for a cover of *AIZ* when he was already living in exile in Czechoslovakia. In the middle column, the legs formed by the SS, the SA (*Sturm-Abteilung*, or Storm Troops), the Imperial Army, and even the simple cavalry officer support the industrial magnate Thyssen in imperial robes and scepter at the top, flying the Nazi flag (with two bags of money containing amounts of 0.00 and 000.0 respectively), while Hitler figures as a lowly drummer at the bottom. Göring reappears as a bear with bat ears, "bloody Hermann," with his two icons, the burning Reichstag and the axe. A fountain spills forth *Volk* communal hearts: the luxury model for economic leaders, and plain ones for followers. Dr. Goebbels's "propaganda-bells" are advertised as the best cure for hunger and joblessness. The acorns on the folkloric German oak have turned to artillery shells, which are vaunted as the most sustaining food for the German *Volk* in the Third Reich, even as a shepherd pipes a peace tune under it. To the right of the house of cards, two pronouncements of Hitler's are printed in traditional Gothic script: "The German way of life has been finally determined for the next thousand years," and "There will not be a revolution in Germany for a thousand years."

The force of this work derives from the stark contrast between the way that the fragility of the house of cards itself contrasts with the classical form of pictorial representation. Even the shadows are carefully laid out to support an aesthetic of realism. The references to painterly tradition are then thematically strengthened by allusions within the cards themselves to Germanic folk tradition. The German oak, for instance, was a well-known icon and was also frequently used in Nazi schoolbooks, while the dancing bear Atta Troll (which appears on the Goebbels card) was a folk character created by Heinrich Heine.[28]

Like Heartfield and others who fought Fascism in the public sphere, Thomas Mann also draws on the fairy tale. In *Doctor Faustus*, he uses the

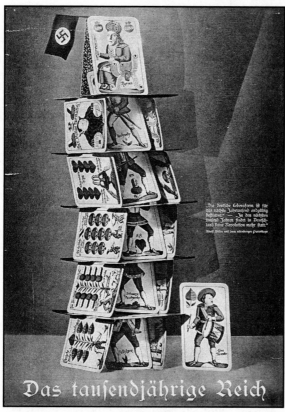

Fig. 16. John Heartfield's "The Thousand-year Reich" (1934). Courtesy of Akademie der Künste, Berlin.

fairy tale to pose a counterweight to Fascist claims on folk traditions. In Leverkühn's conversation with the devil, his demonic interlocutor allegorizes the artist's pain as a variation on Hans Christian Andersen's tale of the "Little Mermaid" who wanted legs so that she could walk on land and win the love of an earthly prince. Like the mermaid, Leverkühn wants to be reassured that he has a soul. He wonders whether his coldness—he has never loved, and his only act of sexual intercourse took place with a prostitute—will even permit him to claim that he has one. Sterility is the danger that threatens to overwhelm him and to make him impotent as a composer. It is for the sake of his art that he makes his "pact."

The devil tempts the composer with the thought that the pains he will feel after he concludes his pact are "pains that one gladly and proudly takes in the bargain with pleasures so enormous, pains such as one knows from a fairy tale, pains like slashing knives, like those the little mermaid felt in the beautiful human legs she acquired for a tail."[29] The pains the mermaid suffers at every step will also afflict Leverkühn as he struggles with his musical compositions within the darkened room of the farmhouse where he has taken refuge during the twenty-four productive years allotted to him by his Faustian bargain.

In presenting Leverkühn's illness as both the motor force of his creativity and the cause of his ultimate breakdown, Mann was able to add yet more layers of allegory to that of the Andersen fairy tale. The dialogue of the "pact" that is offered up by the narrator at the very center of the book (chapter 25) marks the moment in which the various narrative strands will combine into the dominant theme of the Apocalypse. This theme proceeds on every level: the artist's struggle to complete his compositions before the end of his "hour-glass years," which are inexorably running out; Germany's declining fortunes (the bombing of Leipzig in April 1944 is mentioned at the beginning of chapter 26); Leverkühn's successive loss of all those whom he has loved; and finally, rising almost as a counterpoint, the description of his two final musical compositions, the "Apocalypse" and the "Lamentation of Dr. Faustus."

I have already drawn the parallel between the stated ambition of the composer and that of the novelist Thomas Mann—that of "taking back" the great optimistic works of German culture, Beethoven's "Ode to Joy" and the ending of Goethe's *Faust*. Leverkühn's aesthetics elucidate Mann's as well, for Leverkühn practices a poetics of quotation. Zeitblom explains that the "Apocalypse" "attempts to subsume within it, as it were, the life-history of music, from its premusical, elemental, magically rhythmic stages on up to its most complicated perfection."[30] In the violin concerto he writes for his ill-fated friend Rudi Schwerdtfeger, he includes quotations from Tartini's "Devil's Trill" sonata;[31] and in the final composition, the symphonic cantata "Lamentation of Doctor Faustus," he marshals, "precisely as if in a résumé, all the elements of music conceivable as bearers of expression."[32]

In the same way, Mann has used quotations and multiple references from the German cultural past in order to flesh out his composition, from Dürer's woodcuts of the Apocalypse to the chapbook published by Spies in 1587. Some of these may even be hidden. For instance, Mann's idea of linking Leverkühn's artistic creativity to the figure of the "little mermaid" may have originated in a text far older than Andersen's: there is a depiction of a hermaphroditic "sea spirit" in the very collection of Faust materials that Mann consulted during the time of writing his novel. This was the reedition of a

1599 version of the Faust stories by Georg Rudolff Widman and of a book of "Faust's conjurations" (*Fausts Höllenzwang*) published in 1846 in Stuttgart by J. Scheible.[33] The book presents an engraving of a curious mythological figure (fig. 17) that just precedes the *Höllenzwang* section mentioned by Mann in his account of his reading. It appears to be an illustration of a sea spirit that Faust conjured up in order to pry riches from the bottom of the ocean.[34] Three heads—a snarling lion, a large-toothed jackal or wolf, and a human head—are crowned by a ring of fire. The human head is horned and bearded (this contrasts with the large breasts), but the hermaphrodite's expression is serene. In addition to two feathery wings (suggesting that the figure is a "fallen angel"), he/she has two arms and hands that end in snake heads or small duck bills. The two legs are scaly and terminate in a fish tail and a snake. In the background, a bat, a devil riding a goat, a shrouded figure bearing a torch, a burning skull, and various animal and human bones are to be seen. The creature seems to balance itself on the water, perhaps the river Styx. The three heads recall Cerberus, the Roman god of the under-world, while the snakelike endings on the hands and the hermaphroditic breasts and beard make her/him more nearly Protean—a creature who can assume any form.

More than the pathetic image of the fairy-tale mermaid, this image of the merman/mermaid suggests power and control. It suggests the advan-tages that might come from an alliance with demonic forces and also shows the imaginative richness of the mythological tradition out of which Mann fashioned his novel.

Montage Aesthetics in *Doctor Faustus*

Mann's aesthetic strategy in *Doctor Faustus* sprang from the belief that in-vention is often just a rediscovery and rephrasing of a shared mythic cul-ture. In *The Genesis of a Novel*, he writes of his "growing inclination . . . to look upon all life as a cultural product taking the form of mythic clichés."[35] The author's backward reach toward the old folktales of Faust is motivated not just ideologically but aesthetically—as a logical consequence of his be-lief that the mythic past is closer to life experience. There is something of this "return to origins" in Mann's *Doctor Faustus*. In adapting the *Historia*, the author recovers some of the irreverent folk spirit of the Faust tale. For instance, Leverkühn tells Zeitblom of his travels to the depths of the oceans, where he has had the experience of observing aquatic creatures that

Fig. 17. *Jesuitarum libellus*, or the powerful sea spirit. From J. Scheible's 1846 reimpression of *Fausts Höllenzwang*.

live in total darkness unless they create their own source of light, and into other galaxies.[36] These are modeled after the magical voyages of Faust in the folk tradition, which were themselves symptomatic of the dawn of Renaissance humanism and the historical shift away from divine explanations toward scientific observation.

Like Spies's chapbook itself, Mann's work is a compendium of different stories and descriptions of the marvelous. The sense of juxtaposition and layering is intensified by the temporal structure, if only because the time of writing (Mann's and Zeitblom's) continually obtrudes upon the events being written about. Thus, Leverkühn's catastrophic end, which is known from the beginning of the writing (the year 1943), prefigures historical events that had not even come to pass until 1945. Certain passages—such as the dialogue with the devil, which plays such a central role in the structure of the entire work—were, according to their author, "unthinkable without the psychological experience of the Gestapo cellars."[37] This kind of parallelism with the historical circumstance of writing (Mann finished that chapter on February 20, 1945, when the Gestapo threat was still a real one), makes this novel a kind of autobiography of its own composition. It is as though Mann, in writing *Doctor Faustus*, were also writing history.

In fact, it is not just the narrator who protests, "I am not writing a novel";[38] in his diaries and letters from 1943 to 1946, published in the volume *Selbstkommentare*, Mann talks again and again of the "montage" construction of his work. The montage principle in *Doctor Faustus* is evidenced in its almost encyclopedic quality, which presents a compendium of German culture, including Wendell Kretschmar's lecture on Beethoven's Piano Sonata, opus 111; a detailed description of Dürer's first woodcut in the "Apocalipsis cum Figuris" series of 1498; long passages in sixteenth-century Lutheran German (Enfried Kumpf's university lectures, Adrian Leverkühn's letter to Zeitblom about his first encounter with the prostitute Esmeralda, and his final lamentation and farewell to his friends); as well as extended passages on music theory that Mann based on the music of Schönberg and on Adorno's writings on the composer.

Thus montage—in the sense of the juxtaposition of different and even heterogeneous materials out of which the reader is asked to construct an interpretation—is a basic compositional aspect of *Doctor Faustus*. It extends even to the triple temporal frame (narrated time/narrative time/time of the author's composition). Beyond this, the frame has yet another dimension—the time of the reading. This is evidenced by the circumstance that *Doctor Faustus* reads differently half a century after its writing. If Mann could write to his friend Pavel Eisner, in May of 1946, that he had written "a horribly German novel—practically the novel of a Germany that made a pact with the devil,"[39] today Mann's novel, like Goethe's *Faust*, speaks to contemporary issues of intellectual cowardice and artistic compromise that go far beyond national boundaries.

In League with the Devil: *Mephisto* as Novel and Film

A decade before the publication of *Doctor Faustus* by his father, Klaus Mann had explored the theme of the artist's pact with Nazism in his novel *Mephisto*.

The novel, published while the family was in exile in 1936, was made into a film by the Hungarian director István Szabó in 1981. Whereas Thomas Mann depicts the epic struggle of a whole nation around the issues of cultural identity and artistic integrity, *Mephisto* as both novel and film shines a focused light on the particular case of German intellectuals who chose to remain in Germany during the Nazi period.

The novel takes much of its material from the life of the actor Gustaf Gründgens (1899–1963), who was considered one of the greatest actors of the German stage. In the early phases of his career, Gründgens befriended Klaus and his sister Erika (the eldest children of Thomas Mann) and produced two not altogether successful plays by Klaus, in which the threesome also starred. He and Erika briefly married but were already divorced in 1929. Nevertheless, the friendship between the three young artists continued until about 1932.

The Mann family fled Germany in 1933. Gründgens also considered whether or not to return from a film assignment abroad—after all, he was a declared communist, and his homosexuality was well-known. But it was here that he made the crucial decision of his career—the decision that made him into an example of the artist who tries to declare himself above politics. Reassured through fellow actor Emmy Sonnemann, who had married Hermann Göring, that his return was safe, Gründgens accepted the directorship of the Prussian State Theater. Unlike other German cultural institutions that were under the aegis of his rival Joseph Goebbels, this theater came under Göring's jurisdiction in his capacity as prime minister of Prussia; later, Göring further shielded his protégé by naming him a member of the Ministry of State.[40]

At no period of his life was Gründgens a Nazi; even his enemies concede this. During his time of service in the Hitler years, and with Göring's protection, he continued to employ Jews in his theater ("I decide who is a Jew," Göring is reported to have said); and he obtained the release of friends who had been arrested by the Nazis. The actor was rehabilitated rather quickly after 1945 and was allowed to resume his career as early as March 1946.[41]

For Klaus Mann, who had known Gründgens as the idealistic young communist with dreams of creating a "workers' theater" that would revolutionize spectators, the actor's collaboration with the Nazis was a betrayal. His description of the hero of his novel, Hendrik Höfgen, says as much: "He betrays everything that he had heretofore claimed to believe in. He sells his soul for a questionable career rise in the Third Reich. . . . This book is *not* written in accusation of a specific person, rather it accuses *that* careerist, *that* German intellectual who sells and betrays his soul."[42] The Faustian note sounded by the author is all the more appropriate since, like Gründgens, his character Hendrik Höfgen becomes known for his role as Mephistopheles in Goethe's *Faust*. In the end, he fails as an artist as well. When he tries to play Hamlet, the character he is trying to play rises up in his conscience and reproaches him: "You are not Hamlet, you don't have the nobility that only suffering and experience can give. You are merely the monkey of power, a clown to entertain murderers."[43]

Gründgens and his family regarded the novel as a defamatory attack. The novel was published only in East Germany and abroad during the lifetime of the actor. Klaus Mann committed suicide in 1949, shortly after learning that the Berlin publisher Georg Jacobi had decided to renege on his decision to publish *Mephisto*, for fear of offending the famous actor. Mann's letter to Jacobi—one of his last—reflects the bitterness of the artist who has fought on the side of the powerless: "Gründgens is a success: why should you publish a book that could seem to be directed against him? Avoid risk above all! Ally yourself with the powers that be! Swim with the stream! You know where it leads: to those very concentration camps, that you can claim later to have known nothing about."[44] After the death of Gründgens in 1963 (apparently from an accidental overdose of sleeping pills), his adopted son Peter Gorski—who had directed Gründgens in a 1960 film version of *Faust*—successfully sued to prevent the work, which had finally been published in 1965 by the West German firm Nymphenburger Verlagshandlung, from being further published and distributed. It was not until 1981, fifteen years after the death of Gründgens, that the novel was published in West Germany with official sanction. It became an immediate bestseller.[45] The film by Hungarian director István Szabó, made in the same year, won the Academy Award in 1982 for best foreign film.

Szabó's film forcefully poses the questions about power, politics, and art. He goes beyond Klaus Mann's novel in portraying Hendrik Höfgen (played by Karl Maria Brandauer) as an actor who changes his interpretation of his roles depending on who is in power—in Klaus Mann's description, he is a "tragic clown, a diabolical Pierrot."[46] Höfgen's first Mephisto, performed during the Weimar Republic, is a seductive and beguiling corrupter of Faust. "You are what you are," he cajoles, urging Faust to enjoy life to the fullest. His interpretation is the appropriate accompaniment to the creative explosion of Weimar Germany, along with its sense of doom and of time running out.

After Höfgen's return from exile with the help of the prime minister's wife, Lotte Lindenthal, he again secures the role of Mephistopheles. But this time he plays the role more harshly—Mephisto as eternal naysayer and destroyer. Enchanted, the prime minister (Hermann Göring is clearly intended in this characterization) invites Höfgen to visit him in his theater box during the intermission. The novel does not report their conversation; in the film, Szabó moves a later conversation between Höfgen and his protector into this scene. In the novel, the prime minister says, "Hidden in every real German isn't there a bit of Mephistopheles, a bit of the rascal and the ruffian? If we had nothing but the soul of Faust, what would become of us? It would be a pushover for our many enemies! No, no— Mephisto, too, is a German national hero. But it's better not to go around telling people that."[47]

In the film, the screenplay (by Szabó and Peter Dobai) expands on these statements. The prime minister praises Höfgen's portrayal of Mephisto as "holy evil" (das heilige Böse). He claims to have learned the actor's secret: the element of surprise that he works into the performance. "I think I can learn from you," he says. This statement is all the more portentous since, at the end of the film, the prime minister shows that he is planning his own grand production—but one that will take place on the stage of history. Here, Szabó adds a darker note to the role of art at the service of an evil regime— not only can it not remain apart but it actually encourages and inspires the criminal leaders.

Höfgen himself is a *Faustian* Mephistopheles, since he has made a pact with the Nazis in order to remain in Germany. Mephisto is his great role, the one he is destined for and that allows him most completely to express himself. This is what his Jewish colleague Dora Martin tells him, shortly before she goes into exile, without passing judgment: "I never take it amiss that someone is what he is."[48] You are what you are—these are Mephisto's words to Faust (1806).

When Höfgen comes to play Hamlet, he runs into the difficulties mentioned above. Here, especially, the dominant Nazi ideology causes some strange contortions in the actor's interpretation. The screenplay greatly expands the novel's account of Höfgen's lecture to journalists. According to

Höfgen (in the film version), Hamlet will be the "savior of the North, the preserver of blood and race." As a "Nordic man," he kills:

> Generations have made the great error of seeing Hamlet as neuras-
> thenic, as an Oedipal dreamer, as a pathological revolutionary, in
> short, as a decadent type. This is not how I see him. Hamlet is tough.
> It is not just my idea that you will now get to know him as an ener-
> getic and consequent man. Hamlet is also a danger for the German.
> We all are prone to brooding, and we have to overcome it. For the
> hour demands action and not just thoughts, especially not paralyz-
> ing reflections. Hamlet is the tragic contest between action and inac-
> tivity, between hesitation, brooding, and doing; and we, the bearers
> of German culture, know what to make of this. *Hamlet* is a popular
> [*volkish*] work, neither religious nor aristocratic nor bourgeois—it's
> a popular work the way the Greek tragedies were popular.[49]

Höfgen then argues for a "total theater" that will "mobilize" the audience—using the same words that he once used to describe the communist theater he envisioned before the Nazis came to power.

The film medium offers Szabó the chance to make ironic comments on his characters. At the birthday party for the prime minister, the entire theater has been decked out with Nazi flags and insignia (fig. 18). In his speech, Höfgen says that "without patrons, art is but a bird with lame wings"—whereupon the camera draws back to show the eagle of the Reich displayed on a Nazi flag. At a celebration honoring "Nordic" sculpture—giant imitations of classical nudes favored by Nazi cultural potentates—the giant Hellenic statues, emblems of Nazi self-important posturing, dwarf the humans who circulate among them. In this scene, the actor is also invited to sign what purports to be a guest list for the exhibition. Here, Szabó plays up the Faustian theme and subtly indicates that Höfgen has signed a pact with Nazism. Later in Paris, Höfgen meets his former wife, Barbara, who urges him to leave Germany. Wrapping himself in a cloak reminiscent of his Mephisto role, he asks himself, "Freedom—for what?" and then descends into the metro as though into hell.

Parallelism in the shooting and editing of scenes also plays a symbolic role. In his office at the theater, Höfgen is presented with a petition by his enemy, the actor Hans Miklas. Miklas joined the Nazi Party when it still promised to be a socialist workers' party. He is now disenchanted and has

Fig. 18. The actor Hendrik Höfgen (Klaus Maria Brandauer) makes a Faustian bargain with Nazism in István Szabó's *Mephisto* (1981). MOKEP Hungarofilm.

begun agitating against the regime. Now that Höfgen has the upper hand, he decides to curry favor with the prime minister by denouncing Miklas. Soon afterwards, Miklas is arrested and taken to a wooded area, where he is summarily shot in the back. The disdainful way that Höfgen receives Miklas in his office is later echoed by the prime minister's disdain for Höfgen when the actor seeks him out at Nazi headquarters and tries to obtain the pardon of a communist actor, Otto Ulrichs.

Szabó's use of cinematic resources is especially notable in the ending. Both novel and film end with Höfgen's assertion that he is "only an actor." But in the novel, Höfgen utters these words while sobbing on his mother's breast. Despite his public success with Hamlet, he knows he has failed. Coming home from the theater, he is harassed, offstage as it were, by an intruder at his window who threatens him with the coming defeat of the Nazis with whom he is so closely associated. The intruder also reminds him that he has failed to save the life of his friend Otto Ulrichs, who never gave up the fight against Nazism.

Szabó's stronger ending cuts instead from the theater decked out in Nazi flags in celebration of the prime minister's birthday party (the novel actually begins with these festivities) to a luridly lit nighttime scene between the prime minister and Höfgen. The prime minister has Höfgen summarily driven to the newly constructed stadium in Berlin, in complete mystery and in a manner reminiscent of the earlier arrest and execution of Hans Miklas. They arrive in quick march—five SS officers, Höfgen, and the prime minister. Mocking the actor, the prime minister explains that this is where real theater will happen: "What power is looking down on you here? Do you feel the power? *This* is theater! This is where I would put on a performance! Listen to the echo:

Hendrik Höfgen! [The prime minister shouts the actor's name, which echoes loudly.] We will rule over all of Europe and the whole world. We will create the thousand-year Reich!" Like Miklas in the execution scene, Höfgen is ordered to walk away from the armed SS officers. When he reaches the center of the arena, the searchlights come on and blind him. As Höfgen stumbles helplessly about in a crossing of searchlights (which to some alert spectators will appear as the devil's crossroads), the prime minister taunts the artist: "How do you like *this* light? This is the real light!"

A strong wind comes up, and Höfgen, buffeted about and assaulted by the mocking sound of his echoing name, vainly tries to shield himself from the blinding light, not knowing what fate is reserved for him. As he whimpers, "What do they want from me? I'm only an actor!" the film ends. It is 1936, the year of the Olympics and the great Nazi spectacle in Nuremberg—both of which will be filmed by Leni Riefenstahl, another artist who put her art in the service of power and ended up helping the Nazi cause. Höfgen ends where he began—as an outsider to the forces he sought to harness to the chariot of his own fame. Szabó's film offers no solutions but asks whether Höfgen's Faustian bargain was worth it.

Klaus Mann's novel was published a full ten years before his father's *Doctor Faustus*. The letter that the father writes to the son in December of 1936 seems, in retrospect, momentous with literary anticipation:

> Our time has rediscovered evil. . . . The new and signal spirit of our era is a greater clarity and emotional investment in morality, an almost childlike fairy-tale conception of evil. . . . The best and most important moments in your book are perhaps those where the idea of evil is communicated and shown, where the dramatic hero discovers his penchant for it and then sells his soul to it. It is an authentic pact with the devil. That the devil is among us again is surely worth something for literature.[50]

Six years later, the son writes to the father from his U.S. Army post in Camp Ritchie, Maryland, about the latter's new work in progress, without, however, calling attention to his own previous treatment of the Faust theme:

> So you're mixing things musical, which you always loved, with medicine and unfortunately also theology ["Medizin und leider auch Theologie," 355–56]! That will be quite a little brew! Inspiration through illness! Pathology of genius? Art thanks to a pact with the devil? I can

foresee pleasures of a new and bold, but at the same time of a well-trodden and familiar nature. Echoes of "Death in Venice"—*if I am not mistaken?* But everything writ larger and more unearthly, in the style of the gothic-magical . . . outstanding! *I am all for it!* And would not be surprised if this should prove to be your most remarkable brainchild.[51]

The problem of the artist is one that is common to both *Mephisto* and *Doctor Faustus*, and one that runs through much of Thomas Mann's pre-war work, from *Buddenbrooks* to *The Magic Mountain*. The difference of emphasis is as much a matter of the timing of the works' writing and pub-lication as of their approach to the subject. Klaus Mann published his story of Fascist collusion in 1936, in the midst of his activist opposition to politi-cal developments in Germany (his first novel, *Flucht in den Norden* [Flight to the North] had already dramatized the life of an anti-Fascist heroine). The book is intended as a warning to those of his fellow intellectuals who remain in Germany, a way of reaching, through fiction, the same audience that he addressed in lectures and essays. In Amsterdam, before his emigra-tion to the United States, he published an anti-Fascist literary journal, *Die Sammlung* (The Collection), and he also collaborated with his sister Erika in a political cabaret, "The Pepper Mill," that the siblings started in 1933 in Munich and then moved to Zürich in the same year. In 1940–41, he was the editor and publisher of the new literary journal with a progressive agenda, *Decision*. He also reported on the Spanish Civil War and wrote for *Stars and Stripes* during his stint in the U.S. Army after enlisting in 1943.[52]

In 1939, Klaus Mann sent a letter to prominent writers and artists who had remained in Germany, begging them to use their influence to turn public opinion away from war and warning that none of the work they produced under Fascism would have any lasting value: "An author who has remained in Hitler's country has buried himself alive."[53] Among others, the letter was addressed to Gustaf Gründgens.

Honored with the 1929 Nobel Prize in literature, Thomas Mann, while in exile from Germany, was a prominent public intellectual whose opin-ion was widely sought after. His letter to the dean of the University of Bonn upon the occasion of their withdrawing his honorary doctorate in 1936 was widely translated and reprinted; Mann reports that young dissidents in Hitler's Germany learned his outspoken attack on German militarism by heart so that they would not be caught with the compromising text.[54] From October 1940 to August 1942, he broadcast warnings to his compatriots over the BBC, broadcasts that were also listened to in several other German-speaking countries.[55] In the United States, he was a frequent lecturer and commentator on Germany and the war. His essay on Hitler, "This Man Is My Brother," appeared in *Esquire*, while "How to Win the War" appeared in the *Atlantic Monthly*. "The Coming Victory of Democracy," written in Switzerland, formed the basis for a lecture tour throughout the country after Mann moved to the United States in 1938. Mann writes that for him the German distinction between *Dichter* (creative writer) and *Schriftsteller* (writer) does not hold—both roles are inextricably linked; the thoughts expressed in an essay can give rise to a novel and vice versa.[56]

Doctor Faustus comes out of that gestation period of Thomas Mann's active essay-writing, broadcasting, and lecturing about the catastrophic political developments in Germany. Since, however, it was published just after the war, unlike *Mephisto*, it does not constitute a warning against the rising tide of Nazism in Germany and the issue of artistic compromise. It is not the artist but the narrator, Serenus Zeitblom, who lives through the war years in Germany and who exemplifies the intellectual's compromise with Fascism. The artist's descent into madness occurs in 1930 (ironically, the year after Thomas Mann's Nobel Prize!). The last ten years of his life correspond to the rise of German Fascism and the beginning of the war, but by then he has retreated into insanity. This does not make *Doctor Faustus* any less apocalyptic than *Mephisto*—instead, the triangle of artist, illness, and the demonic have an even broader reach. Thomas Mann, true to his prophetic letter to his son that the return of the devil in our time "is surely worth something for literature," has created a work that moves beyond its own time and place to suggest that the end of Hitler does not necessarily mean that catastrophe has been averted.

Jewish Exile: Else Lasker-Schüler

If Höfgen refuses exile because he "needs the German language," Else Lasker-Schüler's play *Ichundich* (I and I—*ich* is the German form of the first person pronoun) dramatizes the tragedy of the uprooted artist. The poet-protagonist wrestles with her Faustian and Mephistophelean selves. The work is at once the expression of the poet's deeply divided and alienated self and an apocalyptic dramatization of Nazi conquest. Written in 1941 at the height of Hitler's campaign for world domination, the play puts the poet's suffering in the foreground.[57] A prologue states that she writes in her own blood with quills pulled from her own feathers—the same feathers that allowed her to fly away from the Nazis. She says that she writes on rusty parchment paper but would prefer to write on her own heart—as it turns out, the theater curtain is heart-shaped, reinforcing the idea that the play takes place within the poet's own soul. The poet explains that the drama that will unfold is the retrospective story of how her divided selves came to be reconciled again and thus comes from beyond her earthly existence—from "the stillness of eternity." As such, it presents itself as a posthumous work.

During her years in Berlin, where she was part of the modernist circle that included Max Reinhardt, George Grosz, and Gottfried Benn, Lasker-Schüler regularly assumed the poetic persona and oriental costume of her alter ego "Prince Jussuf of Thebes." In 1933, an attack by Nazis forced her into exile in Switzerland; and in 1939, she immigrated to Israel, where she lived until her death in 1945 at the age of seventy-six.

The characters that people this poet's soul are eclectic, and the mise-en-scène of *Ichundich* further complicates things by presenting the onstage action as a rehearsal directed by the fabled expressionist German director Max Reinhardt. Moreover, the audience intervenes and comments. This audience is a grab bag of mythical and real personae: it includes the American comedic "Ritz Brothers" team (Al, Jimmy, and Harry Ritz appeared in vaudevilles, musicals, and films in the 1930s and 1940s); the Old Testament patriarchs Saul, David, and Solomon (a serious counterweight to the comedic threesome); Adon Swet (the editor-in-chief of *Ha'aretz*, an Israeli newspaper); the theater's doctor; and others.

The first act takes place near the King David tower in Jerusalem, in a spot that the inhabitants are said to call "the plain of Hell." Acts 2 through 4 move into the palace of hell and then to various surrounding locations, including a park outside the palace. The two selves of the poet are, as it turns out, Faust (who also takes on some aspects of Goethe) and Mephisto. Although the director, Max Reinhardt, makes clear from the outset that they are one and the same, they continually quarrel. Faust wants to be rid of Mephisto but is reminded that that's impossible—Mephisto is Faust's "own" devil. Even though the Nazis are burning Faust/Goethe's books, he is immortal—and Mephisto, for his part, cannot die.

In the second act, Marthe Schwerdtlein appears as a middle-aged version of Gretchen (she sits at her spinning wheel) and is now part blind and hard of hearing. It is she who is in charge of preparing the banquet ("tender, fallen angel wings" are being served) for Faust, Mephisto, and various Nazi personalities: Hermann Göring, Joseph Goebbels, Joachim von Ribbentrop, Heinrich Himmler, Alfred Rosenberg, and others. Mephisto is busy making a deal to supply oil to the Nazis "fresh from the source."

The banquet is interrupted as Hitler arrives in an attempt to stretch his empire over hell itself. But his entire army disappears in a sea of molten lava, still shouting "Heil Hitler." Faust/Goethe asks Mephisto to let him die with his countrymen—this is Lasker-Schüler's critique of the nationalism of German intellectuals during the Hitler era and her version of the pessimism Thomas Mann expressed concerning German culture at the end of *Doctor Faustus*. But Mephisto reminds him once again, "You are immortal, and I cannot die."

Mephisto then gives his own version of the Creation story, situating his own childhood in Eden. He fell along with man, he says, and left Paradise along with him—remaining steadfastly at the side of man after his fall into sin.[58] As Faust's personal devil, Mephisto then claims to belong to the poet's own childhood. When, at the end of act 4, hell is abandoned to the invading Nazis (led by Hitler), the poet's selves reunite into the undivided child that represents at once the poet's soul and the innocent childhood of humanity. The exiled devils ascend to heaven once more.

In the fifth and final act, the "princely poet" (a reference to Lasker-Schüler's Prince of Thebes persona) is sitting in a garden in Jerusalem, talking to a scarecrow and to the newspaper editor-in-chief, Adon Swet (Sigrid Bauschinger intimates that the scarecrow may represent "the spirit of poetry").[59] They agree that the riddle of existence will never be solved here on earth, whereupon the poet gently expires.

Margarete Kupper calls this play "the final attempt of the poet to unify her spiritual-poetic existence."[60] The decades that have passed since its original date of composition now make its collage structure and mixing of characters from different time periods and ontological levels—from the mythical to the fictional and historic—much more palatable. The first editors of Lasker-Schüler's posthumous works judged the play severely and refused to publish it in its entirety on the grounds that it would damage her reputation. Its first stage performance was in 1979 in Düsseldorf, thirty-four years after the death of the poet.[61]

Lasker-Schüler stages her battle between good and evil as a personal drama taking place within one human soul. It is important to bear in mind that this is the work of an exile and also a work that represents the poet's "last words," or testament. The poet's identification with Faust/Goethe is accomplished to the extent that she embodies, in her own mind, the old Faust at the end of Goethe's work—and therefore produces the mise-en-scène of her own death. In the "afterword," the poet who has been witnessing the performed drama survives to give the commentary—yet her final exclamation, "God is *there*," is circumscribed by doubt. Faust, as we well know, also died happily, imagining that he was hearing the sounds of workers' shovels reclaiming new land from the sea—but it was the lemures, digging his grave. There is no solving the riddle of existence on this side of life, the poet reminds us.[62]

The Artist under Fascism

The experience of Fascism is one from which our world has still not recovered. It was the powerful irruption of the irrational into politics, in alliance with capitalist interests who feared, above anything else, the loss of political, social, and economic control to the rising tide of revolutionary reforms demanded by an increasingly articulate and aware working class.

Loss of control means loss of hegemony, if we recall Gramsci's formulation of hegemony as the ability of the ruling class to impose its worldview and to pass off its assumptions about such things as property and morality as "common sense." It's no surprise to see intellectuals, writers, and artists on both sides of this divide in Germany turning to the Faust myth in order to ground their claim to correct thinking, for the lessons of the Faust story already bore the mantle of common sense. Yet as a narrative, it was still open to interpretation. Whoever could most convincingly arrogate for themselves the "good," visionary Faust as precedent would be well on the way to winning the cultural war for legitimacy, sticking their opponent with the onus of the "bad," damned Faust.

Yet even this opposition is complicated by the insertion of Mephistopheles into the debate, a complication symptomatically signaled by Rosenberg's differentiation of the negative demonic (the Mephistophelean Jew) with the positive demonic (the Luciferan German). Thomas Mann will suggest, through his narrator, that the devil that appears to Adrian Leverkühn springs from his inner creative forces—forces that destroy him even as they are the necessary condition for his art. Klaus Mann will have the Nazi minister claim that in every good German there is an element of Mephistopheles as well as Faust. In Lasker-Schüler, the Mephistophelean and the Faustian will embody the artist's split selves.

The figure of the artist stands at the center of many of these works. The artist as maker of worlds is subject to that same impulse with which Goethe imbues the Creator in his prologue to *Faust*: the impulse to test his creation to see if it will withstand the power of his archenemy. In Thomas Mann's *Doctor Faustus*, the composer succumbs to the wager, forfeiting his sanity and his health in order to bring forth his artistic productions; in Klaus Mann's *Mephisto*, the artist compromises with the authorities and proves himself a tool of the Fascist state. The 1936 novel and István Szabó's 1981 film end somewhat differently, but both dramatize the pathetic moment when the actor realizes that he has forfeited not only his integrity but also his autonomy. In Else Lasker-Schüler's *Ichundich*, the poet's soul becomes the stage for the war between the forces of good and evil, and the play ends with the poet's death.

That these opponents of Fascism chose the figure of the artist as the central character of their dramas points to the fact that each of them was an artist who had to pay the price for political opposition by going into exile. Utopian socialists, the subject of the next chapter, privileged the workers or the rulers who allied themselves with workers. Faust becomes a maker of worlds and an agitator for social change in the writings of Anatoli Lunacharski in Russia, Léon Blum in France, and Hanns Eisler and Volker Braun in the German Democratic Republic.

3 Socialist Visions: Faust and Utopia

In the last act of Goethe's *Faust*, Mephistopheles has commanded the lemures, known in classical mythology as kinless and hungry ghosts, to dig a grave for Faust. But Faust, who has just been blinded by Care, thinks that they are building a dike against the sea in order to wrest from it new land for human habitation. In a last, utopian vision, he imagines creating a new Eden, sheltered by the dikes, while the tempest rages outside—not a secure paradise, but one that will need to be continually defended (11575–80).

If this Eden could be achieved, he says, he might finally pronounce the fateful words of the Faustian bargain to Mephistopheles—he might say, to the passing moment, "tarry yet, thou art so fair." In other words, Faust thinks that such an achievement would be worth the forfeit of his soul. Faust expires while holding on to that vision for the future: "Foretasting such high happiness to come, / I savor now my striving's crown and sum" (11585–86).

Mephistopheles now believes that he holds Faust—but he has overlooked that Faust spoke of a future happiness, not a present one. His injunction to the passing moment was a hypothetical one. He dies "striving," and this is what saves him. As the angels descend, they claim Faust's soul: "Whoever strives in ceaseless toil, / Him may we grant redemption" (11936–37).

Although not explicitly socialist (Faust does not articulate how property rights would be distributed in the new "Eden"), Faust's final utopian vision has served as the springboard for socialist thought and literature in Germany, France, and Russia.

The German Democratic Republic: *Faust*, Part 3

The leaders of the newly formed German Democratic Republic (GDR) in 1949 saw themselves as the legitimate heirs of German anti-Fascism. It was in the GDR that political leaders were chosen from among those who had been militant opponents of the Hitler regime. This was a circumstance that lent a particular legitimacy to a Germany stigmatized by World War II and the Holocaust (and which later made it difficult to attack these same leaders when they introduced repressive cultural policies).[1] One of the first tasks was to reclaim German culture and to purify it from Fascist influences. To this end, the writer Johannes R. Becher founded the Kulturbund zur demokratischen Erneuerung Deutschlands (Cultural Alliance for the Democratic Renewal of Germany) in 1945. One year later, Alexander Abusch, another leading intellectual figure, published *Der Irrweg einer Nation* (The False Path of a Nation).[2] Abusch characterized the Hitler years as a major deviation in German history that had been heroically resisted by the German Communist Party, many of whose members had fallen as martyrs to the cause of resistance against Nazism. Both Becher and Abusch subsequently became ministers of culture in the new socialist Germany.

When the GDR came into being in 1949 on the two-hundredth anniversary of Goethe's birth, the connection to German classical culture, and especially to Goethe, became a cornerstone of the official ideology. The year 1949 was filled with celebrations of Goethe's legacy.[3] In a preface to the celebratory Goethe volume brought out by the state of Thüringen, Abusch praised Goethe as "the highest example of the creative human being, of the great worker at his life's work." He also praised Goethe for having contributed to the German spirit of national unity. Becher, who appeared at the Goethe celebrations in Weimar alongside Thomas Mann, called for a "Goethe-renaissance," which, in his words, would be "synonymous with the resurrection of our people."[4]

The new German state was thus firmly rooted in the notion of an unbroken continuity with German classicism. Faust's utopian vision of a "free people" on "acres free" also lent cultural weight to the GDR's policy of reunification (under a socialist government). In 1962, the general secretary of the ruling SED (Sozialistische Einheitspartei Deutschlands), Walter Ulbricht, publicly proclaimed that the GDR constituted the third and as yet unwritten part of Goethe's drama:

> It is only at the end of his days that Goethe allows Faust to realize, as an old man, that the greatest happiness comes from the creative, collaborative work of freed people. . . . Goethe does not say what the collaborative work of the freed people on free land amounts to—he

leaves it open. What's actually missing here is a third part of *Faust*. Goethe couldn't write it, because the time was not ripe. In the developing capitalist order, an order of exploitation, war, and repression, the third part of *Faust* could not yet be written.

It's only much more than a hundred years later—long after Goethe had to put down his pen forever—that the workers and farmers, the clerks and mechanics, the scientists and technicians, and all those who work in the GDR, have begun to write this third part of *Faust* with their work and with their struggle for peace and socialism.[5]

Moreover, a few months before, Abusch had stated that this vision was a mere utopia no longer: "scientific socialism," as exemplified in the Soviet Union and other socialist states united in brotherhood, had made that vision a reality. The marshes that Faust spoke of were those of the old capitalist world that would be dried out and made habitable by socialism. History had proven Marx's dictum correct: human beings are social animals and can only realize their freedom in society. True freedom and the free development of personality are only possible in a society that has eliminated the exploitation of one person by another.[6]

The Russian Revolution: Faust Abdicates to Let the People Rule

The alliance of Faust with socialism was not a new one. Already in 1908, the Russian revolutionary Anatoli Vasilievich Lunacharski had written a play entitled *Faust i gorod* (*Faust and the City*). Lunacharski called his work a "reader's play"—it was not meant to be performed. Written in exile in Italy where he had fled to escape arrest, the play was revised and completed in 1916, just before Lenin asked Lunacharski to return as people's commissar for education in 1917. In its choice of subject, its plot outline, and its poetics, *Faust and the City* contains in seed form many of the conflicts that would eventually shape Soviet cultural policy.

Lunacharski had received a humanist education; even before completing his baccalaureate in 1895 in Kiev, he had gone to study philosophy for a year in Zürich. His revolutionary activities as a member of the Social Democratic Workers' Party, to which Lenin and Trotsky also belonged, led to his arrest in Moscow in 1899. Soon after his release, he was again arrested in Kiev for holding a lecture on the playwright Henrik Ibsen in which he claimed that Ibsen's tragedies reflected the death of individualism. The

German critic Jochen-Ulrich Peters argues that from the beginning, literary and world-philosophical problems were the starting point for his political activity.[7]

Lunacharski considered himself a "poet of the revolution"; exiled in Europe for ten years, he followed the Paris avant-garde closely and wrote reviews on theater and painting for the establishment Russian newspapers. At the same time, he participated actively in Lenin's revolutionary newspaper, *Vpered*. The exposure to the avant-garde was a crucial phase in the development of Lunacharski's aesthetics and was later to have considerable resonance in cultural debates of the new Soviet state. On the one hand, he applauded the avant-gardists' critique of bourgeois art; but on the other hand, it was Soviet policy to claim that the proletariat was the true heir to Russian culture and hence to the humanist tradition. This paradox accounts for many of the problems that faced Lunacharski when he was put in charge of education and cultural policy in 1917.

As the people's commissar for education, Lunacharski instituted a policy of instruction in the humanist cultural heritage, based on the German model of education, alongside technical training. Lunacharski believed that the liberation brought about by the revolution should make the study of literature, art, and philosophy, hitherto the province of the upper class, available to all. At the same time, he avoided the cult of personality that was later to characterize the Fascist appropriation of Goethe. In an essay written in 1932, the year before his death, he emphasized Goethe's conflicted relationship with the feudal and petit bourgeois environment of Weimar. While assessing Goethe's inheritance as "an enormous treasure," Lunacharski is at pains to point out that, as far as Marxists are concerned, his life was not altogether successful. Although he dreamed of a society where individuals could fully develop their possibilities, in reality he suffered from the limitations imposed on him by circumstance.[8] Lunacharski quotes approvingly from Friedrich Engels, who wrote:

> There is a continuing battle within him [Goethe] between the poet of genius who feels revulsion at the wretchedness of his environment, and the cautious offspring of the Frankfurt patrician or the Weimar privy-councilor who finds himself compelled to come to terms with and accustom himself to it. Goethe is thus at one moment a towering figure, at the next petty; at one moment an obstinate, mocking

genius full of contempt for the world, at the next a circumspect, unexacting, narrow philistine. Not even Goethe was able to conquer the wretchedness of Germany; on the contrary, it conquered him, and this victory of wretchedness over the greatest of Germans is the most conclusive proof that it cannot be surmounted at all "from within."[9]

In the arts, Russian culture experienced a flowering of modernism after 1917, as artists rallied to the cause of revolution and sought to produce a revolutionary art. Influenced by French cubism and Italian futurism, the Russian "constructivist" movement organized itself around the Lef group (*Levyi front iskusstv,* "Left Front of the Arts"). The posters (by Alexander Rodchenko, Gustav Klutsis, Vavara Stepanova, and others) that brought the revolutionary message to people in graphic form, or that publicized the films of Dziga Vertov and Sergei Eisenstein, are now recognized as modernist works of the greatest importance.

Lunacharski's policies proved impractical in a country saddled with a 60 percent illiteracy rate. After 1920, Lenin ordered a more practical orientation of education. In the same year, the avant-garde was attacked in the newspaper *Pravda.* It was argued that art should be more accessible to the average person. Yet, as long as Lenin remained at the head of the Communist Party, Lunacharski's position was unchallenged. This was not only because of their early association but also because Lenin himself was steeped in the classical literary tradition. In 1917, he had quoted Goethe's *Faust* (without mentioning that they are Mephistopheles's lines) when outlining the policies that would be necessary to draw the working class into active participation in society: "It is utterly impossible to dispense with the help and the *leading role* of the practical organizers from among the 'people,' from among the factory workers and working peasants. . . . They must understand that . . . the historical moment has arrived when theory is being transformed into practice . . . For 'theory, my friend, is gray, but green is the eternal tree of life.'"[10]

In 1922, when Stalin became general secretary of the Communist Party, Lunacharski's influence began to fade. By 1925 the politicization of literature was declared—henceforth literature was to serve the people. Avant-garde movements like the Proletkult and the Lef group fell into disfavor. In 1928, with the introduction of the first five-year plan, Lunacharski was criticized for his failure to distinguish "between bourgeois and proletarian elements of culture."[11] Lunacharski was forced to resign as commissar in 1929, though he remained as director of a prestigious art institute and a member of the Central Executive Committee of the Communist Party. He died of a heart attack in 1933, just before he was to assume a post as ambassador to Spain.[12]

In retrospect, the play *Faust and the City* seems prophetic, not only of the revolution itself but also of the difficulties that accompanied the Soviets' development of an educational and cultural policy. The first scene finds Faust ruling as Duke of Wellentrotz and Trotzburg over the lands he has won from the sea. Although Faust is loved by his people, there are movements in the land for a democratic sharing of power. In particular, the populace is being stirred up by an old couple, Rebble and Envie (a radicalized and defiant Philemon and Baucis), who point out that the workers are enriching their masters. Faust himself is a benign despot, but his right-hand man Mephisto is hated, as is the incompetent judge whom Faust has appointed.

Faust himself is appalled at the human cost of the labor required to wrest new land from the waters. He is working on the invention of a steam machine that will replace human labor. Faust's dilemma mirrors Lunacharski's own later anguish over his official duties:

> I have built much, I am still building, and I shall go on building. But I am concerned that those who help me, and bear on their shoulders the most ungracious and burdensome part of the work, should be—well, more or less comfortable and contented. . . . But can I make them rich? Can they travel, broaden their minds by reading and art? . . . To my mind, every real man must have luxury as the air he breathes.[13]

Mephisto is intent on acting as the spoiler. He encourages the ruler's son, Faustulus, to abduct a young girl and then to kill the brother who tries to avenge her. The population takes advantage of the opportunity to demand a sharing of power, while Mephisto pushes Faustulus to rebel against his father and demand that Faust abdicate, leaving him to rule. Faust does abdicate, but without naming a successor. Faustulus leaves to raise an army, while the people elect two tribunes and proceed to build a democracy. Faust's daughter, Faustina, deserts her father and marries Gabriel, one of the tribunes.

In scene 8, the most symbolic scene of the play, Mephisto summons the armies of the dead to fight on the side of Faustulus: "The descendants of slaves have raised an insurrection! They mock your degenerate descendants! Come to the succour of Order!"[14] But he is quickly defeated when the celestial figure of Speranza (Hope) raises the more powerful army of the future: "You have summoned from their graves the ancestral oppressors; I will summon the bright descendants of those who seek freedom."[15] Undone, Mephisto claims Faustulus and withdraws from Trotzburg.

The final scene of the play finds Faust living incognito among his people as a plain citizen. He has been won over to the cause of democracy; meanwhile, he still works on his "iron worker," or steam engine. In a last gesture, he appears to the people before he dies and bequeaths them his invention. Rebble and Envie see that there is nothing more to rebel against and leave. Faust has triumphed over Mephistopheles's nihilism in the name of the workers: "We are the builders; you—the dust."[16]

Léon Blum: Faust and the French Popular Front

The reworking of the Faust material from a socialist perspective by Léon Blum, who was to become prime minister of France in 1936, predates Lunacharski's play by almost a decade. His *Nouvelles conversations de Goethe avec Eckermann* is a series of imaginary conversations about politics and society that purports to be a continuation of the original conversations with Goethe published by Johann Peter Eckermann in 1836. First published by the *Revue Blanche* in 1901 without the author's name, the book finally appeared under Blum's name in 1909.[17] In 1937, after Blum's resignation as prime minister, the volume was republished by Gallimard.

Blum situates these imaginary conversations from 1897 to 1900. Throughout, he maintains the historical perspective of a Goethe who would have lived through the historical events of the period since his death—the 1848 revolution, the Dreyfus Affair, and the course of French politics up to 1898 are the subjects of discussion, along with thoughts about social issues such as family life and the status of Jews in France. The Goethe Blum presents is objective, rational, and antiauthoritarian. For instance, Goethe has learned to question the family of his own childhood, where his father's opinions and decisions— like those of military officers or absolute rulers—were accepted without question. In such a family structure, he argues, "the education of children gradually results in a moral blindness. This has serious consequences. . . . Nothing is worse than a lack of discernment, for success in life as for the development of intelligence."[18] Here, Blum gives voice to his own views on education and the necessity for an informed and participatory citizenry.

During a conversation Blum dates to July 7, 1898, Goethe outlines a third part of *Faust*, which will argue for socialism. Faust previously fought for civilization—now he'll fight for justice and against inequality. In this new version, Faust and Mephistopheles will both figure as socialist agitators, with Mephistopheles cast as the pessimistic naysayer, the "pernicious influence which, by imperceptible deviations, derails and perverts all action. Because of it, every one of Faust's acts brings him only deception and sorrow."[19]

Faust attributes the negative attitude of Mephistopheles to his insufficient education; he believes that even rich people can be persuaded to give up their privileges in the interest of all, once they have been exposed to the idea of justice. His Faust, in this new formulation, rejects wealth, power, and bourgeois marriage. He advocates socialism, which, he says, must first assure everyone the necessary conditions for existence: "to be free, one first has to be."[20] Ultimately, the state becomes alarmed at the idea that the rich will be asked to make sacrifices on behalf of the populace, and Faust is thrown into prison along with Mephistopheles and the other socialist leaders. When Faust is released, because of his popularity with the people, this special treatment by the authorities makes him suspect.[21]

In a later episode, Mephistopheles leads the people in burning some newly invented labor-saving machines, on the grounds that workers will lose their jobs. Blum, through his character Faust, condemns this action and the assumption that technological progress and socialism are incompatible. As Lunacharski already suggested in *Faust and the City*, and as will become even clearer in the later writings of Volker Braun in the GDR, it is the ownership and use of technology, not technology itself, that poses the challenge to democratic socialism.

Blum's socialist utopian vision in the *Nouvelles conversations* is especially interesting in the light of the defeat of the Popular Front in 1937. The work almost seems to predict some of the frustrations that Blum would later experience as prime minister. For instance, when Faust enters parliament, his comrades refuse all discipline and division of labor, making the situation chaotic and ungovernable. This was, in fact, what the political leader later experienced, in his failed attempt to get the Socialist, Communist, and centrist parties to work together.[22]

In his *Nouvelles conversations*, Blum implies that Goethe would *necessarily* have reached these new insights from the perspective of 1898. Goethe speaks with Blum's voice when he speculates on why neither Rabelais nor Pascal entertained those very moral and political principles that later seemed so obviously right after the French Revolution. The answer is that we are all creatures of our time: "At a certain historical moment, human intelligence acquires something like a new sense."[23] Identifying at once with a posthumous Goethe speaking in 1898 and an imagined continuation of *Faust*, Blum situates his remarks in the context of the contemporary problems of 1897–1900.

Georg Lukács and the Faustian Dialectic

In his important study of Goethe, the Hungarian Marxist Georg Lukács also puts the Faust problematic in concrete form. *Goethe und Seine Zeit* (*Goethe and His Age*) was published in Bern in 1940, after the author had fled from the Nazis and was living in Russia. Instead of mining Goethe's work for its relevance to contemporary society, however, Lukács wants to uncover the way in which Goethe, in the very structure of his work, revealed his awareness of the social and political contradictions of his time—and most especially, his dawning awareness of class conflict and the problems that would eventually result from capitalism. As Fredric Jameson has argued, Lukács's historical-materialist presentation of Goethe shows how the given social context in which Goethe worked structured his thought.[24] Lukács includes Goethe among the great realist writers like Balzac and Thomas Mann who, despite being members of the bourgeoisie, represented in their works the social contradictions that would inevitably lead to the demise of their class.[25]

Lukács argues that, like his contemporary Hegel, Goethe moved toward a dialectical interpretation of history in which progress would be achieved by the collision of antithetical forces. Yet Lukács argues that Goethe's belief in progress—both that of society and of the "evolution" of the human species toward perfection—still makes him an old-fashioned creature of the Enlightenment. Goethe, he says, was tempted to view European history as the story of progress because he looked at it from the vantage point of the late eighteenth century: the Middle Ages had given way to the Reformation and the Renaissance, and notions of national and political liberty had led, during Goethe's lifetime, to the emancipation of the bourgeoisie, particularly as expressed by the French Revolution. The new ideology celebrated equality and the rights of humanity, along with the belief that human society could transform itself and its surroundings.[26] Although Goethe had been appalled by the excesses of the French Revolution, he regarded its outcome as essentially positive. From recent history, according to Lukács, Goethe drew the lesson that "the unceasing progress of the human species results from a chain of individual tragedies."[27]

Lukács sketches out his approach to *Faust* on multiple levels, from Faust the individual to Faust as representative of the evolution of the human species. In Lukács's view, both Faust and Mephistopheles are complex characters whose personae incorporate elements at war with one another. As a man inhabited by "two souls" (1112), Faust is torn between emotion and reason, a desire to enjoy life versus a desire to attain knowledge; between the urge to unite with nature and the desire to experience the highest forms of culture; between the desire for the highest personal happiness and the search for fulfillment in furthering the collective good of humanity. Moreover, he is not alone in this restlessness. Mephistopheles is also a dual character; he says he is "Part of that force which would / Do ever evil, and does ever good" (1335–36).

Nowhere does this appear more clearly than in the Gretchen episode.[28] Mephistopheles cynically aids Faust in seducing Margarete, but he makes their love impossible by killing her brother Valentin and providing the deadly sleeping potion that Margarete unknowingly administers to her mother. Yet he hasn't reckoned with the changes that this experience of true love will bring about in Faust. For the rest of the drama, she remains his vision of a lost ideal. Even his union with Helen of Troy does not transcend Margarete. This is all the more remarkable since even Faust realizes they never enjoyed perfect happiness—Mephistopheles was always there as the spoiler.

Lukács speaks of Goethe's belief that the realization of human potential is impossible without the experience of ideal love. The doomed love of Faust and Margarete is not just Mephistopheles's doing; it is inevitable in a class-bound society. Goethe, Lukács argues, despaired of his own era, where young men had to marry women from the "right" class to further their careers; true love was impossible since people could not freely choose their partners.[29] In this critique of the Gretchen episode, Mephistopheles appears in the guise that he will assume elsewhere in Lukács's critique: as the personification of the social perversion that comes about through capitalism.

This is not a simplistic equation, however; only when he enables Faust to offer Margarete some precious jewels is Mephistopheles's help directly linked to money. Rather, Goethe implies that the class differences in love create impediments that will ultimately doom that love. Mephistopheles's role as spoiler functions as a metaphor for those impediments.

In the Gretchen episode, Goethe dramatizes the dialectic of personal fulfillment; Faust as an individual has to move beyond what Lukács characterizes as "the small world" in order to realize his full potential. The "great world" becomes the setting for *Faust*, part 2. Here, Faust begins increasingly to assume a symbolic role, in which his evolution stands for that of humanity itself. Lukács argues that Goethe never faltered in his belief in the essential goodness and perfectibility of humankind. Central to this idea is the relation between thought and action (Faust translates the first words of the Bible as "In the beginning was the deed," 1237). Inevitably, people will act in accordance with both good and evil thoughts; but humankind as a whole will suffer the consequences of action. Yet Goethe holds out the hope that good will come out of this suffering.

The character of Euphorion, the son of Faust and Helen, is important here. Euphorion is born full-grown as a warrior poet who dies fighting for freedom in Greece. He was modeled on Lord Byron, who embodied for Goethe those forces that fought against the stifling conventions of his age. His Greek name means "that which carries well"; Xenophon uses *euphoron* to describe a "favorable breeze." Euphorion's death is presented as a necessary stage in historical and social development, enabling Goethe to comment simultaneously on Byron's early (romanticized) death:

> Splendid laurels to be earning
> You were minded—not so Fate.
> Who succeeds? That query dismal
> Muffled Destiny leaves moot,
> When misfortune most abysmal
> Strikes the bloodied people mute.
> Yet afresh new anthems sow them,
> Stand in mourning bowed no more;
> For the soil again will grow them
> As it ever has before.

(9930–38)

Euphorion's striving (like Byron's) ends in death, but new "songs" will come forth from humankind. Euphorion can thus be seen as a personification of human aspiration and perfectibility. The death of Philemon and Baucis in part 2 of *Faust* represents, for Lukács, another stage of social development—the dialectics of history. Faust wants the old couple removed because their tiny house stands on the very place from which he wants to survey his vast dike works. Mephistopheles obliges by burning their place down. Predictably, they perish in the fire; Faust seems to have learned nothing from Mephistopheles's handling of Margarete.

Lukács links this episode to dialectical historicism, noting that although Goethe spent a great part of his life at the court in Weimar, he embodied the spirit of the rising bourgeoisie, which had came to the forefront with the spread of capitalism in Europe. It was only in France and England that this bourgeoisie was revolutionary, however. In Germany, the bourgeois class was still subject to the annoyances of a fragmentary form of government dominated by a multitude of petty princes. Goethe saw the necessity for an economically strong bourgeoisie as a means of overcoming this fragmentation. For much the same reason, he admired Napoleon, whose conquest of the western German territories in Alsace-Lorraine broke the grip of the local princes there. Like the other stages of human development that Goethe depicts, however, this stage too is marked by tragedy. The "small world," this time represented by Philemon and Baucis, has to be sacrificed:

> My lofty title is impure,
> The linden range, the weathered cabin,
> The frail old church are still secure.

(11156–58)

Again, Goethe's choice of names is significant, for in Greek mythology, the old couple Philemon and Baucis were alone in showing hospitality to Zeus and Hermes when they visited earth. As a reward, they alone were saved from a great flood after the gods warned them and told them to climb a mountain to escape it.

The fate of the couple in *Faust*, part 2, symbolically overturns the old values of hospitality and simple goodness. Instead of being saved from a flood as in the classical myth, the couple watches as Faust's massive project makes the ocean recede beneath their dwelling perched high over the sea. Faust regards them as an impediment to progress, a visual blight in his visionary scheme. It's the dilemma between thought and action all over again—"progress" must be achieved through destructive action.

Lukács here makes a bold interpretive move that remains one of his most controversial ones. In effect, he argues that Goethe wanted to show that human progress had to go through a stage of capitalism (with its attendant personal tragedies) in order to create the basis for a subsequent, more egalitarian society. Lukács finds the clue to this in Faust's wish, expressed in the final act, to stand "on acres free" among "free people."

Freedom is thus the ultimate goal of human evolution; but a freedom bought at the price of destruction and individual human tragedy. Lukács assumes that Goethe's historical consciousness coincides with a Hegelian model—humankind evolves into an ever more perfect society. Because of the limitations of his own time, Lukács argues, Goethe cannot see what comes after bourgeois capitalism, but he knows it cannot be the final stage because it is fatally flawed. He discovers, in Lukács's words, "the objective impossibility of separating the Mephistophelean principle from the capitalist development of the productive forces."[30] Lukács sees Goethe as someone who had a dim premonition of a society based on the collective good without actually being able to visualize it concretely. "Goethe does nothing to mitigate the diabolical character of the capitalist form of this progress. . . . He believes in an incorruptible nucleus in man, in mankind and its development. He believes in the salvage of this nucleus even *in* (and above all *despite*) the capitalist form of development."[31] Lukács reads *Faust* as a prescient critique of the capitalism that would not reach its fullest expansion until more than a century later.

The Persistence of Utopia: Dissident Writers in the German Democratic Republic

Of the two socialist versions of a projected third part of *Faust*—conjured up in turn by Blum and by Lunacharski, both of whom were later to become political leaders, Blum's ultimately proved the more prophetic. We can find elements of his scenario, in fact, in two Faust plays from the GDR: Hanns Eisler's *Johannes Faustus* of 1952 and Volker Braun's *Hinze und Kunze*, which was first performed in 1973.

Originally intended as the libretto for an opera, Eisler's *Johannes Faustus* at once became embroiled in controversy. Unlike Goethe's Faust, Eisler's hero is damned at the end. Like the original Faust of the folk tradition (Eisler took much of his plot from the puppet play of Faust), he is a negative example. Eisler made him into a warning of what can happen if working-class leaders fail to identify with, and cast their lot with, the people.

Eisler bases his novel interpretation of the Faust legend on the fact that the historical Faust was said to be the son of a farmer, and that he lived during the time of the sixteenth-century *Bauernkrieg* (Peasants' War). The action begins at a time when Faust's decision to ally himself with Martin Luther, who opposed the peasants, and against Thomas Münzer, who led the peasant uprising, lies in the past. Faust now regrets that decision and tries to rationalize it by claiming that he is interested only in timeless truths. He is willing to make a pact with Mephistopheles in order to escape his nagging feelings of guilt—for instance, one of the terms of the pact is that Mephistopheles will help him forget the songs from the opposing sides of the war, songs that race though his head.

As is to be expected, Mephistopheles does not bring Faust the peaceful state of mind he craves. The scenes from the Bible that the devil helps conjure up (in Atlanta, rather than at the court of the Emperor Charles V, as in the *Historia*) are images of resistance to oppression that remind Faust once again of the struggle he betrayed: David and Goliath, Joseph and Potiphar's wife, and King Nebuchadnezzar's putting to death of the faithful in a fiery furnace. In the last act, Faust finally faces the fact that his betrayal of the peasant class to which he originally belonged is what damns him. He ends his final confession with the following lines (act 3, scene 5):

> Disbelieving in my own strength,
> I gave my hand to the rulers.
> I sank lower than the low,
> And wasted my life away.
>
> For if you give your hand to the rulers,
> Your hand will shrivel up.
> The second step followed the first—
> By the third step I was lost.
>
> Now I find a miserable end,
> And so should anyone
> Who doesn't have the courage
> To stand fast for their cause.[32]

This is a socialist recasting of "Faust's lament" from the *Historia*, a lament that, as we saw in the preceding chapter, figures prominently in Thomas Mann's *Doctor Faustus*; it will be taken up again in Alfred Schnittke's "Faust Cantata."

In the prologue of the play—where Goethe had presented a wager between God and Mephistopheles—Eisler has chosen to present figures from the Greek underworld. Pluto instructs Mephistopheles to tempt Faust with evidence of the nullity of all human effort. Because Faust accepts this and gives up hope—because he refuses to support the socialist project of the peasants—he is damned.

The first review of Eisler's work was extremely positive. Writing in the literary magazine *Sinn und Form*, Ernst Fischer praised Eisler for presenting Faust as "a central figure of German wretchedness [*Misere*]" and for showing "the German humanist as renegade."[33] Eisler's work, he argued, could be considered "the national opera of Germany."[34] Eisler had shown Faust as a traitor to his class and as the enemy of socialism.

Coming so close upon the founding of the GDR in 1949, and considering the official cultural politics of the state, which wanted to reestablish continuity with the grand tradition of German literature after the Nazi hiatus, as well as to pursue a policy of reunification with West Germany on the basis of a common culture, Eisler's *Johannes Faustus* was badly timed. In order to protect its vision of the cultural legacy of Goethe's humanism, the East German establishment was willing to go quite far in preventing other, alternative artistic visions of the Faust legend from being put forth—especially those which distanced themselves from the idea of the heroic Faust's land reclamation projects and Goethe's positive concluding apotheosis.

The first attack came from Alexander Abusch. Recalling the claim of Thomas Mann's hero Adrian Leverkühn, that he wished to "take back" the triumphant and joyous ending of Beethoven's Ninth Symphony, Abusch accused Eisler of wanting to "take back" Goethe's *Faust*. This cannot be done, he argued, since "Faust was and is the great spiritual figure of the bourgeois-revolutionary struggle of the past to know the world and to change it."[35]

Eisler's friend Bertolt Brecht had tried to dissuade him from publishing the libretto before he had composed the music. Brecht himself had run into trouble with the production by Egon Monk of Goethe's youthful draft of the Faust story, the so-called *Urfaust*, at the Berliner Ensemble in 1952–53.

This Faust was not the dignified and wise seer that the ruling elite of the GDR wished to claim as its prophet. In the earlier version, it is Faust, and not Mephistopheles, who acts the prankster in Auerbach's Tavern and makes wine flow from the holes he drills in a table. The *Urfaust*, like *Faust*, part 1, ends with the death of Margarete. In Brecht's production, a narrator then came on stage and recited a laconic, rhymed summary of what was to come in part 2 of Goethe's *Faust*. In statements that he made about the production, Brecht said that this version was chosen because it made it possible to work with the Faust material without being "inhibited by classicism"; if classical works were to retain their relevance, he argued, they had to be protected from a false respect that would turn them into ossified relics.[36] No matter: Walter Ulbricht called the production a "caricature," and the play was panned in the press.[37]

The vigorous critique that was directed against Brecht's production was a foretaste of the acrimonious debate that focused on Eisler's libretto. It was criticized in the official newspaper of the SED, *Neues Deutschland*, and taken up in three sittings of the prestigious literary Mittwochgesellschaft, or "Wednesday Society," that met at the Academy of Arts. The most spirited defense, which also gives a sense of some of the allegations made against Eisler, was articulated by Brecht:

> Has Eisler really tried to destroy totally our classical image of Faust? Has he belied, destroyed, or stripped the soul from a wonderful figure of the German heritage? Has he taken Faust back? I doubt it. Eisler has reread the folktale and has found a different figure—one that is important to him. True, it's important in a different way from the Faust that makes its appearance in Goethe. To me it appears like Faust's dark twin, a great and ominous figure that neither tries to replace or overshadow his brighter brother nor succeeds in doing so. Rather, the brighter Faust shines forth more clearly against the background of the dark one. To write such a work is not cultural vandalism.[38]

At the end of these discussions, Eisler had lost any interest in composing the music for his opera and shelved the project.[39] Two weeks after the final discussion of the literary society, on June 17, 1953, East Germany erupted into a rebellion that was savagely put down by the authorities. The West Germans, in turn, renamed a famous avenue after the date of the rebellion, henceforth known as Strasse des 17. Juni, or "June 17 Street." This accentuates the fierce nature of the contest between the two sides, which were soon to be pawns in a full-blown Cold War—a war in which culture was to play an important part.

It wasn't just Goethe that the East Germans wanted on their side. The May 10 issue of *Neues Deutschland* celebrated the legacy of Hermann Hesse and Thomas Mann, both bourgeois writers. The renewal of German literature was supposed to come not only from a renewal of the classical tradition but from a new workers' literature. The articulation of this policy was achieved at a series of literary conferences held in Bitterfeld, beginning in 1959; hence, the policy has come to be called "the Bitterfelder way." One of the mottoes was "Comrade, take up your pen—the national culture of socialism needs you." Yet, this was not a call for revolutionary art. On the contrary: the classical canon went unquestioned.[40] It is not surprising that this repression of creativity led to few literary productions by the working class.

The story of Faust continued in the GDR, however. Ulbricht's speech of 1962 was echoed in 1968, on the occasion of the Prague uprising, by Minister of Culture Klaus Gysi, who asked, "What is to be our legacy? Faust or Gregor Samsa?" Comparing the "counterrevolutionary" rebels in Prague to Kafka's famous insect from "The Metamorphosis," he restated the importance of following in the optimistic humanist tradition of Goethe's *Faust*.[41]

Volker Braun's 1968 play *Hans Faust* may be seen as an attempt to tease out some of the implications of making Faust a socialist hero. Like the Faust envisioned by Léon Blum, this new Faust works in collaboration with Mephisto, who, as party secretary, is also a socialist leader.

On the occasion of the Goethe celebrations in 1949, Otto Grotewohl, then general secretary of the SED, had spoken of the unresolved contradiction in Goethe's life, a "false idealism" that, he said, had been tearing the German people apart for five hundred years: the contradiction between thought and action. "Power was without spirit and the spirit was powerless."[42] In Braun's play, this contradiction is embodied by his characters Faust and Kunze. Faust is a construction worker who enthusiastically embraces every task assigned to him, but whose strength ultimately fails because he hasn't understood the need for collective action. Kunze, the Mephisto character, is a former resistance fighter and concentration camp survivor ("I come from Hell: the concentration camp") and now a party official whose plans cannot succeed unless he can win Faust for the collective effort.

The pact between Faust and Kunze does not revolve around Faust's soul but instead stipulates that they will collaborate as long as they both remain dissatisfied with things as they are, as long as the world needs to be changed by their actions. After successfully carrying out many tasks, Faust becomes frustrated because he can't see beyond his own individualism. He retires to his scientific studies, which don't serve anyone (reenacting the split between spirit and action, which Grotewohl had identified as the bane of German culture up to that point). But Kunze convinces Faust to return—this time, he'll take part in the planning as well. Their new and more equal collaboration is successful. At the moment of his greatest happiness, when he has found a harmonious way of working with Kunze, Faust dies (this death at the point of highest fulfillment is, of course, reminiscent of Goethe). His successors take up the struggle for a socialist future.

Braun's first version of this play, performed in Weimar at the very moment of the Prague uprising, was never published. The production ran into numerous difficulties. On the one hand, the nervousness of the authorities in the face of the uprising created a tense atmosphere in which criticisms of official policy were barely tolerated. In a fictional account of the controversies surrounding the production, Braun relates how whole scenes were in danger of being censored.[43]

The second version, titled *Hinze und Kunze*, ends not with Hinze's (Faust's) death but with the protagonists' handshake and promise to begin anew. The names of the two protagonists are derived from a German expression meaning "everyman," a bit like the English expression "Tom, Dick, and Harry."[44] Premiered in 1973, the new version is critical of the contradictions that had become apparent in GDR economic planning.[45] In the episode titled "the middle German hole," workers alternately fill in and dig out the same hole as the orders from the planning authorities (ironically referred to as "the Kremlin" or "China") keep changing. At the very moment when Hinze is exulting in the way that the workers multiply his own efforts a hundredfold and make him feel as though he has unlimited powers ("I feel as though I had a hundred acorns on every branch"), Kunze informs him that the authorities in Berlin want to raise the norms of productivity. When the workers, disgruntled that they have no voice in setting production quotas that are supposedly for the benefit of all, want to strike, they're told that they would be striking against themselves.[46]

The play is searching in its examination of the social cost of the change in gender roles. At first, Hinze abandons his wife, Marlies, in order to follow

Kunze. But Marlies doesn't become a victim, like Goethe's Margarete. When Hinze meets her again, she too has joined the factory workers and barely recognizes him. Though made pregnant by Hinze, Marlies decides her work is more important and chooses to abort their child.

The conflict between Hinze, the worker, and Kunze, the planner, is sharply differentiated. Kunze tells Hinze that it's useless for him to work harder than everyone else—the point is for the work to go forward collectively.[47] Kunze informs Hinze that his pride in his individual achievement is a misplaced vestige from an earlier era: "To burrow without thinking is sabotage; to drive yourself without logic is stupid."[48]

Braun's play is consistent with the dialectical theme of much of his work. Realizing that the success of the socialist project will require a change in consciousness and new, internalized measures of personal achievement, Braun deals with the obstacles, both internal and external, that individuals faced in the new order. He is also a merciless critic of muddled bureaucracy. Still, his trenchant critiques—which lost none of their bite as time wore on—were made in the spirit of one sympathetic to the creation of a new, noncapitalist society. This was not the case with the Faust play by Rainer Kirsch, *Heinrich Schlaghands Höllenfahrt* (Heinrich Schlaghand's Descent to Hell). The play was published in the prominent East German theater periodical *Theater der Zeit* in 1973. The Faust character, Heinrich Schlaghand (Strikehand), builds a model city in hell and then has to convince human beings living on earth to inhabit it. The allegory was not lost on the authorities, and the play was not allowed to be performed.[49]

Ten years after the premiere of *Hinze und Kunze*, Braun continued the literary life of his heroes in a series of fragments and aphorisms, *Berichte von Hinze und Kunze*. In 1985, a novel was published, *Hinze-Kunze Roman*. Braun's aphorisms give the flavor of his dialectical thinking and highlight, with bittersweet irony, the contradictions of the Cold War. In the fragment "Hinze's Requirement," he shows how both sides claimed their citizens were "free," whereas, in fact, no one really enjoyed true freedom:

Once when Hinze was in the other part of the country, he was asked why he didn't want to stay, since he had difficulties over there. Hinze answered: This morning I was sitting on the alpine pasture overlooking the city and I was looking down at the lovely land. I wished for the very thing you mentioned. It must be fabulous to look up from one's work and look down there. I'm staying. But, he added, I have a small requirement. The city government will have to collectivize those white factories in the valley, which belong to the wire makers, and take them away from those billionaires. That's my only requirement; the most basic need of my existence is that I can't live if I have to look at private property.[50]

In this little parable, Hinze is still behaving like the Faust of Goethe, who wanted the little house of Philemon and Baucis removed.[51] But now the tables are turned—instead of capitalist development, Hinze wants an unobstructed view of a socialist economy. On the one hand, Braun is making a criticism of those West Germans who think they are the truly free ones. They can't see that the billionaires own almost everything. But Braun's allusion to Faust's arbitrary elimination of the dissident couple who doesn't want to fit into his grand scheme of things is no less critical of the socialist planners of East Germany. In fact, the ideal that Hinze strives after here bears striking resemblance to what Marshall Berman criticizes as "the tragedy of development."[52] Hinze says, "I want to stretch myself out all over the country / And cover it with concrete."[53]

Faust, Technology, and "Progress"

In Braun's *Hinze und Kunze* we have come very far from Lukács's discussion of the dialectic in Goethe. Lukács appreciated Goethe's insight into the contradictory function of evil in history—Mephisto's self-definition as a force that wants evil but creates good.[54] In Braun's play, there is no character who actively tries to bring about evil. If there is a Mephistophelean element, it consists of the seemingly insoluble contradictions that bedevil those who want to start from scratch and create a new society.

For Eisler, as for Léon Blum, on the other hand, evil lies in people's unwillingness to change (this recalls Mephistopheles's self-characterization, in Goethe's *Faust*, as "the spirit that eternally denies," 1338). But Eisler's Faust is defeated, and he recognizes his error. His time has run out, and it is too late for him to correct himself. He is caught by a ruse of Mephistopheles. His twenty-four years have been reduced to twelve, because, Mephistopheles argues, Faust made demands twenty-four hours a day—the equivalent of twenty-four years "on the job." Eisler represents Mephisto as the exploited worker who demands his due! His opera, if it had been completed, would have served as a warning that time for the socialist experiment was limited.

The question of Faust's relation to nature should also be examined. Lukács sees Faust as someone who would master the forces of nature, even within himself. For this reason, the sensual experiences offered by Mephistopheles cannot satisfy him: "Faust has something quite different in mind: not the enjoyment of life (this is only a means and medium) but the realization, the development of all his individual possibilities, so that, by being put to test in the world, he might penetrate, come to know, and dominate reality."[55]

Lukács argues that Mephistopheles represents, in the final act of *Faust*, the capitalist approach to dominating nature.[56] Marshall Berman agrees that the last scene of *Faust* constitutes a critique of development. Berman reads into Faust's death, as he contemplates the new world he has brought into being through the organization of labor, a prophetic statement about the pressure to modernize: "Once the developer has cleared all the obstacles away, he himself is in the way, and he must go."[57] But Berman rightly argues that Goethe's negative portrayal pertains not specifically to capitalism but to unrestrained development as such. After all, Faust spurns money and never shows any interest in amassing wealth. Instead, his critique applies to any process of development—capitalist or socialist—that is cursed with the need to expand and keep on developing. Such development eventually becomes destructive of the very society it was supposed to serve.[58]

This is the side of Goethe that neither the GDR nor the FRG (Federal Republic of Germany) cared to take over into the Goethean or Faustian legacy—the realization that progress cannot be identified with "development for its own sake." Instead, the GDR used the ending of part 2 of Goethe's *Faust* to justify "covering the world over with concrete." The rivalry between the two Germanys, it is now known, led to the kind of ecological disaster in East Germany that Berman associates with unchecked development. East Germany was under pressure to prove its socialist system was better by showing progress in industrialization. Reunification was put on the back burner after Willy Brandt's decision to hold talks with GDR prime minister Willi Stoph in 1970, and henceforth the two Germanys were locked in competition.[59]

In retrospect, Eisler's "dark brother" to Goethe's Faust figure seems a valuable and prophetic contribution to the legend. He could stand for the bureaucrats who failed to side with the people in creating a truly democratic socialism. Perhaps the political and intellectual elite of the brand-new state in 1952 had their own dark ambivalence about the idea of serving the will of the people; perhaps in preventing Eisler's *Johannes Faustus* from coming to the stage, they were trying to prevent the exposition of their own intentions.

The opening of the Berlin wall in 1989 and the subsequent fall of the GDR was followed quickly by reunification in 1990. Ever the dialectician, Volker Braun now found himself caught in a new contradiction, as he expressed it in his poem "Das Eigentum" (Property), rendered here in the excellent translation by Karen Ruoff Kramer:

> I'm still here: My homeland's going West.
> WAR TO THE COTTAGES, PEACE TO THE PALACES.
> I was the one who gave it the boot.
> It casts itself, its meager charms away.
> The ice recedes in tropics of desire.
> And I can go *stay in Timbuktu.*
> My texts now only puzzle you.
> Wrenched off are things I never had.
> I'll miss forever what I didn't live.
> Alluring hope lay in the path, a trap.
> You've grabbed the property that once was mine.
> When will I again say *mine* and mean: us all?[60]

The poem's narrator sees how the whole country is turning toward capitalism ("going West"). The second line is an inversion of Georg Büchner's revolutionary populist proclamation in *Der Hessische Landbote* (1834) and underscores the counterrevolutionary aspect of developments in East Germany. The narrator says he has lost his relevance (his texts have become "puzzling") and feels that his own criticisms of the regime helped to being about its final downfall. He is consigned to the margins of society. To be sent "wo der Pfeffer wächst" (where the pepper grows), as the German original reads, is to be sent far away; the translator has rendered this with the colloquial English equivalent "Timbuktu." The socialism that was never achieved is now no longer possible. This puts him in the position of feeling the loss of a dream that was never realized. He feels betrayed by his own hopes, and his property is now in the hands of others.

This property, or *Eigentum* in the German, is more than material possessions—it includes the idea of cultural inheritance. The new unified German state, like the governments that had preceded it, lost no time in proclaiming itself the heir to Goethe. But the nagging voices of utopian thinkers like Braun murmur in the background:

> Kunze's favorite saying was: Change the world, it needs it. But you couldn't deny that it had changed. Not necessarily in the sense that he meant it, because the forests were dying, hunger was increasing, and the air was getting eaten up. That was too much for Hinze. Your sentence is too short, he said, pulling a long face. Isn't it time to point out that change itself must change? Not so that the world can remain as it is, but so that it can survive at all.[61]

Contemporary Readings of Goethe: Ecological Socialism

Socialists respond to the utopian elements in the Faust myth, rather than proclaiming themselves as the heirs to Goethe's cultural legacy (the practice of Nazi intellectuals) or declaring that Germany, after World War II, had forfeited the right to that legacy (Thomas and Klaus Mann). The socialist thinking that succeeded "first-epoch socialism" after 1989 has gone back to Goethe's *Faust* to find evidence for a model of development that would remain within sound ecological bounds.[62] For Jost Hermand, Faust's unrestrained drive for action exemplifies a negative utopia, an unnatural will to possess: "His existence stands not under the sign of *eros*, but of *thanatos*. And in the wide swath he cuts through life, he leaves behind him almost only broken hearts, casually murdered people, and nature laid waste."[63] Building on a reading of Goethe's natural philosophy, scientific treatises, and literary works, Hermand comes to the conclusion that *Faust* warns against the unlimited freedom to change nature: "Goethe wanted neither unrestrained freedom nor orthodox restriction, but a restrained freedom appropriate to human nature."[64] As evidence, he points to Faust's twin failures in the area of human reproduction: Homunculus and Euphorion.

The homunculus, an artificial human being created in a test tube by Faust's assistant Wagner, dies when he tries to break out of his glass enclosure. Goethe thus problematizes the sort of technological thinking that refuses natural limits. Euphorion, the son of Faust and Helen of Troy, dies when his unbridled enthusiasm—which Hermand characterizes as egoistic and narcissistic—causes him to die, like Icarus, by flying right into the sun.[65]

Hermand's ecological reading of *Faust* offers the hope of retaining the utopian vision of social development, even while reconsidering how progress might be redefined in an era of dwindling natural resources. The Homunculus takes on modern significance in a society where artificial assists to human reproduction have ushered in a new era of ethical discussion in science. Euphorion, on the other hand, can be read as an allegorization of the prevalent economic system that encourages the piling up of money and the expansion of production with no regard for anyone's survival in the long term.

What Hermand does not account for is the rationale Goethe's heavenly chorus gives for Faust's salvation: what is today's utopian form of "striving in ceaseless toil"(11936)? Hermand notes only that Faust's form of unscrupulous activity leads to death. Here, he echoes Marx, who considered unthinking capital accumulation to be a version of Faust's credo: "In the beginning was the Deed" (1237).[66] But Goethe reminds us that we cannot fight the destructive forces of development by consigning people to inactivity. Instead, progress and development need to be redefined in ways that are compatible with a better way of life for all. Utopian vision is now more urgent than ever before, but it will require, as Volker Braun writes, that we "change change."

4   Gendering Faust

S ocialist Fausts have heretofore remained male—this suggests a re-
luctance of socialist utopian thinkers to rethink issues of gender
and relations of power between the sexes. Isn't this a failure to think
through all the implications of the Faustian bargain? Goethe's
Faust, after all, demands to experience "what to all of mankind is apportioned" (1770–71). Shouldn't this include experience as a woman as well as
a man? In his two Faust plays, Goethe briefly flirts with the idea of gender
transformation. Mephistopheles does undergo a female metamorphosis in
part 2 of *Faust*, changing himself into one of the Phorkyad deities. He sees
it as a shameful disguise: "They'll call me a hermaphrodite" (8031). His metamorphosis enables him to appear as a female adviser to Helen and to convince her that Menelaos means to sacrifice her. As Phorkyas, she/he suc-
ceeds in uniting Faust with Helen, who flees for her life and takes refuge
in Faust's medieval castle. Mephistopheles's female identity as an ugly old
woman with only a single eye and tooth is a disguise that doesn't really
explore the politics of gender—Helen trusts Phorkyas precisely because her
appearance and manner conform so exactly to the stereotype of the wise
crone. Elsewhere, Goethe even purposefully avoids transgender issues: the
Homunculus that his assistant Wagner creates in a test tube is clearly marked
as male, though in the tradition of alchemy, this would normally be a hermaphrodite. Spinning through the air in his glass enclosure, the Homunculus crashes his glass upon spying the beautiful female figure of Galatea,
who rises from the sea (8472–73).

There is only a hint of cross-gender sexual dynamics in the two parts of
Goethe's *Faust* in the relationship between the two main protagonists. The
exasperation Mephistopheles expresses at Faust's continued dissatisfaction
might be read as a lovers' quarrel. At the moment of Faust's death, the devil
comments, "No joy could sate him, no delight but cloyed, / For changing
shapes he lusted to the last" (11587–88). This hint about a possible *queering*
of Faust—where the relationship between the two antagonists might be seen

as a reciprocal seduction with erotic tensions—has yet to be fully explored. The *feminization* of Faust has, however, been developed in several ways in twentieth-century expressionist theater, in Weimar cinema, in French *écriture féminine* of the 1970s, and in modern fiction.

A Precursor to Feminism: Louisa May Alcott

In 1866, Louisa May Alcott, daughter of the Concord educator and transcendentalist Bronson Alcott, wrote the first of two novels that she titled "A Modern Mephistopheles." The second was published in 1877; the first was recently discovered among her unpublished manuscripts and appeared in 1995 with the title *A Long Fatal Love Chase*.[1] Rosamond, the heroine of *A Long Fatal Love Chase*, is a Faustian spirit whose first utterance is that she feels as though she would gladly sell her soul to Satan for a year of freedom from the reclusive life she lives with her grandfather. Soon a mysterious visitor named Tempest appears, who promises to marry her and take her away. From the beginning, Rosamond is struck by Tempest's resemblance to a portrait of Mephistopheles that hangs in the house. After a year of happiness, she learns that Tempest is already married and resolves to flee. The greater part of the novel relates the heroine's many hair-raising escapes from various hideouts, with her seducer in hot pursuit. Whether she goes to Paris, to a convent, to Wiesbaden, or to Staffordshire, where she lives in the same household as the first Mrs. Tempest and her son Lilo, Tempest relentlessly tracks her down. At the convent, Tempest disguises himself as her confessor; in Wiesbaden, he prevents her from marrying an aristocrat by telling the prospective husband that Rosamond is mad; and when Rosamond resolves to return to her island with her protector from the convent, the friar Ignatius, Tempest manages to separate them by subterfuge. He tries to drown Ignatius by running down his boat, only to discover that it is Rosamond whom he has killed.

Although Rosamond shows a remarkable independence and resourcefulness for a heroine of her times, she deploys all her ingenuity to rescue what amounts to a very traditional notion of a woman's "honor." Moreover, she does love her "Mephistopheles."[2] Her Faustian bargain is real enough, although Alcott makes her unaware, at first, that she has sold her soul.

Mephistopheles is by far the most interesting character in the author's second Faustian novel, *A Modern Mephistopheles*. Helwyze (hellwise), the demonic hero, has just finished reading Goethe's *Faust* and decides to play

Mephistopheles to a despairing young poet, Canaris. He makes a bargain with him, whereby Canaris agrees to live with him; in return, Helwyze will advance Canaris's career. An old flame, Olivia, once spurned Helwyze and now loves him; he enjoys rebuffing her and using her as the passive audience to the real-life drama he has set in motion. Canaris is ordered to marry Gladys, a young, innocent girl. To Olivia, Helwyze mockingly remarks how Canaris and Olivia resemble Faust and Gretchen, whereas the two of them play the roles of Frau Marthe and Mephistopheles. Olivia reproaches him for indulging in what she judges to be his obsession with wielding power over others.[3]

The reader does not know what the terms of the bargain are until the very end, when it is revealed that Helwyze, rather than Canaris, has written the literary works for which Canaris is celebrated. Gladys suffers a miscarriage from the shock and dies; Canaris slinks off to an uncertain fate; and Helwyze, devastated by the death of Gladys, waits only for death: "Goethe could make his Satan as he liked; but Fate was stronger than I, and so comes ignominious failure. Margaret dies, and Faust suffers, but Mephistopheles cannot go with him on his new wanderings. . . . In loving the angel I lose the soul I had nearly won; the roses turn to flakes of fire, and the poor devil is left lamenting."[4]

In some way, Helwyze seems an embodiment of the transcendentalists' view of Goethe, a detached, godlike figure who in this instance sets real-life people in motion as though they were figures in a tragedy of his own invention. Ralph Waldo Emerson considered *Faust* to be "the most remarkable literary work of the age."[5] His essay on Goethe, in *Representative Men: Seven Lectures*, is also an essay on the purpose and function of art. Writing should not just mirror nature but should put things in a new order, the order of "truth." For Emerson, Goethe "has the formidable independence which converse with truth gives."[6] He is the greatest example of the writer's life, whose purpose is to express his own truth: "There lies the burden on his mind,—the burden of truth to be declared,—more or less understood, and it constitutes his business and calling in the world, to see those facts through, and to make them known."[7]

Emerson's admiration is echoed in the article on Goethe that Margaret Fuller published in the *Dial*, the transcendentalist magazine she founded in 1840. For both, Goethe exemplified "genius," the quality of mind that breaks with convention and seeks its own laws. Yet both were also scandalized by what they considered to be Goethe's immorality and were put off by his cool detachment. Remaining consistent with the transcendentalists' call for self-realization, Fuller formulated her criticism of Goethe with the notion that he "failed to reach his highest development."[8] Emerson, too, chided Goethe for stopping short of the highest artistic attainment, for being a "lawgiver of art" rather than an artist who could "surrender to the torrent of inspiration" or even find an "eternal truth" that was greater than himself.[9] Reading Emerson, one feels that he located Goethe's greatest achievement in the creation of the demonic personality of Mephistopheles. Emerson understood Goethe's devil to be "pure intellect applied . . . to the service of the senses" and went on to praise him as "the first organic figure that has been added for some ages."[10] In Emerson's formulation, it is Mephistopheles, even more than Faust, who exemplifies the dissident, self-reliant personality and who chooses to live by his own laws.

Concerning Helwyze, the novel's narrator comments, "He had not planned to ruin the youth, but simply to let 'the world, the flesh, and the devil' contend against such virtues as they found, while he sat by and watched the struggle." But, like it or not, Helwyze is drawn into his own drama by his growing attachment to Gladys. This, too, is consistent with the transcendentalists' critical view of Goethe's many love affairs and perhaps reflects Alcott's wish that even he should get his just deserts in the end. Most important of all, however, is the fact that Alcott does not condemn Helwyze—he is necessarily Mephistophelean because that is his "true" nature. Because of this, he makes a most fascinating transcendental hero. His final words are those of an unrepentant demon: "Life before was Purgatory, now it is Hell; because I loved her, and *I* have no hope to follow and find her again."[11]

Indeed, Helwyze perfectly embodies the idea of freedom as it is expressed in the essay "Prophecy, Transcendentalism, Progress," published in the *Dial* in 1841: "Man's freedom is the essence of his being; and the nearer he is to a state of absolute independence of will and action, the more perfectly will his whole nature be developed, and his destiny on earth accomplished."[12] Helwyze has accomplished his destiny on earth perfectly, but it is a demonic destiny.

Helwyze, of course, is no Faust—but ironically, his uncompromising spirit contains much of what later becomes identified with Faustian striving. Indeed, Alcott's second novel, for all its melodrama, sets forth a character who seems out of place in the nineteenth century and more at home in the destructive modernization of the twentieth and the twenty-first.

In *A Long Fatal Love Chase*, Rosamond prefigures a type of rebellious independence that will have to wait another hundred years to be widely expressed. In *A Modern Mephistopheles*, Alcott's heroine turns the tables on the devil, who ends up vanquished by his desire—a theme Portuguese director Manoel de Oliveira will return to in his 1995 film *O Convento* (*The Convent*). Alcott is also among the first to explore the idea that an artist might make a Faustian bargain in order to win fame, a theme that will also enjoy fuller development in the twentieth century. As Elaine Showalter writes, "Both stories suggest her guilty sense of having bartered her womanhood and art in the name of financial expedience, to achieve literary and commercial success."[13] In this regard, it is interesting that *A Modern Mephistopheles* was first published anonymously in 1871 in the Roberts Brothers' No Name series. Evidently, Alcott believed by 1870 that the authorial persona created by the success of *Little Women* was inconsistent with her more audacious and sexually explicit writings.[14] Showalter notes that contemporary reevaluations of the female gothic have discussed the way that this genre allowed for the expression of the taboo subject of female sexual desire and sexual freedom: "For many nineteenth-century American women readers and writers, the Gothic suggested independence, adventure, narrative boldness, and self-reliance. It allowed writers otherwise subject to the narrative restrictions of gentility and patriotism to find overt outlets for their sexuality and to imagine exotic or European settings for their transgressive plots."[15] Alcott's Faustian heroine bends her whole will toward escaping male domination, whether of the grandfather or the lover. Though she is ultimately destroyed in the struggle, she never once gives up.

"Let Me Live as a Man": Wedekind's *Franziska*

Alcott's rebellious heroines find a powerful echo in a play by the expressionist playwright Frank Wedekind (1864–1918), who was supremely scornful of the sexual politics of his day. His explorations of the erotic life were so controversial that many of his plays were banned either before ever seeing a performance or a few days after opening. Although Wedekind is best known for the 1891 *Spring's Awakening* (which put the controversial subject of sex education for children on the stage) and the 1894 *Pandora's Box* (whose femme fatale character was immortalized by Louise Brooks in the silent film of the same name by G. W. Pabst in 1929), his oeuvre includes a constellation of dramas—*Earth Spirit* (1894), *Death and the Devil* (1905),

Marquis von Keith (1900), and *Franziska* (1911)—that have the Faustian theme as their main emphasis. Peculiar to each of these is a "masquerade" scene in which the characters put on a play within the play; the subject of the masquerade in each case is the nature and role of gender.

In *Franziska*, Wedekind makes Faust into a cross-dressing hermaphrodite who changes from a woman into a man and then back into a woman again. Franziska thus wins for herself the wide field of human activity and aspiration that Goethe had mostly reserved for men. The play is a prescient acting out of the kind of politicized transvestism that Marjorie Garber has described in *Vested Interests*. Rather than being merely a form of masquerade, she argues, transvestism can operate as a "third term" that threatens and disrupts the dualism of gender.[16] In the wake of French philosopher Michel Foucault's painstaking delineation of sociosexual practice as a form of social control, Wedekind's work now seems prophetic.

Part of the difficulty of assessing Wedekind's *Franziska* today has to do with our unfamiliarity with the expressionist theater. This is a theater of very strongly delineated central characters who embody ideas and passions without much psychological depth. In their wake, they leave destruction, since the nature of their progress through the world is to cut off the options for the weaker characters who cross their path. Many of these minor characters commit suicide, and this sacrifice is seen in the play in a completely unsentimental way, as a confirmation of the dominance of the strong characters.

Power (including erotic power) is the main theme of *Franziska*. In the opening scene, the eighteen-year-old heroine explains to her mother that she refuses to marry the man who made her pregnant because she hasn't yet had time to find out who she is. From the beginning, she appears to be a person who makes her own rules. As soon as she is back in her own room, her Mephistopheles climbs through the window: Veit Kunz, a professional arts manager who promises her she can have anything she wants for two years if she will agree to be his wife/mistress/slave afterward. But she wants more than the utmost in freedom and pleasure that he offers to her as a woman. She wants to be a man. Kunz agrees to let her experience a man's capacity for pleasure and freedom for the appointed period and predicts that afterward she will willingly fall into his arms, because it's the law of nature. But Franziska warns him that these so-called laws are put forward by men.

As a man, Franziska resembles many of Wedekind's other strong, rapacious characters (such as Lulu in *Pandora's Box*), characters Klaus Mann characterized as "feral."[17] She leaves devastation in her wake. She marries Sophie but pretends to have an affair with Lydia so that her lack of male equipment won't be discovered. This gives her the pleasure of imposing the double standard on a fellow woman. She explains to her "wife," "With us men unfaithfulness in marriage is a luxury; with you women it's betrayal and cheating."[18] Kunz informs Sophie that great male artists need suffering wives, and Franziska chimes in: "The suffering wife acts as a quickening medicine for the man, tightens up all his nerves and muscles."[19] Meanwhile, Franziska discovers that Kunz, whose mistress she has become, has made her pregnant. Even before Sophie discovers the pregnancy of her "husband," however, her own brother informs her that she has married a woman. Sophie shoots herself, but it is typical of Wedekind's dramaturgy that this moment is not dwelt on (nor does he explain what happened to Franziska's first pregnancy). Instead, Kunz and Franziska proceed to their next adventure at the court of the duke of Rotenburg.

Wedekind has described how, in his portrayal of the marriage of Sophie and Franziska, he wanted to provide a caricature of what he saw as the norm, namely the unviable nature of marriage based on the woman's subordination.[20] The literary model remains, of course, the Gretchen episode in *Faust*; but the gender politics is rendered especially stark when one considers that it is not her sex but her role as "husband" that enables Franziska to exploit Sophie's masochism. Thus, Wedekind suggests that sadomasochistic relations are built right in to the institution of marriage.

At the court in Rotenburg, the issues of gender and power are explored in a larger arena. Veit Kunz arranges for Franziska to appear to the duke in his garden as a mysterious spirit who discusses philosophy with him. The duke doesn't realize that she is the same Franziska he has cast in his play along with his mistress, Gislind. Kunz explains to Franziska that this is another part of her education, and that he is intent on making her over into an accomplished sexual slave who (in an ironic paraphrase of Goethe's *Faust*) will have experienced everything a human being could want to experience.[21]

In the play, Franziska, in medieval dress, is paired with Gislind, who is clothed only lightly in a transparent veil. The women in the play embody truth (Franziska) and earthly love (the naked Gislind). As it happens, the duke, under Kunz's influence, is trying to create a sociosexual revolution by gaining acceptability for the idea that young women should go naked in public, casting off what he calls their "slave dresses." In the play, a two-headed dragon threatens the two women, and the duke then appears onstage as Saint George to defend them. All this is too much for the local police chief, who is unaware of the duke's role and wants above all to put an end to the public display of Gislind's nakedness. He interrupts the performance, and in the ensuing confusion, Gislind finds out that Franziska has been meeting the duke secretly at night in the guise of a philosophical spirit. Shamed by the realization that the duke despises her lack of intelligence, she kills herself with the sword that is lying around as a stage prop. This second suicide is no more remarked upon than the first.

Kunz now prepares the final stage of his education of Franziska by having her assume the role of Helen of Troy in the mystery play in which he has cast himself in the role of Christ. The plan is to dramatize the visit of the Redeemer to hell, where he is to pick a few heroes from the Old Testament and Greek antiquity and take them back to heaven with him (the elect are Adam, Noah, the three Patriarchs, Socrates, Plato, Aristotle, and Samson). But Samson refuses, initially, to leave without Helen of Troy. Helen pleads for herself with Christ, pointing out that they were both child prodigies, are similarly illustrious, and, in fact, equals.

The role-switching in this mystery play is another example of Wedekind's way of making a point by pushing his dramaturgy to extremes. Franziska/Faust becomes Helen, and Kunz/Mephistopheles becomes Christ, as Kunz reaches for the dramatic juxtaposition of what he considers the ultimate in female and male mythic achievement: perfect beauty and perfect power. This is what makes Helen and Jesus equals in his eyes. But he has made an error that nearly proves fatal to him. Franziska has never been interested in the "eternal feminine." In the middle of the rehearsal, she leaves him for another man, the actor who plays the role of Samson. A third suicide attempt is now in order, as Kunz tries to hang himself but is saved at the last moment by an old admirer of Franziska's.

The final scene takes place some years later. Franziska appears as the mother of a four-year-old boy. She decides to marry her new protector, the painter Karl Almer. She says that she has discovered "god." They prepare to live happily ever after. The end.

As in his better-known plays *Pandora's Box* and *Spring's Awakening*, Wedekind reveals himself in *Franziska* to be a social pessimist. His characters can't seem to escape playing vicious power games with sometimes fatal outcomes. If he holds out any hope at all for humankind, it is that the

Faustian spirit will reject the "law of Nature" and make its own laws. This is what Franziska does in rejecting Veit Kunz, her mentor and seducer, in order to reintegrate herself in society as a mother and wife. The fact that this is a "traditional" female role does not necessarily mean that Wedekind essentializes woman as wife and mother. In the first place, Franziska, even though a woman, has reached this contented state only because she has already experienced "all the pleasure and freedom that a man can experience." Halfway through the play, Kunz says to the duke, "Women of manly strength, men with womanly gentleness and mildness have been since the beginning the most perfect embodiment of peace on earth."[22] This brings up the question of hermaphroditism and transvestism, not as disruption (Garber) but as harmony. Yet, even this is suspect, since it is Kunz, the Mephistophelean figure, who speaks the lines. For Sabine Doering, a central theme of the play is "the inability of men to gain any lasting control over women or even to understand their nature."[23] This does seem to explain Kunz's ultimate failure to exercise any control over Franziska.

Wedekind's plays can be said to starkly outline the darker side of sexual and gender politics without offering any solutions. We cannot even be sure that the ending of *Franziska* is not an instance of Wedekind's humor and irony. In his long poem about marriage, which was recited as a prologue to a performance of *Franziska* in Munich, he had the following to say:

> It's neither charm, celebrated by the poets,
>   nor wealth and happiness, that brings two together
>   and most securely guards their covenant;
>   rather it's a stronger magic
>   which also sprouts in misery and captures head and heart:
>   that's what guides them, protesting all the while, down the
>   same road.[24]

As a play about a Faustian woman, Wedekind's *Franziska* shows an awareness of the limitations to self-realization that society imposed upon women in his time. It is all the more remarkable that he explores this theme not because of any sympathy with feminism but because of a prescient awareness of the relation of power, gender, and sexuality. Wedekind points us to an understanding of gender identity as a discursive practice. In Nancy Fraser's words, "To have a social identity, to be a woman or man, for example, just *is* to live and to act under a set of descriptions. . . . To understand anyone's feminine or masculine gender identity . . . one must study the historically specific social practices through which cultural descriptions of gender are produced and circulated."[25]

Wedekind understands gender identity as theater, and masculinity and femininity as roles that Franziska can embrace or discard. Even though gender is essentialized in Wedekind (men strive for control, women are willful and passionate), he presents the decision to assume one gender or another as a matter of choice. His presentation of the Faustian bargain thus avoids any implication that women, in their humanity, desire differently from men—although Franziska does seem to want different things, depending on whether she has decided to assume a male or a female persona. The exposition of those very differences, though, constitutes a critique of conventional notions of gender. Like the socialist utopian writer Ernst Bloch, who will be discussed in my concluding chapter, Wedekind considers "woman" in his own historical time to be an incomplete project, due to the material and psychological limitations that are imposed on her.

Writing the Faustian Feminine: Hélène Cixous

If Wedekind understands gender as role-playing, Hélène Cixous sees it as inscribed in language. The transgressive thrust of her works is to attack language and the historical weight of cultural myth as an enforcer of gender power relations. Her 1975 *Révolutions pour plus d'un Faust*, written in the wake of the social upheavals of 1968, is a whirling star cluster of discourses that try to spin their way out of the male universe, while referring back to revolutions past, present, and future.[26] *Révolutions* is an epic in which the Virgilian guide is "the madman" or "fool" (*le fou*), a kind of demon or companion who finds the narrator and the reader in a "discontinuous ballet, the dance of structures, the spontaneous carnival of the effects of culture." He takes them on a voyage through "creation, nature, theory, criticism and their mirror images." But the reader and the narrator are wiser than everyone they encounter, because they are searching for the not-yet-known.[27]

In this search, all the referenced texts are written by men, and women writers are strangely absent. This notable absence recalls the statement by Luce Irigaray, a practicing French psychoanalyst who also holds doctorates in linguistics and philosophy, to the effect that man cannot even see woman's otherness because he has reduced her to his mirror opposite, which is a kind of sameness.[28] Cixous's strategy is to break the mirror so that the female self can emerge.

Cixous turns the invisibility of women back against men, who become the "other of the other" and hence are canceled out, just as women have been. In her project of rethinking the patriarchal basis of Western civilization, she has created an "open" book whose recurrent theme is creation and creativity. In its thematic development, it moves from creation myths to various "workshops" that exhibit different aspects of creativity—and then to political revolution.

Part of Cixous's strategy for making masculine culture invisible is to present her narrator as a grammatical transvestite—that is to say, the narrator refers to herself in the masculine. She also eschews conventional narrative structures and grammatical syntax, moving from space to space with the logic of a dream. Cixous's writing style corresponds to the radical rewriting that Irigaray calls for:

> Turn everything upside down, inside out, back to front. Rack it with radical convulsions, carry back, re-import, those crises that her "body" suffers in her impotence to say what disturbs her. . . . Overthrow syntax by suspending its eternally teleological order, by snipping the wires, cutting the current, breaking the circuits, switching the connections, by modifying continuity, alternation, frequency, intensity.[29]

Cixous engages extensively with Goethe, whose two *Faust* works are personified as the "first Faust" and the "second Faust"; they're ludicrous, clownish creatures who go about shouting famous lines and sounding off like stuffed shirts. The great land-reclamation project of *Faust*, part 2, is called into question as the workers (Cixous calls them slaves) ask who will profit from their labor.[30] Challenged, Faust grows to huge proportions and becomes the embodiment of his own grandiose schemes. Faust is a negative force, eternally unsatisfied, continually desiring.[31] You just can't get rid of Faust, the madman/fool explains: "There will always be another Faust." The scene then turns into an ideological theater in which Faust trades sound bites with Socrates and the pre-Socratics. The effect is an emptying out of their authority, which is subverted by the author's satirical representation of male posturing.

The masculine creative principle is seen as destructive and violent, and the scene of Faust's vast earthworks project abruptly turns into a brutal war. Before succumbing, a young woman abandons her male infant, "emblem of the revolution," in the narrator's arms. In the melee, she loses sight of the child, only to see it creeping over the dead on all fours with the rapidity and agility of a hare, presumably to survive and wreak destruction another day.[32]

Cixous's narrative is branching rather than linear, so that in the end, the reader remembers not a coherent progression but strings and knots of images. In one striking scene, an army of ants, representing the forces of order, tortures human lovers by eating them alive. In this scene, Cixous describes even the male lover as "maternal," since as a member of the loving couple, he is seen in a positive light. The two lovers smile at each other "outside of repressive structures, of families, of states and ministries"; but they are brought down by repression "in the form of long masked ants, of stiff robes, of columns and processions of police and orthodox priests with high capuchins; the excited black suits hurry, precipitate themselves, fall over each other, their veils thrown back over their black boots and their long black penises furled."[33]

Cixous complicates matters, though, when her narrator declares herself in love with the Unsatisfied—"amoureux de l'Insatisfait"—thereby making her claim to be another Faust (who, as I have pointed out, refers to herself in the masculine, *amoureux* and not *amoureuse*).[34] She admires the Faustian spirit as Goethe conceived it because it belongs to humanity as a whole rather than to masculine culture. The madman/fool explains, once again, that Goethe's works are superior to their (limited) creator: "The man-mother, who knows nothing but the pregnancies of his spirit, who forgets to think about himself and the historical dimension of his work; who multiplies without becoming, who ceases to exercise his intelligence—he ends up producing works that surpass him, and about which he can have ridiculous opinions." The madman/fool contrasts the *homme-mère* (man-mother, but also the Greek epic poet Homer) with the *homme-guerre* (man of war) who does not create but only destroys.[35]

In Cixous's version, the real Faustian spirit is one of continual creation, reproduction, and multiplication. This is why, I think, she devotes the first part of *Révolutions* to myths of creation in which the multiple puns on seeing and the eye express the urgency of the need to "turn everything upside down, inside out, back to front."

Change d'yeux
Change dieu
Change! Dieu!
[Change your eyes
Change god
Change! God!],

the madman/fool says, and promptly stages a show in which the narrator finds herself at the center of creation, confronted with the *nombroeil* (from *nombril*, "navel," and *oeil*, "eye"):

Now there's an immense net trembling with hair with eyes with threads with navels with eyelashes with eggs which is doing up and undoing its knots. Suns get caught in it. A heart struggles and becomes uterine, its tubes chase human stars. The disparate members throw themselves into the net, that a sexual organ instantly attracts, then another. Here bodies hesitate that could be mine! From my astonished sex organs several brand new souls escape and go down there to incarnate themselves without me. I am not simple. Everything that comes out of me also enters me. I fecundate and am fecundated. What if the net were me in some other fashion? Then all my eyes are looking at me! From the knots that hold it back, a being so bright that I can't identify it at once, loosens itself, in the shudder of a rich cascade of flames and threads. It's a *nombroeil!*[36]

In Cixous's creation myth, the narrator is urged to imagine a feminine principle that can fecundate itself; the progress of the epic is an "opera" (in the Latin sense of "works") of research into what hasn't yet been thought of. "Dare to be the unknown," the madman/fool says.[37]

As I have already mentioned, a large section of the opera/work involves a visit to various workshops, which function almost like autonomous, possible worlds that work according to a fixed principle. These include the "workshop's workshop," the "workshop of passages," the "workshop of numbers," followed by the "non-dialectical workshop," the "heliopolitical workshop," the "matrix workshop," and the "workshop of the Other." The first five workshops each exhibit a different cultural aporia that must be left behind in the narrator's quest. The apparitions of Faust already cited appear in the second, the "workshop of passages"; in the first workshop, the madman/fool brandishes a white piece of paper that the reader is warned against interpreting as an allusion to a pact.[38] This is as close as Cixous comes to mentioning a Faustian "bargain." Instead, the paper is truly blank, to represent the opera (work) of rewriting that will be required as the madman/fool, the narrator, and the reader progress though the text.

The "heliopolitical workshop" proposes one of Cixous's most visually arresting myths. Two cities, Heliopolis and Hermopolis, are trying to get the "great eye" for themselves; they are pulling at it, one from the north and one from the south, with cables that are buried beneath the sand. Each city is fighting for who will own the "real" (the eye). The two machines to which the cables are attached speak in enigmas: The first one inquires, "Who is the one who exists for himself and who is preceded? Who is the son who kills the father? Who is the daughter who bears the mother?" The other machine asks, "If the egg that is deposited in the ocean of Chaos contains the author who creates the ocean, who creates the egg; then who creates the author?" The argument ends with the appearance of a huge phallus: "Hero of the Hero, mortal, Father of all phantasms."[39] As the "new phallus" advances, he shoots the "eye" that blocks his progress. The "eye" is covered with cuneiform letters, and yet another "new phallus" is born. The reader who is alert to French feminist theory will have recognized the "machines" as the generators of patriarchal myths that are posited on the phallus-as-presence.

In the sixth workshop—that of the matrix (with its maternal root inscribed in its name), the narrator begins to create an alternative language, to correspond to the third term that will insert itself between the male-as-presence and its blank mirror-opposite, the traditional feminine. *Idée* (idea) becomes *Idieu* (combining *idea* and the French word for *god*). Now the narrator addresses the reader, asking her to become the maternal author of her work: "Am I not folded into your breast which I dream of transcending thanks to you?"[40] Finally, the reader, the madman/fool, and the narrator all arrive at the last workshop, that of the "Other." Here, they (we), as "the adventurers of the heteron," are all meant to feel quite at home:

> In this workshop the need to create accelerates the rhythm of Compositions, precipitates transferences, activates the identification of opposites, and you, reader, rip the silks of Signification and take my place, move with the speed of sight and conjugate your force with

mine in order to break me through to the light, here, here, here, here. . . . And you, bastard of mine and the world's, reader-eye, open yourself; I enter where I already am, at the speed of light, in the transparent company of a madman/fool. Let's tear down the veils! Let's burn the Signifiers! Whatever the cost, let's intrigue against meaning![41]

The "maternal" Goethe reappears and is said to have had a good delivery. A pathetic figure, he chases the echo of his own voice and narcissistically falls in love with it. But he is unable to explain the meaning of his work. Instead, Faust proclaims that his works (the "sons" of their creators, or *oeuvres-fils*) are not meant to be read but to be learned by heart.[42]

It is interesting that at this stage in her writing, Cixous indicts not the text produced by patriarchy but the way it is read (or memorized, as in this case). In place of rote acceptance, she proposes the *Lisant*, an active reader whose work will perform the work of cultural understanding. The narrator discovers her own shadow in the margins of an illuminated manuscript, "neither woman, nor man, nor being pleasing the eye, but knavish, pliable, elastic, and capable of crossing rivers at a single bound. He's the one who makes a charade between the fault and the eye [*faute* and *oeil*, which is also a play on *fauteuil*, the reader's cozy armchair]. It's the *Lisant*, he who reads himself."[43]

In *Révolutions*, the concept of the feminine is not entirely positive. Since Cixous's project is to rethink patriarchal culture, she includes some of the negative representations that have served as the guideposts of that culture. The first section of the book ends with the image of the stinking grandmother who gives birth to wars and, through war, to the epochs of history.[44] Cixous's negative female images correspond to Faust's encounter in *Faust*, part 2, with "the Mothers" who hold the web of time and whom he has to confront in order to summon forth Helen of Troy. In *Révolutions*, even when goddesses make a brief appearance as embodiments of the "eternal feminine," they are associated with death. "Your love gives me life," the goddess replies when the narrator declares herself willing to follow her even if she is Death itself.[45] The second section of the book is a further exploration of this equation of woman/death/history, an equation that Irigaray situates within patriarchy: "She is wholly devoted to giving life, then, source and re-source of life. To being still the restoring, nourishing mother who prolongs the work of death by sustaining it; death makes a detour through the revitalizing female-maternal."[46]

The second part of *Révolutions* starts out with the four horsemen of the apocalypse, which are said to represent the four movements of humanity in history: birth, construction, destruction, and death. The madman/fool explains that existence is a struggle: where there is war, there will be life. He invites the narrator to survey history from a balcony. From this vantage point, she observes, on the one hand, an army arising from a receptacle where all the world's seas have been stored; and on the other, a young woman and on old woman facing each other in "hateful complicity":

> Thus old age observes its youth and youth defies its old age, and each silently menaces and replies to the other: years separate them, time unites them, the marriage of wars and of the dead, goddesses of sterility: they give birth to monsters, to the spirits of murders, to phantasms of castration, to the great barbaric Instincts that depopulate and they stand rigid on the beach of the beaches in front of the army. The old woman is pregnant, the young woman is cold and dry.[47]

The madman/fool explains that the young one is "the universal non-mother," she who devours her own breasts; she destroys what she produces, vomiting forth dismembered cadavers. The old woman presides over the ritual self-castration and self-mutilation of an entire army and then walks along the beach collecting the severed testicles and penises that have already been rolled in flour and cooked. The narrator reflects that the old woman is the one who weeps for history.[48]

The fool/madman then shows her two scenes from history: the 1968 massacre at My-Lai by U.S. troops, and the Brazilian dictator Marshal Arthur da Costa e Silva who took power in Brazil in 1966. These two historical instances are intended to show her that the Real is unavoidably cruel. Yet, out of oppression, the new generations inevitably arise—from the cadavers of My-Lai, "millions of babies crawl toward us, naked, still humid, they roll over one another in their advance."[49]

The narrator is now ready to encounter Faust in his final incarnations. The concluding episode from history meshes the French Revolution, the struggle between the red and white factions in the Russian Revolution, and May 1968 in a symphonic finale. Faust reappears and wears, successively, the masks of Freud, Mao, and Zarathustra. He then splits into a red and white Faust, "mythical twins, sun and moon, the before and the after." The white Faust recedes to a dreamy horizon, and the narrator notices that he limps (this could be a reference to Oedipus, or Satan, or both). The red Faust advances, armed with a machine gun and a kind of hammer. The white Faust now wears a face "neither male or female, neither old nor young, but of an average human."[50] Frenetically, this Faust makes and destroys, while consulting an image that he wears on a watchband. It's supposed to be the image of Helen, but on closer inspection, it's just a picture of Faust himself. He can't find her for all his frenzied searching because he can only narcissistically find his own image. Finally, the white Faust sits by the sea and, using the water as a mirror, tries to paint the face of Helen over his own face, without, however, being able to change his eyes. It's a powerful image of the trap Irigaray describes, the result of the feminine being seen as the negative image of the masculine, rather than as an "other" in its own right: "Four centuries have passed. I've lived like a widower: after death. I am buried in the depths of these dead eyes. . . . I've lost the desire for myself and I haven't found the desire for the other."[51]

When the red Faust encounters the Chinese Revolution and suddenly believes that he has found Helen of Troy, it transpires that the madman/fool has been Faust all along and that the insatiable desire of Faust has been the desire for revolution. Cixous then unfolds a revolutionary theater in which *l'Ardent* (the ardent one) plays a major role, moving between the French Revolution and May 1968. In the end, though, the people are beaten back by the counterrevolutionary monster: "Except for his haunches he consists only of serpents. His arms reach out in several hundred kilometers in every direction. His horrible testicle pierces the sky, his hairy wings veil the light, his eyes throw bombs, his mouths and his penis spit flames that reduce entire regions to burnt coals."[52]

In the wake of the failures of 1968, Cixous ended her book with the images of failed revolution. She holds out hope by saying that the interminable, forking paths of history continue, and the "people" strive toward the future as "an eye-work, an eye-force, and History enters with great luminous waves in the matinal pupil."[53]

We can look back to a moment in Cixous's text when she offers an image of the "true" revolution that humanity should be striving toward: this is the image of Euphorion, the son of Faust and Helen, as imagined by Goethe. Like Goethe, Cixous presents a figure that, true to its name, disappears into the "euphoric" sky and cannot be held to earthly existence. But she also suggests that Euphorion represents a "third term" between the current definitions of masculine and feminine that might offer a way out of the endless mirroring that entraps current gender distinctions. The madman/fool describes Euphorion as

> neither vision nor allegory. . . . pretty, though not a girl; strong, though not a boy; it's the body-soul, the one who makes himself while laughing, and laughs to make himself, he is born from the acme of desire, his growth is never finished, he is the Se-Duction, he bursts forth wherever men weaken, he recharges the languid members, he enriches desiccated souls, the Splendid One, the essence of immaterial Goods, the Inexhaustible One. From lack, he makes desire, from the void aspiration, from absence the most brilliant phantasms; give him what you do not have, and he'll give you what he is; but first, ask yourself if your throat is not rusty, and whether you can scream with joy.

The sight of this hermaphroditic creature has a corresponding effect on the narrator, who collapses in a euphoric orgasm: "I dissolve, I burn, I evaporate, I freeze with love." Then she falls back into the real world "where men are like animals."[54]

In Cixous's 1975 work *Sorties*, the male intertext has been almost entirely replaced by women: Helen, Penthesilea. Reading *Sorties*, the reader is struck by how this is a seamless, evolutionary change, as though *Révolutions* were the first stage in a project of rewriting culture that was mapped out beforehand with broad strokes. Some passages of *Sorties* read like a gloss on *Révolutions*; consider, for instance, this statement about woman's "selfhood":

> If there is a self proper to woman, paradoxically it is her capacity to de-appropriate herself without self-interest: endless body, without "end," without principal "parts"; if she is a whole, it is a whole made up of parts that are wholes, not simple, partial objects but varied entirety, moving and boundless change, a cosmos where eros never stops traveling, vast astral space.[55]

Susan Suleiman has shown how the idea of the encounter of the ideal masculine and the ideal feminine is a recurrent theme in Cixous's work.[56] In later works, these forces take on further mythological embodiments: Achilles and Penthesilea (in *Sorties*), Chlorina and Tancredi (in *Coming to Writing*). Suleiman has also, quite aptly I think, seen the connection between Cixous's writing style and the "automatic writing" of the surrealists.

The author's recurrent play on the theme of perception and the eye also recalls the famous scene in Buñuel and Dali's 1928 film, *Un Chien Andalou*, in which the spectator's perception is assaulted by the slicing of an eye. In other ways, too, she often seems close to the images of surrealist film. For instance, the separation of the lovers by the forces of repressive authority in *Révolutions pour plus d'un Faust* might remind her readers of the scene in Buñuel's 1931 film *L'Age d'or* in which two lovers roll passionately in the mud during a ground-breaking ceremony. Forcefully separated by representatives of the church and state, they keep trying to reunite during the film.

The union between ideal male and female qualities is also a surrealist concept—one, moreover, that the surrealists themselves derived from alchemy.[57] It would be consistent with Cixous's Faustian theme to explore alchemical metaphors, because the figure of Faust has been linked with alchemy since the beginning. Ultimately, Cixous's optimism is based on the idea that the unending quest of the narrator and the reader through the history of the world, which is said to be "interminable" (the last word of her book), will lead to the discovery of a spiritual or at least immaterial "gold." As the madman/fool reassuringly states, "the heart of the earth is of gold."[58] The link with surrealism and with alchemy enables us to gloss Goethe's own final lines—"Das Ewig-Weibliche / zieht uns hinan" (Woman Eternal / Draw us on high, 12110–11)—as a reference to the unification, in alchemy, of energies symbolically depicted as male and female. Faust's ending thus becomes depersonalized, and rather than ending on a note of individual salvation, his death and return to the earth represent the cycle of creation itself. The "endless striving" that brings about Faust's redemption is not that of an individual but of the elemental forces in which, as a part of nature, individuals participate.

Faustine: Surrealist Dream Imagery

The influence of surrealism is felt in yet another work that feminizes Faust, British novelist Emma Tennant's *Faustine* (1992). Her novel is a haunting work that moves oneirically between the different layers of consciousness and memory of the main character, Ella, and then juxtaposes these with the "tales" of other characters. At the start of the novel, it is the year 1989, and Ella is twenty-six. Raised in Australia by a friend of her mother's, she has returned to a large country mansion near Stonehenge, England, where she remembers her grandmother having lived. As Ella tries to piece together her past from her memory fragments, to "make a pattern where before there was only the blank space of absence and trying to forget," a recurrent image floats in and out of her consciousness.[59] Her recollection is dreamlike: "What I remember may be as invented or as real as a dream. Did I really see the trees in a park 12,000 miles away, straining in a great wind, and see the fear on the face of the man who was pushing me in my pram?"[60]

For the reader who reads this novel within the Western cultural tradition, this passage may evoke surrealist imagery, similarly constructed on the logic of dreams. This image of the child threatened by external forces is suggestive of the surrealist world of Max Ernst and has an eerie quality similar to his 1924 collage, *Two Children Menaced by a Nightingale*. In the painted part of this work, a young girl with a knife runs, her long hair flowing behind her. A dead girl lies on the ground. At the apex of the roof, a painted figure seems to be kidnapping a child. The dreamlike quality of the representation is heightened by the collage of wooden elements in other parts of the picture: a small painted shed is topped by a projecting wooden roof, while a wood knife is attached to the front of the shed. The picture plays with its frame: a knob joins the painted canvas to the wooden frame, suggesting that this representation is a decorated door onto another reality—that you can go behind the painting to another space. Also, to the left of the girls, a wooden gate opens out onto the picture frame; it is attached with tiny metal hinges to a wooden post—another reference to opening, to the articulation of space. In this way, Ernst's work oscillates between the representation and the frame that separates it off from the world, a metaphor perhaps for the oscillation in dreams between memory, construction, and the lightning connections of what Freud called "the dreamwork." In Ella's memory, this threatening memory image recurs obsessively until she finally interprets its import.

At the English mansion, people seem to expect Ella, even though they don't welcome her. Prevented from leaving by a demonstration of hippies at Stonehenge, she wanders about the mansion, meeting a surly couple who serve as caretakers, then Jasmine (the "nurse"), who was an old friend of her grandmother's, and finally her mother, Anna. Tennant interweaves the stories of these two new encounters with Ella's own memories until time becomes twisted and circular. What are hippies doing at Stonehenge in 1989?

The mystery that Ella is trying to unravel is why her grandmother abandoned her and left her to be raised in Australia. She seems never to have developed a relationship with her mother, a feminist publisher who was willing to put her professional interests ahead of her daughter. Ella feels betrayed only by the grandmother, whom she adored. As she moves about the mansion, Ella notices that several rooms have been set aside as a shrine to a 1960s pop star, Warhol model, and successful media executive, Lisa Crane. The shrine celebrates Lisa's youth, beauty, and power. Ella finds herself fascinated by Lisa. At twenty-seven, Ella is already feeling that she never wants to grow old, and as she looks at the young people protesting at Stonehenge, she reflects ruefully that she never really had a chance to enjoy her youth.

Eventually, the different tales coalesce into the story of Muriel Twyman, the grandmother. The central moment of the story is Ella's dreamlike image of the pram in the thunderstorm, for it was at this moment that Muriel signed a pact with the devil in exchange for twenty-four years of youth, beauty, and power. The grandmother is, in fact, Lisa Crane, whose time will run out on Ella's second night at the mansion. She will revert to her old self and regain her real age—seventy-two years old.

Tennant's final images at the mansion are oneiric. The scene she now describes is one of stasis and waiting, with the sense of an impending climax. For the reader familiar with surrealist painting, this scene may evoke a memory of René Magritte's 1927 painting *L'Assassin menacé* (The Menaced Assassin); in that painting, the corpse of a woman, unblemished except for blood that flows from the mouth, lies on a table in the middle of a room. The impeccably suited "assassin" leans toward a victrola; the needle seems near the end of the record. Outside the window in back of him, three suited men watch and wait. On either side of the door, two more men in dark suits and bowler hats are lurking—one with a club, another with a net. The faces of these six men are all expressionless, as though lost in thought at the music. They wait for the music to finish; their eyes are unfocused. It is a moment of suspension, of timelessness: after the murder, before the arrest?

In Tennant's mise-en-scène of a similarly lugubrious waiting game, the dinner table has been set for six, but as the guests move toward the table, they undergo transformations. Anna and Jasmine wait at the table. A man walks up the drive. A young woman begins her descent to the hall. A hand knocks on the oak door, which is opened by the young woman. A wind comes in with the visitor.

At this point, the image of the young woman and the visitor is doubled, as they are both seen once again walking arm in arm up the drive. This is Ella, in company with the devil. The previous chapter has informed us that she looks identical to Lisa Crane: "The mirrors in the room show her face and mine—like two halves of an apple."[61] The reader is given to understand that Ella has also decided she never wants to grow old, and that she, too, will make a pact with the devil.

In that moment, though, Lisa must turn into the seventy-two-year-old Muriel Twyman. This happens in yet another surrealist image: "It can only be the effect of light and shade from the moon—the swirling party colors from the windows of the house—that gives the impression that an old woman, huge in the faint glow from the fires in the woods, is running up the drive after them."[62] This leaves the reader with one more mystery—why is the table set for six and not five (Ella, her mother, her grandmother, Jasmine, and the devil)? Does the devil have two places at the table—or will Lisa Crane and her former self, the seventy-two-year-old Muriel Twyman, both be seated as ghostly doubles? Tennant's oneiric imagery makes clear that this is a dinner party that can never take place, caught as it is in the circularity of time; it is a meeting toward which the strands in the plot move without ever arriving.

In *Faustine*, Tennant attacks contemporary consumerism and mass culture, showing that women are tempted to want to stay young forever lest they become "invisible" to the society around them. The author uses dark humor to probe her characters' wish to deny the aging process: in his coda, "The Devil's Tale," the devil refers to the forty-eight-year-old Muriel Twyman as the "sad menopausee" and describes her as an "easy prey" for his flattery. Yet he also reflects that the materiality of the quest for youth and beauty is inconsistent with the very idea of a soul.[63] In the end, the devil himself is frustrated—the women he makes pacts with slip away from him, their souls wiped out by superficiality. In the end, he stands for Chaos, the apocalypse, as Ella darkly surmises when she glimpses him: "He turns and sees me. At that moment I know the earth is very old, and cannot much longer endure the chaos and ruination brought upon it."[64]

Ella's journey is, in fact, a kind of descent into hell: she describes the old caretakers as the guardians of a "Cerberus gate-room to the life-in-death chamber of Lisa Crane."[65] Hell is the place where the generations are out of diachronic succession, where the quest for youth turns your grandmother into your younger sister. Consumer society, from Tennant's perspective, is hell on earth, for women at least.

As *Faustine* makes clear, the problem for writers who conceive of a feminine Faust lies with the vexing question of femininity itself. Irigaray has shown how femininity in our culture is invariably defined as the "other" of maleness and hence has no independent characteristics of its own; as it is traditionally conceptualized, it is "a sort of inverted or negative alter ego— 'blank' too, like a photographic negative." If femininity is simply the opposite of maleness, this leaves women "off-stage, off-side, beyond representation, beyond selfhood."[66]

This is, in fact, what happens to Emma Tennant's women. Lisa Crane's power comes from the fact that others desire her; what she herself might want, other than their desire, doesn't enter the picture. Tennant can see through her character, but she can't see a way out of Lisa's, or later Ella's, predicament. This is what Irigaray would have us expect: "Woman would thus find no possible way to represent or tell the story of the economy of her libido. Just as man would find no possible meaning in 'female libido.' The libido is masculine, or at any rate neuter."[67]

Tennant's novel is an effective exploration of the implications for women of one facet of the Faustian bargain: the desire for youth. For Goethe's Faust, youth provides the possibility not only for romantic conquest but also for an active role in the world as an adviser to the powerful. For Tennant's female Faust, youth is linked to the woman's wanting to remain an *object* of desire, along with the power and fame that accompanies that status. Yet this doesn't necessarily mean that Tennant fails to imagine women could want anything else. The surrealist, dreamlike atmosphere of her novel suggests rather that she depicts women whose unconscious is profoundly colonized and accepting of women's traditional social roles. Her Mephisto figure mocks the vulnerability of women who accept being defined in terms of youthful attractiveness, characterizing his victim as "the latest convert to the cult of eternal youth." But even the devil ends up asking the exasperated question, "What the hell do women really want?"[68]

Faust and Feminism

In these feminist texts, the Faust myth plays a counterhegemonic role. To propose a female Faust goes against the historical and cultural assumption that Faust is male. Wedekind and Cixous explode received notions of masculinity from within. Franziska experiences both sides of the gender divide, while Cixous's hermaphroditic narrator-protagonist and shifting grammatical gender markers subvert the way Western discourse reinforces male dominance. Tennant, widening the path opened by Alcott, proposes rebellious heroines who make Faustian bargains in order to claim independence and power. Though they retain certain traits that are traditionally ascribed to femininity, their active and obsessive pursuit of their desires sets them apart. Like Else Lasker-Schüler in *Ichundich*, they make a claim for women's full participation in what Goethe's Faust claimed as "what to all of mankind is apportioned" (1770).

In sum, the twentieth century saw not one but many "feminisms." Western cultural feminism, which sought to rethink women's traditional role through historical myth, language, and narrative, could not ignore the Faust story that has been so influential in its definition of Western "man." The Faust legacy, especially after Goethe, also served to define the role of "woman," variously conceived as object of desire and as mediator between man's transgressive self and the meliorative conscience he personifies as his god. The feminist engagement with the Faustian allowed writers to explore issues such as essentialism (the extent to which the feminine is bound up with the female body), transgender identity, and gender socialization.

Nancy Fraser's writings have been influential in suggesting that to posit any set of attributes/desires as feminine runs the risk of falling back on the old Freudian model according to which anatomy is destiny. The ambitious project of writing a female Faust comes up squarely against the major issues of French and American feminist thinking, with all their cultural, social, and psychoanalytic ramifications. Recent writing has also stressed the differences between women from different classes, races, nationalities, religions, and partnering preferences.

In this respect, Weimar cinema, and in particular Murnau's *Faust*, deserves another look. For one of the aspects of that cinema was to offer female spectators a viewing experience in which feminine desire could be acknowledged and even flattered. Janet Bergstrom has noted how the sensual attractiveness of the young Faust figure in Murnau's film is an example of a "clearly-coded feminine displaced onto the body of an aestheticized male-gendered character."[69] Bergstrom suggests that female spectators are asked to identify with the old Faust's desire for his younger self, a desire almost immediately headed off by the vision of a transparently veiled woman that Mephisto presents to Faust as the kind of erotic experience to which he will thenceforth be entitled. For the woman spectator, this vision, which puts woman back in her place as object, legitimizes the female spectator's experience of same-sex desire: "Given all this narrative and stylistic machinery, the viewer is left to enjoy the beauty of the young Faust without thinking twice."[70] Along the same lines, Patrice Petro has written about the way that Weimar melodrama reinforces the spectatorial enjoyment offered by Murnau's feminized Faust figure and "opens up a space for female subjectivity and desire, where the contemplative gaze is inseparable from an alternative conception of female spectatorship and visual pleasure."[71] In the end, one of the most important uses of the Faust myth for feminism has been its transformation, in the interest of a female readership, to reflect forms of feminine desire that are not linked to that of being an object for someone else's libido.

This is not to say that cultural feminism as an emancipatory project has been superseded. As Beatrice Hanssen cogently argues, "we need to see the different feminisms standing side by side . . . so that a so-called cultural feminism that demands the recognition of identity claims can cohabit with other branches, for example, those concerned more specifically with economic redistribution."[72] Today's plural feminisms may perhaps offer new Fausts, socialist feminists who will put their imprimatur on Faust's active principle and prove themselves agents for revolutionary social change.

5   Anti-Fausts and the Avant-Garde

Georg Lukács saw Goethe's *Faust* as the expression of "the destiny of all mankind," an attempt to synthesize in a single work the history and identity of Western humanity.[1] But Lukács also saw that Goethe stood on the brink of a new world he could not be a part of. His synthesis looks backward. At the end of part 2 of *Faust*, Faust is blinded and cannot step into the modern world he has helped to create. The two parts of *Faust* stand as summations of the inquiring and irreverent humanism that began with the Renaissance and the Reformation, continued through the Enlightenment and the Sturm und Drang, and ended with Goethe's unique mixture of measured classicism and self-affirming romanticism.

By the beginning of the twentieth century, new spirits were stirring as literary and artistic avant-gardes turned their ire against bourgeois society and its institutions. Faust reappears in avant-garde works as the enemy of reason, the necromancer who sets himself up as the opponent of those very humanist values with which the myth had traditionally been associated.

In *Theory of the Avant-Garde*, Peter Bürger delineates the way that the avant-garde attack on the institutions of art stems from the artists' concern that artistic conventions had removed art from life. Using various strategies of transgression, artists sought to reaffirm the connection between art and the social world. To this end, it was important to avant-garde artists to avoid creating works that were complete in themselves and thus closed off from the real world. Bürger argues that the avant-garde used two strategies to break out of the conventional mold. The first affected the aesthetics of form, in that montage became the most important component in avant-garde works: by fitting together disparate elements that lay bare the constructed nature of their joining, the appearance of a closed totality is avoided. The second has to do with strategies of reception: the spectator/reader/listener becomes an active participant in the work to the extent that he/she experiences the fragmented construction of the work as a shock.[2]

Both strategies are deployed in those twentieth-century avant-garde works that seek to challenge the role that the Faust legend has played in Western cultural traditions. When Faust appears as a character, he is so unlike the Faust of classical humanism that a shock effect is produced. Instead of Goethe's sublime and energetic striver, we are presented with dreamers living on the margins of society. Alfred Jarry's Faustroll practices the science of "'pataphysics." Gertrude Stein's frustrated Faust sells his soul to the devil in order to invent electricity and then realizes he could have done just as well on his own. The French surrealist Georges Ribemont-Dessaignes offers a comic Faust, henpecked by his cook Mephistopheles. And Michel de Ghelderode's Faust ventures outside his laboratory in the sixteenth century only to discover that an actor is playing him onstage in the twentieth.

The shock effect of the work can also be brought about through its formal construction. Avant-garde works break away radically from the accepted norms for art. Alfred Schnittke's "Faust Cantata" and Faust opera superimpose musical citations from several epochs and styles onto the damnation scene from Spies's sixteenth-century chapbook. *Votre Faust*, an opera composed by the Belgian Henri Pousseur with a libretto by French author Michel Butor, seeks to actively involve the spectator by enlisting the audience's participation in choosing from among several different possible plotlines. The four Faust films by experimental filmmaker Stan Brakhage in the United States are part of that filmmaker's lifelong project to help the spectator unlearn visual codes and learn new ways of seeing.

A Precursor of Modernism: Alfred Jarry

Alfred Jarry's *Les Gestes et opinions du docteur Faustroll, 'pataphysicien* was written in 1897–98, when the author was twenty-four, and published posthumously in 1911 after Jarry had become the darling of the Parisian avant-garde. The hero, Faustroll, is presented in mock-scientific terms as the inventor of "'pataphysics," or the science of particulars; in other words, the laws that govern the exceptions to the rule: "'Pataphysics is the science of imaginary solutions, which symbolically accords to features the properties of objects described by their virtual nature."[3] To see how such a science might work, Jarry invites us, through his character Faustroll, to imagine that objects do not fall according to the laws of gravity. Instead, the void rises up around an object, making it appear to fall. As whimsical as this may seem, Jarry criticizes the anthropocentric view of the world that Stan Brakhage will take issue with almost a full century later in his experimental films. When Faustroll changes himself into a small insect in order to observe the entire universe reflected in a drop of water,[4] he prefigures Brakhage's insistence that we have to relearn how to see.

Removed from his apartment by the bailiff Pamulphe for nonpayment of his rent, Faustroll talks the official into navigating across Paris with him in his bed. Faustroll explains that the boat/bed cannot sink for the simple reason that it will remain on land. Setting out with twenty-seven volumes of literature and a monkey whose only spoken words are "haha," the two men set off for places whose sources are literary and whose description amounts to a dense, intertextual network of citations.

The play is a frontal attack on social conventions and institutions. Jarry's text is laced with modern versions of Faust's exploits, in mock-scientific language; it concludes with a final section of Faustroll's (posthumous) writings in the "'pataphysical" spirit, including a meditation on "ethernity" (*ether* + *eternity*) and a geometry of the divine ("God is the shortest distance from zero to infinity").[5] In Jarry, we can already observe the turn away from rationalism and the Enlightenment tradition that was to be so important for Dada and surrealism. Both would, in fact, hail him as a precursor. Like them, he turned away with disgust from bourgeois society and celebrated self-expression at the expense of logic.

Absurdism and Surrealism: Michel de Ghelderode and Georges Ribemont-Dessaignes

In the Faust drama of Michel de Ghelderode, absurdism is combined with a pessimistic critique of the way masses of people can be manipulated for destructive purposes. Ghelderode (born Adémar-Adolphe-Louis Martens in 1898 in Ixelles, a suburb of Brussels) drifted into theater from cabaret writing. Because he was interested in folk stories and the marionette theater (which is a sophisticated art form in Belgium), he was soon able to find regular employment as a playwright with the Flemish Popular Theater (Vlaamsche Volkstoonneel). Although he wrote in French, the performances of his plays were in Flemish. *La Mort du docteur Faust* (*The Death of Doctor Faust*) was written in 1925.

Ghelderode's international fame did not come until after World War II, when he was "discovered" in Paris by the somewhat younger practitioners of the "theater of the absurd" (Eugene Ionesco, Arthur Adamov, and Samuel

Beckett). Although not officially part of this movement, his works are most easily understood in this context. In *The Death of Doctor Faust*, the boundaries between illusion and reality become fluid and interchangeable. The historical Faust meets his modern "other," with catastrophic consequences for both. As Ghelderode said in an interview conducted in Ostende, Belgium, in 1956:

> Of course I modernized the Germanic fable: Faust no longer regrets the life he has missed and aspires to a renewal, a metamorphosis. Instead, it's a drama about identity. My Faust looks into himself, wants to know who he really is. In order to realize this identity—because until now, on the threshold of old age, he has been only a fake and conventional person—he decides to live in a vulgar manner, like an ordinary person. He wants to live by his senses and with his feet on the ground, not on the ceiling! So Faust begins a human adventure. He goes looking for himself. In the end, he finds himself, but on the threshold of death; and the experiment, naturally, ends badly.[6]

Ghelderode's play is subtitled "A Tragedy for the Music Hall." The playwright has constructed a work that only masquerades as a farce. Underneath, there is a tone of pessimism, even despair. As the play begins, the sixteenth-century Faust ventures forth from his study for the first time, only to find himself in the same Flemish city in the twentieth century during carnival. He wanders into the Tavern of the Four Seasons where a Faust play is about to be performed on a cabaret stage. Watching the proceedings is the devil Diamotoruscant, who is up to all kinds of mischief before the play begins. He throttles a human loudspeaker/news announcer, argues with a poet about the devil, recycles the announcer's news as a cinematic variety show, and then hypnotizes the customers into unmoving figures before the play begins on the cabaret stage. In the tavern, the sixteenth-century Faust meets a twentieth-century Marguerite, a servant girl. The Faust play doesn't please either one of them, and they leave to go to the fair. Diamotoruscant stays behind to heckle the actor playing the devil. Losing all control over his lines, the actor announces the end of the world to the reawakened customers, and the first act of Ghelderode's play ends in chaos. In the second act, Faust is trying to rid himself of Marguerite, whom he has raped. Outside the hotel, Marguerite makes a public scene and accuses him of betraying her. Diamotoruscant, who has been waiting next to a nearby movie theater, responds to Faust's call for help. He convinces the shocked bystanders that Marguerite's protests are only an act, put on as a public advertisement for the Faust play to be staged that night in the Tavern of the Four Seasons. In despair, Marguerite then commits suicide by throwing herself under a streetcar.

For the third act, the stage is divided into two spaces on which the action takes place simultaneously—inside Faust's study and outside in the street. The street scene is filled with townspeople and policemen who are looking for the culprit in Marguerite's suicide. A screen projects headlines announcing the circumstances of the girl's tragic end. The actor Faust is forced to flee and takes refuge in the sixteenth-century study. There he is amazed to be addressed as Faust by Faust's disciple Cretinus. When the sixteenth-century Faust arrives, he discovers his double there, along with the cabaret actress who played the role of Marguerite onstage. Diamotoruscant looks on while the two Fausts confront each other. Statements by Faust lead the actor Faust to believe that the actress Marguerite has betrayed him, whereupon he rushes outside (back into the twentieth century) only to be caught and lynched by the vengeful crowd. Back on the other side of the stage, with Diamotoruscant's encouragement, the "real" Faust shoots himself (like Balduin in *Der Student von Prag*). Dying, he wonders aloud, "Tell me where is Faust? Where does he begin? Where does he end? Is he a fiction? . . . I am following a shadow. Am I going to murder phantoms?"[7]

Douglas Cole traces the influences on *The Death of Doctor Faust* from the early modernist plays of Guillaume Apollinaire and Jean Cocteau, as well as the movement in France "to purify the theater by restoring to it the elements of spectacle, music and fantasy which had been ignored by the conventions of the well-made play and salon comedy."[8] Indeed, the play-within-a-play structure, the allusion to the cinema, and the emphasis on costume and disguise do recall *Les Mamelles de Tiresias* (Apollinaire, 1917) and *Les Mariés de la tour Eiffel* (Cocteau, 1921). James Ensor's maskers are specifically alluded to in the play, as they move through the crowd and across the cabaret stage as carnival figures. But perhaps more important, Ghelderode's violent ending looks forward to Antonin Artaud's "theater of cruelty," which had its roots in Dada and surrealism. From Dada, Artaud took the total rejection of tradition, and from surrealism, the idea that art should express the ideas of the unconscious. The murder of the actor Faust by the enraged masses and the "real" Faust's suicide might be viewed retrospectively as symptoms of the widespread rejection by artists and writers of the 1920s of the Western cultural values that had led to the slaughter of World War I. In *The Theater and Its Double* (1938), Artaud was to outline his ideas for a radical new theater: "The theater will never find itself again—i.e., constitute a means of true illusion—except by furnishing the spectator with the truthful precipitates of dreams, in which his taste for crime, his erotic obsessions, his savagery, his chimeras, his utopian sense of life and matter, even his cannibalism, pour out, on a level not counterfeit and illusory, but interior."[9]

In his "Second Letter on Cruelty" (1932), Artaud sounds like Goethe's Mephistopheles: "I employ the word 'cruelty' in the sense of an appetite for life, a cosmic rigor and implacable necessity, in the gnostic sense of a living whirlwind that devours the darkness, in the sense of that pain apart from whose ineluctable necessity life could not continue; good is desired, it is the consequence of an act; evil is permanent."[10]

Ghelderode's Faust leaves his sixteenth-century study in the spirit of this "appetite for life," with tragic consequences. Ghelderode intimates how the public can be influenced by mass media to dispense summary justice that often mistakes the real culprit. In this modern era, the devil has become a master of illusions who serves up the news as cinematic entertainment and cynically panders to the thrill-seeking crowd. Alternately hypnotized and violent, the crowd offers a prescient picture of Fascist manipulation. Faust himself has lost his footing in this modern world; mistaken for an illusion, he ends up wondering if he even has a soul. The "real" Faust is at first a comic figure that sallies forth to satisfy his sexual desires; his darker side is revealed when he rejects Marguerite once she has satisfied him because he doesn't want to spoil his image as a scholar. On the other hand, the actor dies from taking his role too seriously and rushing out into the crowd claiming he is Faust.

Ghelderode's pessimism is allegorized in the stalking masqueraders—the figure of death that visits Faust's door and the three maskers who wordlessly haunt the cabaret stage. The pessimism is made clear in other ways as well. The characters in the play are afflicted by a constriction of space—there is nowhere to flee, as the actor Faust discovers. Whether on stage, in Faust's sixteenth-century study, or among the vengeful twentieth-century crowd, there is no escape from death. Yet even the dying in the play suffer from illusion—caught in the web of appearances and role-playing, the dead do not even die as themselves. Even as they expire, they wonder who they are or whom they have been taken for (and Marguerite, of course, is the victim of the illusions of others).

Written six years after Ghelderode's *The Death of Doctor Faust*, Georges Ribemont-Dessaignes's *Faust* (1931) is surrealist in inspiration. We find examples of "automatic writing" generated from the onomatopoetic repetition of sounds, as in "je n'entends rien à son croah de corneille nourrie de calculs" (I understand nothing of his crow's croak nourished in calculations), or surrealist images pulled from distant realities, as in "melancholy as the blade of a knife."[11] True to the irreverent attitude of surrealism for received masterworks of the past, Ribemont-Dessaignes's play parodies Goethe. The disciple is a wise crow educated by Faust who resumes the whole world in a single croak and who has learned all the sciences: "botany, chemistry, pharmacy, a real doctor," Faust brags. (This also recalls Dr. Faustroll's monkey who only says "haha.") The great project at the end of *Faust*, part 2, is turned into a public works project for communal garbage collection. Goethe's nay-saying Mephistopheles becomes Faust's cook Ophidie, whose delight is to contradict him at every turn. Faust knows she is the devil because she is able to distinguish good from evil, whereas God and human beings have lost this capacity.

Goethe ended his Faust works with a paean to the feminine; the founder of surrealism, André Breton, made the quest for the "feminine" one of his guiding principles. His ideal was the hermaphrodite that would unite male and female. Ribemont-Dessaignes's *Faust* is typical of surrealist productions in that the women become the dominant focus (as in, for instance, Breton's novel *Nadja*). Marguerite, true to the surrealist valorization of spontaneity, rejects the proposal of an accountant's clerk who offers her bourgeois marriage with four children, Sunday outings, a piano, and a sewing machine; but she falls victim to Faust's faithlessness and kills herself. Helen, on the other hand, becomes cynical and accuses Faust of sleeping with her not for her own sake but for the sake of her good looks. Faust is stoned and beaten to death by the villagers who take revenge for Marguerite's suicide. This is a play stripped of any religiosity: Ophidie, the devil-cook, stands over Faust's corpse and announces that "there is but one demon, and it's the one that takes us by the hand to the empty void of death."[12]

It should be said that, this parody notwithstanding, Breton drew the second part of Goethe's *Faust* into the surrealist pantheon of myths in the 1947 exhibition "Arcane 17." Each of the twenty-one steps up to the exhibition hall was associated with one of the trumps of the tarot and with one "proto-surrealist" writer from the past. Step 15 (The Devil) was assigned to Alfred Jarry, and the following one (The Tower), to the second part of *Faust*. Along-side Goethe's role as a cultural icon—a role that the surrealists were eager to question—Breton seems also to have recognized the transgressive and liberating aspect of Goethe's work.[13]

Gertrude Stein and Contemporary Multimedia

Composed just before the outbreak of hostilities in World War II, Gertrude Stein's 1938 play *Doctor Faustus Lights the Lights* is at most an oblique response to the coming crisis. Stein's concern for avant-garde production outweighs any political interpretation one might want to place on this work. As both Henri Pousseur and Stan Brakhage were later to do, she mixes the myth of Orpheus with that of Faust. Conceived as an opera libretto with interspersed ballet scenes (the work was commissioned by the British composer Gerald Berners, who was unable to complete the score), *Doctor Faustus Lights the Lights* has only been performed as a play. Nevertheless, music is important to an understanding of the work, particularly in light of the Orpheus theme. In addition, Stein's internally rhyming sentences, constructed as a montage or collage of fragments, create a verbal mix that is highly incantatory and rhythmic. Her verbal assemblages in *Doctor Faustus Lights the Lights* have their own harmonies and dissonances, intensities and serene moments.

If musicality is important to the piece, so is mise-en-scène. Doctor Faustus, presented at the outset as the inventor of electric light (an accomplishment for which he has sold his soul to the devil), appears in his doorway with a blaze of electric light behind him. Later, the heroine, "Marguerite Ida and Helena Annabel," appears in her own halo of light. The ballet sequences are described in terms of lights going on and off, or simply as "a ballet of lights."

When the play opens, Faustus has decided his invention is a curse. He believes he could have invented electricity without the devil's help: "If I had not been in a hurry and if I had taken my time I would have known how to make white electric light and day-light and night lights and what did I do I saw you you miserable devil I saw you and I was deceived and I believed miserable devil I thought I needed you, and I thought I was tempted by the devil and I know no temptation is tempting unless the devil tells you so."[14]

Faustus is also tormented with the idea that perhaps he was tricked—

perhaps he didn't even have a soul to sell. Besides, he now longs for darkness ("now there is nothing more either by day or by night but just a light").[15] Faustus asks his dog (who keeps saying "thank you") and the boy who comes to play with him to leave him alone, and he begins to dream of a woman, "Marguerite Ida and Helena Annabel." Her composite name combines the names of Goethe's two Faustian heroines. But Marguerite Ida and Helena Annabel, when she appears in scene 2 of the first act, is also Eurydice.

Bitten by a viper, she is instructed by an old woman to seek Doctor Faustus so that he can cure her. Like Faustus, who is confused about whether he has a soul, Marguerite Ida and Helena Annabel is confused about her identity:

> Do vipers sting do vipers bite
> If they bite with all their might
> Do they do they sting
> Or do they do they bite
> Alright they bite if they bite with all their might.
> And I am I Marguerite Ida or am I Helena Annabel
> Oh well
> Am I Marguerite Ida or am I Helena Annabel.[16]

In scene 3, Faustus cures Marguerite Ida and Helena Annabel, thus saving her from going to hell ("as my soul has not been sold I Marguerite Ida and Helena Annabel perhaps I will go to hell"). Like Orpheus, who could not look on Eurydice without losing her to the underworld, Faustus is instructed by Marguerite Ida and Helena Annabel not to look at her ("you have the light cure me Doctor Faustus cure me do but do not see me, I see you but do not see me cure me do but do not see me I implore you").[17] Faustus is successful, and the chorus sings in the distance:

> Who is she
> She has not gone to hell
> Very well
> Very well.

Meanwhile, the heroine rejoices, "I am Marguerite Ida and Helena Annabel and enough said I am not dead."[18]

The second act is a bit of an interlude. The rescued heroine appears, bathed in light. Her light is described as a halo of candlelight, and she has begun to draw pilgrims who come by sea, land, and air to see her. There is a "ballet of lights" in celebration. A man comes "from over the sea," accompanied by a boy and girl. He sings a love song: "I am the only he and you are the only she and we are the only we. Come come do you hear me come come, you must come to me." However, Marguerite Ida and Helena Annabel rejects her suitor once she recognizes Mephistopheles standing behind him. Brandishing the artificial viper she holds in her hand, she tries to ward off the devil: "Lights are all right but the viper is my might." Mephisto only laughs and taunts her with the insufficiency of her candlelight: "Where is the real electric light woman answer me." He rushes off, warning, "if I work day and night and I do I do I work day and night, then you will see what you will see, look out look out for me."[19]

Act 3 brings all the characters onstage along with the chorus and ballet. Faustus learns from the chorus that Marguerite Ida and Helena Annabel can turn night into day, although she does it not with electric light but by ruling the sun and the moon. Instead of being jealous, Faustus is delighted, because now he can hope to enjoy darkness and perhaps even go to hell. He will no longer have to be alone and aloof with his invention ("never again will I be alone"). A reverse Orpheus, Faustus now wants to go to hell with his Eurydice. Mephistopheles agrees to rejuvenate him so that Marguerite Ida and Helena Annabel will love him; but he insists that Faustus must commit a sin before he can be accepted in hell. Faustus sets the viper on the boy and the dog and then takes the credit for killing them. But once again the devil shows himself the master of deception. Marguerite Ida and Helena Annabel refuses to recognize Faustus in the young man he has become through Mephistophelean magic and chooses the "man from over the seas" instead. Faustus is claimed by Mephistopheles and "sinks into the darkness" alone as the voices of the boy and the girl call out in vain to the viper that Marguerite Ida and Helena Annabel had once brandished as a countervailing force to evil: "Please Mr. Viper listen to me he is he and she is she and we are we please Mr. Viper listen to me."[20]

The thin protesting voices of the two children read a bit like the note of hope that Zeitblom hears at the end of Leverkühn's musical setting of Faust's damnation. Although Stein's apolitical stance during the buildup of Nazism and the war years (which she spent in Vichy France) reveals an intellectual blind spot, she seems to have been strongly affected by the intensity, violence, and irrationalism of those times.[21] Like Thomas Mann, she sends her Faustus to damnation, although like Goethe, she saves her heroine, whose multiple names and mythic identities make a claim on the idea of the mythic feminine, as opposed to the masculine principle embodied by the overly controlling figures of Doctor Faustus and even the "man from over the seas." Mephistopheles himself sees his power limited to control over men—despite his threats, he holds no sway over the heroine.

The premiere of Stein's *Doctor Faustus Lights the Lights* did not take place until 1951 at the Cherry Lane Theater in New York, with incidental music by Richard Banks.[22] More recently, New York's Wooster Group Theater in SoHo presented its multimedia adaptation of the work, *House/Lights* (directed by Elizabeth LeCompte), to considerable critical acclaim.[23]

The collage/montage effect of Stein's poetic language was augmented in *House/Lights* by the splintering of the stage action onto multiple image layers, with the use of video monitors, a video camera, and a computer that appeared to orchestrate the different image sources. Stein's idea for a "ballet of lights" was carried out onstage by electric lights strung on poles that could be raised and lowered, while her humorous take on male domination was amplified by the insertion into the action of a low-budget sadomasochistic cult film of the 1960s, Joseph Mawra's *Olga's House of Shame*. The film's voice-over presentation of successive women who are being beaten and tortured (in a mise-en-scène so obviously fake it becomes unintentionally funny—no one even actually gets slapped in the film) makes a surprisingly efficient parallel to Stein's phonic repetitions. In this stage adaptation, Olga, the head dominatrix, was merged with Stein's Mephistopheles (Suzzy Roche), while Faust's role was mirrored in the film by Elaine, who makes a "deal" with Olga and becomes her second-in-command. The lines from Stein's play were read by Faust/Elaine (Kate Valk) at a microphone that distorted them with a synthesizer and made them sound mechanical. At times, the actors passed in front of the onstage video cameras so that their pantomime merged with the action of the film displayed on the monitors (fig. 19). In another remarkable staging, there was a frantic attempt on the part of the live actors to mimic a shot sequence of the film depicting a sex scene. The effect was hilarious as the actors struggled vainly to get into the positions shown on the screen and thereby demonstrated the film's total lack of realism. The layering effect was further enhanced by the inclusion of scenes from Busby Berkeley films and 1960s rock music.

Fig. 19. Suzzy Roche (as Mephistopheles) and Kate Valk (as Faust) in Elizabeth LeCompte's mise-en-scène of *House/ Lights* (New York City, The Wooster Group, 1999). Courtesy of The Wooster Group, copyright © Mary Gearhart.

House/Lights transformed the gender politics of Stein's play—all the major characters were played by women. Much emphasis was placed on Mephisto/ Olga as the seducer of Faust/Elaine, particularly in the viper scene where Mephisto bites Faust's leg. In addition, the monitors played a scene from *Olga's House of Shame* that suggested that Olga is sexually attracted to the women she controls. The choice of women actors required some shifts: Faust rebelliously announced that she could "go to hell all alone" (while Stein's male Faust feared to go alone). Also, when the Faust in *House/Lights* killed the boy and the dog, there was a hint of the "gun crazy" female killer of film noir who can't be restrained. *House/Lights* was at once a feminist work and an avantgarde work. Its sexual politics included a Mephistophelean female dominatrix as well as a Faustian liberated female libido, while its multimedia staging modernized the technological theme of Stein's original play.

Stan Brakhage's Four Faust Films

When Stan Brakhage died in March 2003, he had been at the forefront of avant-garde filmmaking in the United States for fifty years. The *New York*

Times obituary commented, "Like the work of many artistic radicals, his is often described in terms of what it is not: working in a photographic medium most commonly defined by storytelling and the reproduction of real-world objects and events, Mr. Brakhage made films that usually had no narrative, were often not representational and at times even dispensed with photography altogether."[24]

Brakhage drew inspiration from, among others, Gertrude Stein, as he makes clear in a lecture titled "Gertrude Stein: Meditative Literature and Film," presented at the University of Colorado in 1990 and later reprinted in *Millennium Film Journal.* The lecture's central thesis is that film, following the example set by Stein in literature, should free itself from referentiality:

> Film must eschew any easily recognizable reference. . . . It must give up *all* that which is static, so that even its stillnesses-of-image are ordered on an edge of potential movement. It must give-over all senses-of-repetitions precisely because Film's illusion-of-movement is based on shot-series of flickering *near*-likenesses of image. . . . The forms within The Film will answer only to each other.[25]

Another influence was Méliès, whom he praises for being able to "exteriorize moving imagination" and also to discover an "alien world beneath the surface of our visibility." Brakhage may even have been inspired by Méliès's Faust films in his own choice of the subject; he praises the French filmmaker for borrowing "the trappings of all western man's converse with demons."[26]

Like the surrealists, Brakhage argues that imagination is strongest in childhood. He is most interested in recovering the freshness of visual perception before the developing child learns to categorize shapes and colors into named objects and qualities. In his writings and interviews, he opposes "open eye vision," or what we are directly conscious of, with what he calls hypnagogic vision, moving visual thinking, peripheral vision, dream vision, and memory feedback:

> *Hypnagogic vision* is what you see through your eyes closed—at first a field of grainy, shifting, multi-colored sands that gradually assume various shapes. It's optic feedback: the nervous system projects what you have previously experienced—your visual memories—into the optic nerve endings. It's also called *closed-eye vision. Moving visual thinking*, on the other hand, occurs deeper in the synapsing of the

brain. It's a streaming of shapes that are not nameable—a vast visual song of the cells expressing their internal life. *Peripheral vision* is what you don't pay close attention to during the day and which surfaces at night in your dreams. And *memory feedback* consists of the editings of your remembrance. It's like a highly edited movie made from the real.[27]

Brakhage's project is a utopian one that aims to recover the lost capacity for vision that characterizes adulthood and thus to offer resistance to society's suppression of imagination: "It seems to me that the entire society of man is bent on destroying that which is alive within it, its individuals (most contemporarily exemplified by the artist), so that presumably the society can run on and on like the machine it is at the expense of the humans composing it."[28] For Brakhage, the project of filmmaking is, in itself, Faustian: "If you accept the full adventure of this course [filmmaking], you will surely lose your mortal soul: you will be tortured by demons (physically pained by them, mentally-anguished to the point of suicidal thought): you will be stretched to the orders of angels more terrible than demonic force, set tasks by them beyond all comprehension or imaginable accomplishment."[29]

Between 1987 and 1989, Brakhage made four films that take up the Faust theme.[30] In fact, they represented the culmination of a forty-year project for the filmmaker, who wrote a grant proposal for what he termed a "Faust in reverse" as early as 1955 and a scenario for an unfinished "Faustfilm" in 1957. Although the early scenario bears little resemblance to the four finished films, the grant proposal states, in outline form, some of the themes that would reappear more than forty years later. The initial situation was to represent the dreams of a young man living alone in a cold-water flat. He is loved by a woman whom he rejects and who then leaves him; confronted by his own selfishness, he "makes a pact with his devil-self in the mirror" and hangs himself. Grown old and white in a "frozen room turned white as winter," he then struggles from death to rebirth. The theme of self-knowledge, of Faust's love for another, of rebirth or at least assimilation into the world, and the motif of whiteness are elements that eventually made their way into the four Faust films. Perhaps even more important, this short text contains Brakhage's eloquent statement about his goals as a filmmaker:

I am after pure film art forms, forms in no way dependent upon imitation of existing arts nor dependent upon the camera used as the eye. I do not want films to show, as in existing documentary (the only direction film has taken to free itself from photographed drama) but to transform images so that they exist in relation to the film only as they flash onto the screen . . . exist in their own right, so to speak.[31]

The four Faust films are at once a continuation of Brakhage's lifelong quest for a synesthetic cinema that would, in Gene Youngblood's words, represent "the totality of consciousness, the reality continuum of the living present," and a radical departure from his previous films.[32] They remain consistent with Brakhage's other work in that many of his familiar techniques require the spectator to recognize repetition and self-referentiality in order to experience the films as coherent. Some of these techniques include the superimposition of multiple images, out-of-focus shots, washing out images by shooting directly into light sources or underexposing the shot so that the image is dark, shooting through a prism, "all-over" dispersal of visual information so that the viewer has difficulty establishing a hierarchy for processing it (a technique taken from abstract expressionists like Jackson Pollock), interruptive flash frames, pulsation, shooting through painted glass, shooting in fog and downpours (the "filters of the world"), as well as handheld camera movement that simulates body motion.[33] All of these filmmaking strategies make the films hard to describe in words (Brakhage's intention) and render shot-by-shot analysis almost meaningless. The filmmaker objectifies the film image *as* image and prevents any absorption into the narration. Brakhage's artistry seeks to use film as a way to liberate the spectator's learned visual conventions.

The four-part structure is a recurrent one in the filmmaker's opus: the early masterpiece *Dog Star Man* consisted of a dreamlike "prelude" followed by four parts, and *The Dante Quartet*, made up of images painted directly on film, was made in 1987 at about the same time that Brakhage started part 1 of his Faust series. Another four-part series, *Tortured Dust*, was made in the 1980s.

In many ways, however, the Faust films constitute a radical departure. In three of the four films, Brakhage speaks his own poetry in a voice-over narration. The films are accompanied by sound and music, whereas most Brakhage films are silent. There are actors who murmur lines that the film viewer strains to overhear. Most unusual of all, Brakhage introduces characters: Margaret, Faust, and Faust's friend (his demonic counterpart). Here, we find the filmmaker at his most mythic, at least since the *Dog Star Man* series of the late 1960s. In that film series, part 1 shows the father figure (Brakhage) struggling up a snow-covered mountain to cut firewood from a tree that the filmmaker links allegorically to Ygdrasil, the world tree; part 2 celebrates/shows the birth of the filmmaker's son; part 3 mingles visceral shots with lovemaking scenes intercut with shots of nature; while the coda depicts a conflagration and catastrophe. In the Faust series, there is a progression from the introverted Faust of part 1 to the poem on love and art that makes up part 2 and the fusion with the world in part 4 (part 3 constitutes an interlude, a "Walpurgisnacht" of music, dance, and the words of actors, with no narrative voice).

At the same time, the Faust films, because of the techniques of interruption outlined above, succeed in being "presentational" rather than "representational"—that is, they challenge the viewers to construct their own cognitive maps. Brakhage's Faust films do not tell a story—they are like filmed poetry or the equivalent of abstract expressionism in painting. The filmmaker's narrative voice amplifies, rather than explains, the images, with comments that relate more to the themes of vision and perception than to Faust's attempt to negotiate his sense of place in the world. Rendered in lines replete with onomatopoeic associations and rhymes, the spoken words constitute another voice that accompanies the images, along with music (much of it by Rick Corrigan) and *musique concrète*, or rhythmically arranged music/sounds that suggest objects not depicted on the screen (a film projector, water, a muffled bell, hammering, etc.).

The four parts of Brakhage's Faust films are nevertheless distinct in their content and focus. Part 1, *Faustfilm: An Opera,* is shot almost entirely in a low-key blue light. At times, it is hard to make out Faust's figure as he moves about in the semidarkness, plays his French horn, meets Gretchen, and finds the friend for whom he yearns. Through the narrator, we learn that Faust is divorced and living alone in the house of his father, raising his young son by himself.

The narrator explains that Faust needs workmen to tend the light so that he can find his way around the darkened house; and that by the same light, he occasionally warms his hands. Light is a continuous theme in *Faustfilm*, and the narrator explains that Faust is not the master of it: "The light with its peripheral sparks had a life of its own." When Gretchen appears, she dances a shadow dance on a sheet hung above the bed, re-creating a film screen within the screen of the spectator's viewing. Other objects—soap bubbles, a paper lantern in the shape of a sun—exist as objects to catch and refract light. Faust and Gretchen also move in front of or behind a painted scrim, or transparent screen, that patterns the light against them and double themselves in mirror reflections. Brakhage's explorations of light here recall Faust's realization in part 2 of Goethe's *Faust* that he cannot bear to look at the sun directly; he is compelled to turn away from the sun and see light reflected in the rainbow ("life is ours by colorful refraction," 4727). Like Faust at the beginning of part 1 of *Faust*, Brakhage's hero in *Faustfilm* suffers from estrangement (the narrator calls it "asidia, estrangement from God") and is so alienated from himself that his "absolute wish," as expressed to the friend Mephistopheles, is that he "could have fulfilled his every life's task without having to live through the intervening years of tedious accomplishment . . . become an old man, every sense of completest of destiny, whitest of hair." The depth of Faust's despair, before the appearance of Gretchen, is rendered rhythmically by overlaying fragments of conversation ("awful thought . . . deadlines . . . absolute wish . . . losing ground") while the image also breaks up continuity through images that flash by in rapid montage.

Gretchen, when she appears, is described as Faust's "dream woman" who "finally becomes flesh to his imagination." Some of the shots with Gretchen break with the predominately blue lighting of the film, which is now interrupted by ocher and red. The vegetal forms painted on the scrim behind which the couple appears and disappears recall Goethe's scene of Gretchen and Faust in the garden—even though this first part of Brakhage's *Faustfilm* remains completely indoors. Once again, there are fragments of conversation: "Your soul and mine," says Faust; "I'm not understanding you," says Gretchen. In the final shots, the friend/Mephistopheles suddenly appears naked between Faust and Gretchen, who sit on the bed. The friend reminds Faust of his "pact" and agrees "philosophically" with Faust's wish for "aged redemption." This first part concludes with the vision of the friend come between Gretchen and Faust, who blow soap bubbles at one another against a blue screen/bedsheet lit from the back.

The second of Brakhage's Faust films, *Faust's Other: An Idyll*, moves explicitly into the realm of art and aesthetics. Here, Faust is a musician (Joel Haertling) who lives a romance with a woman painter (Emily Ripley). The narrator's bittersweet commentary suggests that the "idyll" of the title was or is to be short-lived; in his notes on the film, Brakhage also derives the title from the Greek *idein*, "to see":

Just draw, scrawl or anything,
straight line, square block,
round ring circle will be fine.
If you please to do so I—
That piece of me or you
well hid in the soft white lie—
drum rag of skin.
See things you can't
or we together cannot know.
So softly now plant pencil lines on paper scraps
When the little mindly maps lay neatly out,
You and I and me
we'll shout our bitter share of joy,
And find within our sleep blue-blown eye
The boy—you know, the one that once we knew.[34]

Faust plays his horn while the woman painter paints—the canvas is red,
green, and ocher, while the color of the other shots remains blue, as in the
first film. While images repeat and succeed one another in rapid montage,
creating rhythmic intensity, the theme of vision comes to the foreground
in the narrator's recited poem:

All is atremble
the waves of light,
the eye itself impulsed and continuously
triggering its moods, the jelly of its
vitreous humor, the first bend of light,
the wet electrical synapse of each transmission,
the sparking brain;
but then comes the imagination of stillness
midst the meeting of incoming light
and discrete sparks of nerve feedback;
the pecking order of memory which
permits cognizance of only such and thus such
and imposes on each incoming illumination
an exactitude of shape and separates
each such with a thus;

distancing in the imagination
it thereby creates the dance of inner
and incoming light imaginary tensions;
these tensions then in taut network
containment of these shapes
constitute warp woof of memory's
pick of shapes acceptable
to the imagination.

Here, Brakhage echoes another passage from Goethe, namely Mephistopheles's ironic commentary on God's creation in part 1 of *Faust*, where
he notes that light is only visible when it is reflected off objects:

I am but part of the part that was whole at first
Part of the dark which bore itself the light,
That supercilious light which lately durst
Dispute her ancient rank and realm to Mother Night;
And yet to no avail, for strive as it may,
It cleaves in bondage to corporeal clay,
It streams from bodies, bodies it lends sheen,
A body can impede its thrust,
And so it should not be too long, I trust,
Before with bodies it departs the scene.

(1349–59)

The filmmaker, whose art depends even more on light than the poet's, expands the discussion of vision by bringing up the question of memory images ("warp woof of memory's pick of shapes") and their relation to the
imagination.

The second Faust film corresponds to the Gretchen story in Goethe's
Faust, and it is here that the narrator (always in Brakhage's voice) expounds
on his ideas about love:

What we call loving may be no more than empathy's ultimate
    and infinitely affectionate
layering of rainbow-like aura ordering;
it can certainly be nothing less;
. . . Those moves of reciprocity or whorls of self some each,

> each slide of skin beginning and end this one,
> if armed and unarmed at once one knows the limitless limit
>   midst such ambiguities;
> just exactly as hug presses closure to open it bodying forth,
> that there be no being, feeling such buzz of another so loved—
> so too is aura oracular and picture at once.

The narrative voice suggests that love is a *shared perception* of the world in which reality appears clothed in a kind of aura that both lovers can experience simultaneously. In this, the filmmaker remains true to his recurrent claim that authentic experience lies not only beyond words but even beyond convention-bound visual perception—Ripley's painting and Brakhage's interruptive techniques are directed toward the goal of reflecting some of that aura back into the viewer's perceptual field.

Brakhage has described his *Faust 3: Candida Albacore* as the daydream of Faust's Emily. His ambition was to allow a woman to have "something of her ritual included in the myth of Faust."[35] This is the most lighthearted of the four films, although it begins with a disturbing image of a broken doll lying on the ground. Goethe's Walpurgisnacht scene in part 1 of *Faust*, with its medley of witches and warlocks, provides the source. The actors are dressed up in bizarre and colorful ways: a woman in a bishop's miter, a woman in a lace dress with white leggings, a woman in a fez wearing a mask on the back of her head, a man in oriental garb spinning a globe. A woman dancing with two swords reappears from the second film, inviting the viewer to judge that earlier image as anticipating its fuller development in this film. Faust, still playing his French horn, now wears a gas mask. The soundtrack mixes circus music, *musique concrète*, taped dialogue played in reverse, chimes, drums, and brass instruments. The color white, which is referred to in the title, is developed thematically in the costumes: a spinning white umbrella and repeated "whiteouts" of the image. This is the shortest of the four films and reads like an interlude before the final film, *Faust IV*. As a celebration of the feminine, *Faust 3* resembles the surrealist film *L'Etoile de mer* (1928) by Man Ray and Robert Desnos. Brakhage may even be playing intertextually on this film through the twirling white umbrella and spinning globe, which bring to mind the split and multiplied screen images of twirling starfish and bottles in the earlier film, or the twirling umbrellas in the Odessa Steps sequence of Eisenstein's *Battleship Potemkin* (1925).

Brakhage's fourth and final Faust film moves into geologic space; like Murnau in his shots of Faust's and Mephistopheles's aerial flight in his 1926 film *Faust*, Brakhage takes his camera into the air and films roads, the ruins of the Mesa Verde Native Americans, landscapes, and cityscapes from a flying perspective. Images from the first and second films flash by as memory traces, interspersed with these views. In this way, Brakhage sets up a referential universe within the Faust films, which become complete in themselves—like the imagined worlds of Méliès. The narration brings Faust into the larger world, as part 2 of Goethe's *Faust* had done:

> This is the ore of Faust's vision and meditation
> and the error of all his envisioned meaning;
> this is the land mass that fed his flesh,
> the very marrow of his unformed bones,
> the raw electrical connects of all he was ever to have known;
> these then are the symbols of human hubris that tricked him
> out,
> the engineered play at mastery over earth and all and the
> glistening sea,
> the dread darks thereof; the very air, sun's white and molten
> whole,
> these the synaptical sparks of Faust's brain dreaming finally of
> stars.[36]

The final tone is conciliatory, as Faust fuses with the world, yet the voice is exhausted and has many more stops. There is a sense of ending, of perhaps making a final statement:

> What is it to be a rill, be rock, take a stance—
> a honeycomb-wise delirium weaves designs at one with brain
> and all that *was* known is now newly known
> The inquiring cathedral brain takes care to be there
> where the eye's nerves are.
> Multitudinous mountain shapes vie with inner cloud geometries
> so that what *was* is now reborn One.
> To where the curve of earth itself—bee-weave
> bear black's incrustation of one's closed
> known old illusional buzz of being—what one was

is now one's end-zone.
Gone to ground being then the very soft teeth of the combs
sown between sky and mind.
The wild mountains of eyes' irregularities—
and all that *was* known *be* now then one's own.

Brakhage suggests that Faust's redemption is the total knowledge that
comes about through the fusion of vision and memory. The head and shoul-
ders of the blue, meditative Faust are repeatedly superimposed onto the
other images, reversed, and then doubled (fig. 20). The final eight minutes
go by in silence, as the soundtrack falls away, leaving only landscape. For
Brakhage, however, this is not silence but rather a return to the "musical
or sound sense" of the silent films.[37] Much of the filmmaker's subsequent
work has, in fact, dispensed with a soundtrack.

The spectator of Brakhage's four Faust films is not invited to identify with
Faust or any other character; instead, the films try to take the spectator through
an aesthetic and cognitive experience. In the first film, we are plunged into
darkness and are asked to find our way around the visual images presented,
in much the same way as Faust has to grope around his dark house. The
"servants" who help him have their counterpart, for us, in the projector,

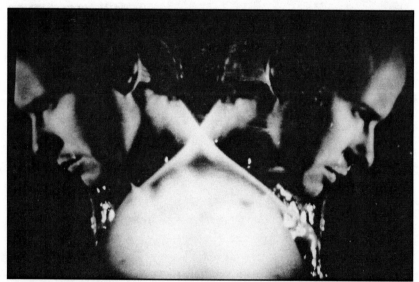

Fig. 20. Faust (Joel Haertling) doubles himself in Stan Brakhage's *Faust IV* (1989).
Courtesy of Stan Brakhage and Marilyn Brakhage.

screen, and film that are there to "aid" us. In contrast, *Faust's Idyll* and *Candida Albacore*, with their respective themes of painting and theater, celebrate light and texture. In the end, however, these are shown to be utopian moments (*Candida Albacore* is even said to be a dream), just as Goethe showed Faust's happiness with Gretchen to be only a stage in Faust's evolution. By the end of the tetralogy, in *Faust IV*, the spectator planes above the landscape as a liberated camera eye. The intended fusion of the spectator with the camera's vision of mastery mirrors Faust's own ascension; Brakhage explains that Faust becomes one with "the hypnagogically visible cells of his receptive sight and inner cognition" and that this was "all I could give him of Heaven."[38] In lieu of presenting us with a Faustian *narrative*, Brakhage actually invites us to share in his vision of the Faustian *experience*.

The Faust films were a lifelong project for Brakhage, as indeed the Faust drama was for Goethe, who left the second part of *Faust* sealed on his desk, to be opened after his death. The Faust films also represent Brakhage's "testament." Here, he may have been following Cocteau, whose film *Orphée* he credits with showing him at a young age that "'the movies' MIGHT/(possibly) be an Art Form."[39] At the end of his filmmaking career, Cocteau made *The Testament of Orpheus* (1959), a summation of his life's work and philosophy. Although Brakhage continued making films for another fifteen years after 1989, he seemed to be following in Cocteau's steps with his Faust films. They constitute a summation of the artist's lifework in that they can be understood on four levels: the autobiographical/everyman, the aesthetic/philosophical, the perceptual/cognitive, and the performative/somatic. Above all, in setting forth Brakhage's own narration on topics such as love, friendship, perception, and aesthetics, they are unique in his oeuvre.

On the autobiographical level, P. Adams Sitney has suggested that the four Faust films span the period of Brakhage's breakup with Jane Collom and his falling in love with Marilyn Jull, who was to become his second wife. Certainly, part 1 does mention Faust's divorce, while part 4 seems to move beyond what Sitney calls the "psycho-drama" of parts 1 and 2 (with their enclosed spaces) into a broad view that encompasses the natural world. (Sitney calls this a shift in genre to the "moving vehicle lyric" that Brakhage had already perfected in his earlier films).[40] Yet even on a personal level, these films move beyond the autobiographical to meditate on human experience (friendship, love, personal destiny) and the individual's place in the world. In the "60th Birthday Interview" with Suranjan Ganguly published in 1994 in *Film Culture*, Brakhage describes part 4, which incorporates many images he filmed on a road trip with Marilyn through the West and the Midwest, as an attempt to "inherit the landscape again" and to free himself from psycho-drama: "Part 4 is the obliteration by single frame of the memories of the past in the swell of the earth and the desert. . . . In Part 4 there is no story really—but a going to the desert to rid myself of these 'pictures' and encompass the whole spectrum of sky and earth and what lies between the two."[41]

The whole life cycle is meant to be experienced in the four Faust films—Faust is described as "young" in part 1 and looking forward to the completion of his destiny. By part 4, the narrator's voice sounds exhausted, as though coming to final conclusions about life and art. The broader vision also corresponds to the high mountains in Goethe's drama, where Faust has the vision of wresting land from the sea.

The Faust films also constitute a summing up of Brakhage's aesthetics, even as they appear to resonate with insights gleaned from the particular predecessor whom the filmmaker seems to have had in mind, namely Goethe. One need look no further than Goethe's *Faust* for the mix of poetic styles and genres, the mingling of narrative and philosophy, and the interplay of dance, music, and poetry. In addition, Brakhage seems to have paid some attention to Goethe's scientific work in the area of color theory. The film-maker's descriptions of what he calls hypnagogic vision and memory feed-back recall some of the German writer's observations on "physiological colors" produced by the retina in reaction to strong stimuli (and encom-passing such phenomena as retinal traces, afterimages, and the generation of an opposite, compensatory color in response to a strong color stimulus).[42] Goethe's pioneering work on the *subjective* experience of color (and his observation that we perceive color only as it bounces off objects) corresponds to Brakhage's description, in *Metaphors on Vision*, of "the eye's flight dis-covery of its internal ability to produce prismatic sensations directly, with-out extraneous instruments. . . . Fixed by effortless fascination, akin to self-hypnosis, my eye is able to retain for cognizance even those utterly unbanded rainbows reflecting off the darkest of objects, so transitory as to be completely unstructionable, yet retaining some semblance in arrangement to the source of illumination."[43] Part 2 of the Faust film series restates some of these ideas, which were also later elaborated in such essays as "In Consideration of Aesthetics" (1996). Here, Brakhage accepts as the best definition of film the title of a book by William Wees, *Light Moving in Time*, and writes:

Imagine(n)ativity: too much takes over from the eye as mind in what then becomes fantastical. How to separate out from in and the in from innard's error—there was/is always an original imprint of light on eye's outer surface. There is instanter than elaboration of bent light sparking optics within the minding eye which triggers eye cell response immediate at optic nerve ends and also from brain's biological limits.

The possibly memorable of each instant's input is as if weighted or charged for fullest electrical retrieval, images forced to biologic shaped gnoscent to memorabilia.[44]

What's important to Brakhage is to retrieve the innocence of what Goethe calls "physiological vision," an aspect of seeing we don't pay attention to because we have become accustomed to processing our optic experience into conventional categorizations.

Brakhage's filmmaking aims to restore some of this lost vision to the spectator by means of perceptual strategies. For instance, in *Metaphors on Vision*, he describes seeing spots before his eyes when watching a child being born.[45] Goethe also wrote about "subjective halos" and considered that they resulted from "a conflict between the light and a living surface": "From the conflict between the exciting principle and the excited, an undulating motion arises, which may be illustrated by a comparison with circles on water."[46] Goethe was also fascinated by rainbows (Faust notes with delight the rainbow's "shimmering arc," 4722) and conducted many experiments in order to study them. In his second birth film, Brakhage writes about trying to communicate his subjective vision by experimenting with light in order to convey that optic experience.

Finally, like much of Brakhage's other work, the Faust films are performative in that their movement is tied to body movement, and the camera dances in order to convey a somatic experience on a human scale. One of the intertextual interfaces here is with the poet Robert Duncan, in whose house Brakhage stayed in 1953 and 1954 and whose play *Faust Foutu* he mentions in *Metaphors on Vision*.[47] In Duncan's play, produced in a dramatic reading in San Francisco in 1954 at King Ubu's Gallery, Faust is a painter. The play contains a hymn of praise to the human body: "Dear Human Body, ruthless arbiter. Even in rage I address you. In all your shifting guises, male and female seductions. Eternal fisher of men. In your ripe bosom, lustrous pear-clear breasts, abundant, or in your pectoral splendors with nipples like young grapes among the hairy leaves of the vine. Eternal museum of our desire. My burning face, my trembling hands, exalt you!"[48]

Bruce Elder has written that Brakhage's attempt to achieve, in the mind of the spectator, an experience of the present moment (a quality Brakhage admired in the writing of Gertrude Stein) is linked to the body: "The unceasing present is also the time of internal somatic awareness."[49] In part 2 of the Faust films, the camera "dances" with Emily, and in part 3, the camera assumes the perspective of one more performer among the dancers and musicians. Brakhage has never retreated before the body, filming the births of his children, sexual acts, and even viscera in such works as *Dog Star Man* (1961–64), *Window Water Baby Moving* (1959), and *Wedlock House: An Intercourse* (1959). Yet there would seem to be a conflict here, between these representations of the body and Brakhage's aesthetic claims, in which he reiterates the desire to move beyond representation: "Much of my life's work constitutes an attempt to subvert the representation photography is by creating a sense of constant present-tense in each film's every instant of viewing."[50] After the Faust series, Brakhage turned away more and more from photography, writing in 1996:

> I no longer photograph, but rather paint upon clear strips of film—essentially freeing myself from the dilemmas of representation. I aspire to visual music, a "music" for the eyes (as my films are entirely without soundtracks these days). . . . [I] now work with the electric synapses of thought to achieve overall cathexis paradigms separate from but "at one" with the inner lights, The Light at source, of being human.[51]

In the Faust series, that search for inner light is still held within the narrative of the Faustian, yielding one of the most remarkable syntheses between myth and film form to be achieved in cinema's first one hundred years. This is perhaps most evident in part 2, where Brakhage's voice "argues the logic of loving" over images of Emily dancing with her shadow as Faust offers her a drink:

> We can calm become then
> and en-auraed each his/herself
> as always fish in water with it,
> but now at one within the entire aurora of it

be enabled to see unseizing this that,
yes but also the, *the* globe, moebic, whole of light's life
through to the particularity of its being
shimmering us as phasual essences,
essential neither to of from
but rather timely with it
rhyming the entirety from of it[52]

The circumstance that Brakhage shifted increasingly away from sound and photographic representation after the Faust series enhances the role of these films as a sort of last word or testament. Like Goethe, who has his Faust ascend into the light at the end of the drama, Brakhage melds human aspiration with light, and love with the experience of shared aura, just as, in his earlier films, birth was associated with color spots and rainbows. *Faust IV* ends in silence and with a sunrise, in a landscape from which traces of the human have all but disappeared. For Brakhage, this absence, which presages his turn away from representation, is an expression at once of dread—the coming dark age that will descend upon humankind because of its neglect of and alienation from nature (to quote part 4 again, "the engineered play at mastery over earth and all and the glistening sea, the dread darks thereof") and of hope, as he writes in his essay on Bruce Elder in 1994: "I empty Film of its referential means, as best I'm able (holding language and narrative drama especially at bay), because I would receive this great new gift/Film in the light of its Light-life—that it may grow into its greatest possibilities."[53]

Fragmented Realities: Michel Butor and Henri Pousseur

As with Brakhage's Faust tetralogy, audience participation and involvement is central to *Votre Faust*, an opera that resulted from the collaboration of French author Michel Butor and Belgian composer Henri Pousseur in 1960–67. The opera's business is itself musical: Henri (the Faust character) is hired by the Mephistophelean theater director to write a Faust opera. The impresario also tries to induce Henri to break off his love affair with Maggy, a waitress, and take up with a singer. At five junctures during the performance, the audience is asked to vote on how the plot should proceed. Should Faust go to the fair with Maggy, with her sister Greta, or with the singer? Should the scene at the fair be interrupted so that Faust can return to his room? Should Maggy recover from her illness and accompany Faust to the port?

This "variable fantasy in the guise of an opera," as the subtitle calls it, is aleatory in other ways as well. Pousseur uses citations from Webern to Monteverdi, from Varèse to Schumann,[54] while Butor provides an equivalent rich tapestry of literary citations, particularly in the Faust marionette play inserted in the scene at the fair. What is to be played by the twelve musicians, sung by the four singers, and recited by the five actors (some of them taking on several roles) depends on the plot choices the audience has made. Pousseur's comments on the different versions of the marionette play give an idea of the interplay of the musical and literary citations:

> In the second version, it's the ballad of the king of Thule [from Gounod] that appears more or less periodically during the spectacle, a bit like a phrase of the chorus in a Bach cantata; in the fourth version, [Butor] used long fragments from Marlowe's *Doctor Faustus* in the original English. In that version, the text is very rich and continuous for a precise reason: in the other three versions the texts are recited by speaking actors (who assume the role of the marionettes with hand-held masks) while the counterpoint is sung; in the fourth version, the actors only mime the words, and the whole text is sung by the singers.[55]

The correspondence between the different locales—represented by projected images—and the verbal and musical citations is carefully worked out. Each locale—Faust's room, a cabaret, the street, the fair, and the port—has its corresponding color and set of musical quotations. Each locale also adds one additional language, so that the lines of the cosmopolitan port location end up being spoken in five different tongues. For instance, the cabaret scene—lit in green—is in German and French; the music is "bergodebussyist tinted with modern-jazz quartet" and features, among other things, a jazz version of Marie's lullaby in Alban Berg's *Wozzeck*, bird songs based on Pierre Boulez, and fountain sounds that recall Debussy. On the other hand, the scenes at the fair—where, as mentioned previously, a marionette version of Faust is staged—are in French, German, English, and Italian and feature music by Gluck, Mozart, Wagner, and Monteverdi. Here, the lighting is predominantly red.[56]

Votre Faust was first performed in 1969 in Milan, in a production that lasted almost three and a half hours. A critic noted that the aleatory aspect of the composition remained somewhat unexplored, as the audience's choices didn't differ noticeably from performance to performance. Rather, it was the collage technique (in both music and dialogue) that lent the piece its special character.[57]

Sigrid Wiesmann expounds on the philosophical import of the work's form: "It is a world without meaning, without center, without God. Fundamentally, everything is derivation and variation." Wiesmann judges the work to be an important cultural expression of the 1960s because of its multiplicity, eclecticism, and intellectualism.[58] Pousseur also links the work to the spirit of the times; it is startling to read that already in 1969 he was referring to what we now call the "information age" ("le milieu informationnel dans lequel nous vivons"). The composer's statement to the effect that "everything is citation . . . we accept that we exist in a collective network of creation, that we are just the agents of creativity,"[59] now seems like a prescient commentary on what we have come to call "postmodern pastiche," in which different historical registers and styles are mingled in a single work.

In his commentary, Pousseur states that one of his goals was to liberate music from modern serialism that, in his opinion, had degenerated into a mere academicism.[60] Indeed, Butor and Pousseur do not limit themselves to formal experimentation. Henri's situation in *Votre Faust* is in itself a critique of the commercialization of art—the theater director has the power to decide that the commissioned work will be a Faust opera. In the end, Henri decides not to comply, and the "deal" falls through. The emphasis on aleatory plot choices is an allegory of free will. Pousseur underscores the fact that the choices offered to the audience amount to a Brechtian strategy—Brecht had wanted a theater that would make the spectator reflect on life outside the theater, but he didn't write a play in which the audience could find different solutions. It was Pousseur's idea to supply such a work.[61]

Wiesmann has noted the similarity between the organizational principle of the Pousseur and Butor opera and the plays of Gertrude Stein, in which "life is presented as something that is not subject to definite causality, but rather remains repeatable and variable within a limited set of possibilities."[62] In one version of the cabaret scene, for instance, the four singers, supplemented by a tape recorder, perform a multilingual collage that mixes citations from other works with recapitulations of previous dialogue from *Votre Faust*:

Tenor: Qu'est-ce que vous prendrez?
Alto: Un Champagne

Soprano: Et pour Monsieur?

Bass: Ein whisky und ein Martini

Tape Recorder: Je ne savais pas que vous aviez fait aussi de la musique
d'église les eaux des yeux il faut que cela soit un Faust les vagues
des yeux c'est que nous n'avons pas encore abordé la question du
livret les algues des yeux.[63]

The tape-recorder passage uses both montage (the abrupt joining of gram-
matically disjunctive sentence fragments) and collage (the piling up of word
sequences, identifiable as belonging to distinct voices or registers, liberated
from their immediate context) in a verbal construction whose dominant
organizational principle is rhythmical.

For the recorded version, both collaborators developed a way of retaining the aleatory possibilities by distributing a deck of cards along with the
record. The listener is invited to use the cards to rearrange the order of playing the different tracks and also to vary the balance between the right and
left speakers. (In the recording studio, careful attention was paid to stereo-
phonic sound, so that different aspects of the work come forward according to the balance of the speakers during playback.)[64]

The polyphonic structure was not new to Butor when he began his collaboration with Pousseur. One of his early novels, *Passage de Milan* (1954),
relates the different activities and interactions, during one night, of a whole
building full of apartment dwellers. The period of his collaboration with
Pousseur was one of intense formal experimentation in his other literary
works. In *Mobile: Étude pour une représentation des Etats-Unis* (1962), he uses
a technique of enjambment that purports to give a portrait of the United States
by linking cities of the same name from different parts of the country. But it
is the layered linguistic texture of different voices in *6 810 000 litres d'eau par
seconde: Étude stéréophonique* (6,810,000 Liters of Water per Second: A Ste-
reophonic Study) that more nearly approximates the compositional strategies of *Votre Faust*. That work constructs a verbal and aural representation of
Niagara Falls through the interweaving voices of visitors, travel descriptions,
sound effects, and literary texts. The book is divided into twelve chapters that
correspond to the twelve months of the year. As a composition in multilay-
ered voices, in which the voices of the narrator (the "speaker") and the reader
occupy the center of the page while other voices are placed either on the
right or left, it invites reading aloud. If recorded, the balance between left

and right channels could be exploited in ways similar to the recording of *Votre Faust*. In a further approximation to music, Butor also indicates seven different levels of sound intensity. Finally, the reader is invited to read the text following ten different paths or reading strategies.[65]

Paradoxically, for Butor as for Pousseur, the formal experimentation of *Votre Faust* can be understood as a quest for greater realism in music and literature. Pousseur reintegrates serial music with the mythic content composers like Schönberg had turned away from, while Butor stresses the importance of finding new forms in order to represent our ever-changing reality:

> The world in which we live is changing at a rapid pace. The traditional narrative techniques are incapable of integrating all the new relations that arise from those changes. The result is a perpetual anxiety; we're incapable of mentally arranging all the information that assails us, because we don't have the necessary tools. It is thus that the search for new forms of the novel that will help in this process of integration serves a triple role in developing our awareness of reality: that of denunciation, of exploration, and of adaptation.[66]

Alfred Schnittke's "Faust Cantata"

The search for new forms of the novel finds its musical parallel not only in Butor's collaborator Pousseur but also in the Russian composer Alfred Schnittke (1934–98). If Thomas Mann based the hero of his novel on Arnold Schönberg, today it is Alfred Schnittke who stands as the twentieth century's most "Faustian" composer. The parallels are truly remarkable, for not only was Schnittke's final work a Faust opera but his use of musical quotation and stylistic heterogeneity seems an illustration of Mann's own descriptions of what were (at that time) fictional musical works. Moreover, in his published notes to the 1989 recording of his "Faust Cantata," Schnittke stated that he wanted to create a "negative Passion . . . hence the reliance upon the Passion form with a narrator (tenor), Faust (bass), Mephisto (two-faced and two-voiced: hypocritically servile counter-tenor and triumphant deep female voice), and choir." In its musical form as well, the cantata recalls Adrian Leverkühn's desire, in Mann's novel, to "take back" the musical heritage.

Schnittke's choice of the Faust theme was related to his reading of Thomas Mann's novel, which he had encountered as a youth, and to the experience of Fascism:

It is the eternal demonic figure that is always reappearing. . . . The people were seduced by the way Hitler talked. . . . Millions of people participate in the Satanic theater. For years they are hoodwinked. Then they gradually reflect and speak about it. After the apparent victory of humanism, what has happened since the nineteenth century is inconceivable. All at once this darkness, a darkness more dreadful than any in the whole history of mankind.[67]

Twenty years in the making, Schnittke's *Historia von D. Johann Fausten* is a pessimistic mise-en-scène of the Spies *Historia.* The last movement, which sets to music the chapters describing Faust's damnation and death, was composed and first performed in 1982–83. Fourteen years later, after having suffered two strokes, Schnittke wrote the first two acts, in the form of operatic recitative mixed with choral passages. The work premiered with the Hamburg State Opera in June of 1996, two years before the composer's death.

In the reviews of the opera, critics were unanimous in their opinion that Schnittke's concluding "Faust Cantata," which, in fact, was the earliest section he set to music, is the most compelling part of the work. The chorus of students to whom Faust addresses his confession sings the most haunting music; the devil splits into two voices, Mephostophiles and Mephostophila, who, in offering Faust false consolation, amplify their terrible predictions with tango rhythms suggesting a "devil's dance" and with rock music (supported, in the Hamburg production, by the composer's son on a synthesizer).[68] This section best exemplifies Schnittke's theory of "polystylistics," a form of composition in which a single work assembles different musical styles and quotations from a variety of historical periods (reminiscent of Leverkühn's ambition, in Thomas Mann's *Doctor Faustus*, of combining "all the elements of music conceivable as bearers of expression"). The composer creates a remarkable musical portrait of the devil as seducer who appears in two material guises before Faust—as an adolescent male and a glamorous woman—to take him to hell. A description of this passage by composer Yakov Gubanov, professor of musical composition at the Berklee College of Music, will give an idea of Schnittke's polystylistic mode of composition. Describing the devil's seductive song, he writes: "The religious loftiness of Johann Sebastian Bach's arias is combined here with the sensuality of Richard Wagner's harmony; the kindheartedness of Schubert's songs is interwoven with the mysterious and penetrating intonations of Tchaikovsky; allusions and reminiscences of Mahler and Brahms, Gounod and early Schönberg are the components of the unprecedented embodiment of the devil."[69]

The first sections of the full opera (most commentators agreed that it could not be called a "finished" work), as performed in Hamburg, departed from this rich interweaving of musical textures and styles to adopt, instead, the minimalist style the composer exhibited in works written after his first two strokes. It is mainly in the form of an oratorio.[70] The last notes of the cantata, coming in the form of simple bars played on the piano, seem like a kind of farewell to music: "a headless sonic remainder, a dispersed plaint, a repeated dim-dada, dim-dada of the piano."[71] Is this cynicism, the world ending with a whimper, or a final "hope beyond hopelessness, the transcendence of despair," as Thomas Mann's narrator interprets the last note of Adrian Leverkühn's "Lamentation of Dr. Faustus"?[72] Perhaps this is up to the individual listener.

What Adorno said about "new music" in his essay "Schönberg and Progress" applies to Schnittke as well: "It gives up the deception of harmony, which has become untenable in the face of a reality that is tending towards catastrophe."[73] Schnittke's Faust work is one that also addresses social issues; moreover, its very incompleteness was something Adorno would have taken as proof of its relevance: "The only works that count today are those that are not works at all."[74]

Hermeneutics and the Avant-Garde

Peter Bürger's description of the reception of avant-garde works is appropriate for the avant-garde works discussed here—there is a renunciation of the interpretation of meaning. Instead, the spectator/viewer/reader becomes attentive to the principle of construction of the works.[75] The question of just how this enables the audience to reconnect art with life remains to be addressed.

There are two concerns here. The first is that the audience will come to the avant-garde work expecting to be shocked and thus will become, in a sense, consumers of shock in the same way that they were previously consumers of meaning in non-avant-garde works.[76] The second concern is that the very institution of art attacked by the avant-garde establishes the parameters for the political effect that art can have, including avant-garde art. Bürger argues that since "art in bourgeois society continues to be in a realm that is distinct from the praxis of life," the avant-garde has, in fact, largely failed in its agenda to change life through art.[77] The positive contribution of the avant-garde has remained within the realm of art itself—it has succeeded in destroying the notion of aesthetic norms.[78] As Bürger notes, "The intention to revolutionize life by returning art to its praxis turns into a revolutionizing of art."[79]

Yet, there is another way in which these works can be construed as political. Most of them constitute, either implicitly or explicitly, a parody of Goethe's hero. As Linda Hutcheon states in *The Politics of Postmodernism*, parody can have a political content because it shows us how distant we are from the totalizing representations of the past: "Through a double process of installing and ironizing, parody signals how present representations come from past ones and what ideological consequences derive from both continuity and difference."[80] Many of these avant-garde works break out of the strictures of revolutionary *art-making* to question the way all *representation* is constructed. This is as true for Brakhage, who wants to change our everyday visual perceptions, as it is for Pousseur and Butor, whose aleatory composition is a response to the tumult of sounds and messages we are exposed to in the information age; for Schnittke, whose stylistic heterogeneity constitutes both a summation and a farewell to Western musical tradition, as it is for Stein, whose radical poetics cannot be dissociated from her gender politics.

These avant-garde works also offer varied responses to the question of the Faustian self. Jarry still insists on a self-proclaiming and eccentric individualism as a bridge between the nineteenth century and the twentieth. In Ghelderode, the twentieth-century actor Faust displaces the "original" Faust, who in any case is no longer sure of his real identity, while Ribemont-Dessaignes presents him as the henpecked victim of his Mephisthophelean cook—hardly a heroic figure. In Gertrude Stein's play, he is a worried and frazzled inventor who frets about the unnecessary deal he made with Mephistopheles. Brakhage presents him as a mind screen, a dreamer traversed by landscapes, colors, and light and attending to inner visions. Pousseur and Butor serialize him, making him the nodal point of aleatory possibility. Schnittke retells his end in a polyphonic homage to Western music, ending on a single, plaintive note. Within the twentieth-century avant-garde, along with Faust's fall from heroism, we can see a progression in the Faustian self from division to multiplication and eventual dispersion. In every case, avant-garde artists played off the hegemonic status of the Faustian hero, subvert-ing his role as model, his traditional humanist aspirations, and his authority.

As with feminism, the challenge of Faustian humanism as the represen-tative of the established social order was one to which the avant-garde re-sponded with transgressive strategies. Faust and Mephistopheles have pro-vided an endlessly fascinating subject matter for avant-garde artists who have wanted to unsettle the conventions of their art and the accepted ways of thinking in their societies.[81] In a sense, their choice is similar to that of the first filmmakers—the Faust story provides a familiar conceptual frame that ensures that we will puzzle over their creations and try to see how they re-late to the past history of Western culture, even as, like Jarry's playful and fractious adventurer, they embark on uncharted seas.

6   Oneiric Fausts: Repression and Liberation in the Cold War Era

The feminization of Faust passes through the oneiric in order to open up language in new configurations and to explore the possibilities of reimagining a different reality. In the avant-garde, dreams play a role in surrealist versions of Faust and in the turn from rationality that characterizes artists as diverse as Brakhage, Jarry, and Ghelderode. In another link between Faust and the oneiric, reality takes on the character of a bad dream on both sides of the Cold War divide—in American film noir and in Mikhail Bulgakov's novel *The Master and Margarita*. In the United States, the dark vision of the Faustian gets displaced, albeit briefly, by the liberating strains of the Beat writer Jack Kerouac, who recasts the Faustian motif in a more celebratory and optimistic mode. The return of nightmarish visions in films and other expressions of popular culture in the 1980s and 1990s might be seen to reflect a renewed disillusionment and cultural anxiety in the United States, while the psychological ravages of the post–Cold War era on the other side of the divide are rendered in filmmaker Jan Svankmajer's surreal *Lekce Faust* (*Faust*).

American Film Noir

At the conclusion of World War II, the Truman administration decided that it would have to build up a European bloc to counter the potential economic power and ideological appeal of the Soviet Union. The idea of a communist military threat was created, as Senator Vandenberg advised Truman, to "scare hell out of the country." Thus, the stage was set for European reconstruction in exchange for trade policies advantageous to American capitalists. As Richard Freeland notes, the Truman administration was convinced that "the mobilization of broad public support for its foreign policies depended on a dramatization of the communist threat to the United States."[1]

The official policy of anticommunism led to specific governmental initiatives aimed at creating a Western bloc and an Eastern bloc, which became the two sides in an ideological and economic Cold War. In Europe, money funneled through the CIA was used to create anticommunist labor organizations, thus weakening European popular support for the Soviet Union and strengthening trade relations with the United States.[2] At home, anticommunist rhetoric served to limit labor victories, since labor leaders could be accused of being communists. In 1947, the attorney general published his list of subversive organizations. Federal employees were required to take a loyalty oath beginning in March 1947. Franklin D. Roosevelt's vice president, Henry Wallace, was dropped from Roosevelt's third reelection ticket in 1944 on the grounds that he was pro-Soviet; in 1948, his Progressive Party was labeled communist when he ran for president as a third-party candidate. In the same year, the administration perpetrated a hoax on the American people (the "War Scare"), claiming the Soviet Union was planning an invasion of Western Europe.[3] On February 9, 1950, Senator Joseph McCarthy accused the State Department of harboring communists.

As early as 1947, Hollywood itself was drawn into the anticommunist campaign when nineteen writers were summoned before the House Un-American Activities Committee (HUAC). Ten of them were charged with being members of the Communist Party and were eventually jailed in 1950 for refusing to cooperate in naming fellow writers (Bertolt Brecht and Hanns Eisler, both of whom were called before the committee, left the country shortly afterward). By the end of the second round of hearings in 1951, between 250 and 300 writers, directors, and actors had become effectively blacklisted and could no longer find employment.[4] Many of the blacklisted artists would not work again in the film industry until the 1960s, and many of them never returned. Of necessity, the hearings served to discourage union organizing in the entertainment industry itself. A description given in 1953 by John Howard Lawson, one of the original "Hollywood Ten," conveys the nightmarish quality of Hollywood's atmosphere in those times:

> As the lists of the "politically unreliable" persons multiply, motion picture workers have no way of knowing whether or not they are included among the suspects. Actors who are not called for jobs, writers who are no longer sought out for assignments, can only speculate on the possibility that sometime, somewhere, they have signed a petition

or attended a meeting or engaged in an indiscreet conversation. The testimony of informers can rest on gossip, rumor, or personal spite. ... In the smog of fear that hangs over Hollywood, studio employees are like people in a plague-ridden city, carefully avoiding contact with anyone who might spread the contagion. The prevalence of fear is the best proof that there is no safety for anyone in this fetid atmosphere.[5]

It is striking how closely Lawson's description resembles the world of film noir. On the one hand, film noir expressed anxiety concerning the hostility with which politically progressive film artists in Hollywood were being viewed by conservatives; on the other hand, some of the characteristics of film noir—the confusing plots and oneiric quality—were the direct result of the need to approach social issues of concern to the left—such as a critique of capitalism—obliquely.[6]

In the classic noir style, Italian neorealism was added to the look of German expressionism. Where the German influence contributed heavily to the look of noir, neorealism assured the presence of gritty urban settings: "From alleys filled with brimming garbage cans and back streets, the mise-en-scène might move to the docks and waterfronts, or interiors characterized by narrow corridors—physical expressions of the claustrophobic unconscious."[7] Yet the influence of German filmmakers went far beyond style. In his masterful study *More than Night: Film Noir in Its Contexts*, James Naremore demonstrates how the influence of German expatriate filmmakers brought with it also a critique of capitalism and a hostility to the mass culture exemplified by Hollywood films—in effect, transposing Weimar ambivalence toward America into the heart of the studio system. Noir is inflected with the sensibility of modernist art, especially surrealism's emphasis on the unconscious as the instrument for sounding psychological depth. Naremore argues that the look and atmosphere of noir films is profoundly influenced by modernism: "Like modernism, Hollywood thrillers of the 1940s are characterized by urban landscapes, subjective narration, nonlinear plots, hard-boiled poetry, and misogynistic eroticism; also like modernism, they are somewhat 'anti-American,' or at least ambivalent toward modernity and progress."[8]

Some of the original Hollywood Ten were directors or screenwriters for noir films: Albert Maltz was the screenwriter for *Naked City* (1948), and Dalton Trumbo worked under an assumed name after 1947 to write the scripts for *Gun Crazy* (1949) and *The Prowler* (1951). Edward Dmytryk, who later turned "friendly witness" and testified against others, directed *Crossfire* (1947) and *Murder, My Sweet* (1944).

The second round of hearings encompassed actors and directors as well as writers. Once again, there is a correlation between the blacklisted artists and the noir films they directed, wrote, or acted in before 1951. Thom Andersen, the author of an influential essay titled "Red Hollywood," lists thirteen other noir films, characterized by greater psychological depth, that were directed by a "second wave" of film artists who were blacklisted after 1951. Among them, he counts Robert Rossen's *Body and Soul* (1947), Abraham Polonsky's *Force of Evil* (1948), and John Huston's *The Asphalt Jungle* (1950).[9] John Garfield, the star of both *Body and Soul* and *Force of Evil,* was also blacklisted.

Film noir presents protagonists who struggle alone in a hostile world either as victims or victimizers (or sometimes both). Often these films present characters who are confronted with a "Faustian bargain." Sometimes the bargain takes the form of a crime they are tempted to commit in order to live securely (and, they promise themselves, honestly) afterward; or else they are drawn by love into a pact with a partner who proves to be demonic. Frequently, they are put in the position of being asked to "sell their souls" by committing acts that go against their deepest sense of decency and self-respect.

Directed by John Farrow in the year following the HUAC hearings of the Hollywood Ten, *Alias Nick Beal* (1948) is a rare instance of a noir film that deals explicitly with corruption in politics. The film exhibits many aspects of noir stylistics as laid out by Paul Schrader in his influential essay.[10] Many scenes are shot at night with chiaroscuro lighting that models faces into expressive masks. Like many other classic noir films, this film is shot tightly, and its emphasis on verticality and obliquity avoids the epic sweep of other genres, such as the Western. One senses the environment (which is usually urban) closing in, becoming almost a prison for the characters. As is characteristic of other noir films, *Alias Nick Beal* also contrasts the loyal wife or woman friend with the femme fatale who encourages the hero to betray his own sense of right.

Since this film is not in distribution (it exists in an archival nitrate print at the UCLA film archive), its plot will need some exposition here. Like other noir films that eschew a linear narration, it is narrated almost entirely in flashback. The first shot shows Joseph Foster (Thomas Mitchell) climbing some steps while the voice-over comments, "In every man there's an imperfection; you discovered that in eight short months when you climbed from a district attorney to a governor's mansion." The second shot is already a flashback, as the camera tracks from the "District Attorney" sign on Foster's office door to the conversation inside.

Alias Nick Beal is also the most overtly Faustian of all the noir films—"Old Nick," after all, is a common name for the devil. In the film's first scene, District Attorney Foster courageously faces down gangster Frankie Faulkner who threatens him. But Foster has a weak spot—he is a passionate do-gooder and desperately wants to oust the criminal elements in the city. After Frankie leaves, Foster talks to his second visitor, the Reverend Thomas Garfield, about the Garfield Boys Club. Left to himself, Foster then agonizes about a gambler named Hanson and utters the fateful words: "He's an octopus, sucking the blood of every small businessman in the city. I'd give my soul to nail him." Having said that he would sell his soul, Foster doesn't have to wait long.

While visiting the boys' club, Foster is handed a note that offers to help him fight against Hanson. The China Coast Café, where he is to meet the sender, is a quintessential noir hangout on the waterfront, complete with a neon sign, a foggy atmosphere, and the whistles of offshore boats. An elegantly suited man appears from out of the fog—Nicholas Beal, "agent." In the chiaroscuro of the café, Beal offers Foster help against Hanson.

Beal leads Foster to the old cannery where the records incriminating Hanson are found. When Foster hesitates in taking them without a warrant, Beal reminds him that he said he would sell his soul for them. Foster takes the records—the first step in his gradual corruption. In yet another noir moment, Beal suddenly vanishes, and Foster, searching for him with a flashlight, winds up staring close-up at a rat. The next shot shows the newspaper headlines announcing "Foster Triumphs; Hanson Guilty."

Like other Faustian characters before him, Foster has initially sold his soul for a noble goal. But he soon realizes that he is in the power of a force that will bend him toward evil. Wanting to compromise Foster even more, Beal offers to help finance his gubernatorial campaign, especially when it looks as though Foster is going to make a "clean breast" and confess to the illegal search of Hanson's books. When Foster hesitates, Beal picks up the alluring, misguided Donna Allen at the China Coast Café and throws her at Foster. Donna, equipped with a sable coat, jewels, and a fancy apartment with an erotically suggestive Daliesque mural (another imprimatur of noir's debt to modernism), proves irresistible to Foster. She gets him to accept Beal's money, and he is soon running as the Independent Party candidate. Beal arranges with machine politicians to secure the election in exchange for favors once the governor is in office.

By now, Foster is feeling the heat of the deals he has made. At dinner, he tells his wife that he feels trapped into collaborating with the "Foster machine," since giving the victory to his opponent (a villain named Kennedy) amounts to "selling the state down the river." It's another Faustian moment, for his wife replies, "I'd rather have you sell the state than yourself."

Meanwhile, the reverend suspects that Beal is the devil. This realization comes just in time, for Beal has framed Foster for a murder he committed himself (Henry Finch, the bookkeeper at the Highwater Cannery). Beal threatens to get Foster arrested unless he agrees to make Beal "Keeper of the State Seal" (which would give him unlimited power) once Foster becomes governor. If he reneges on the deal, Foster has to agree to follow Beal to the island of "Almas Perdidas" (Lost Souls). This, finally, is the scene of the pact, and the lighting is correspondingly dramatic: Beal's eyes gleam in the chiaroscuro atmosphere. Foster signs the contract.

We're back to inauguration day—where the film began. In a dramatic reversal, rather than accept the governorship on Beal's terms, Foster publicly confesses his corruption and resigns in favor of the lieutenant governor. He must now go to meet his fate at the China Coast Café. However, the reverend shows up just in the "nick" of time and saves Foster with a Bible.

Although most noir films are not so explicitly Faustian, many of them do refer to the selling of one's soul.[11] Take one example from Robert Montgomery's 1947 *The Lady in the Lake*, in which a literary agent describes to her boss a short story written by the main character, Philip Marlowe: "This isn't the ordinary blood and thunder yarn . . . this has part of Marlowe's soul in it. I would say it was worth five hundred dollars as souls go these days." Interestingly, this dialogue does not occur in the novel by Raymond Chandler, where Marlowe is summoned to a maker of expensive perfumes rather than to a literary agency.

The Faustian theme can be detected in film noir whenever the heroes make "deals" for success, power, money, or love that go against their sense of their true self or moral integrity. Inevitably, the characters with whom

the heroes strike the bargain later trick them, and in the usual Mephistophelean double-cross, prevent them from realizing the gains for which
they have bargained away their self-respect. Finally, many of the characters
die just after they appear to have attained their ultimate goal. Like Goethe's
Faust, they are thwarted at the point of their greatest success. Others, though
they may be saved, have to give up the prize for which they had bargained.

The repentant "Fausts" include not only the hero of *Alias Nick Beal* but
also Charlie Davis (John Garfield), the boxer in *Body and Soul* (1947) who
has put himself in the hands of a corrupt manager. When instructed to "fix"
his upcoming fight by losing, Charlie at first agrees. But then he learns that
he has become a neighborhood hero to the Jewish community where he
grew up. The neighborhood is betting on his victory, even as he himself has
staked his money on losing. At the last minute, he decides to win the fight
after all, a move that destroys his career and ruins him financially. He has
given up the "body" for the "soul."

Most Faustian bargains in film noir end badly. Robert Siodmak's *The
Killers* (1946) begins with the execution by two hired gunmen of the hero,
Swede, who refuses to defend himself because he realizes that he cannot
escape the terms of his pact with the film's demonic femme fatale, Kitty
Collins.

As in *The Killers*, the femme fatale of film noir is often the Mephistophelean character. This is as true in Jacques Tourneur's *Out of the Past*
(1947) as it is in *Gun Crazy* (1949), directed by Joseph H. Lewis and written (under an assumed name) by the blacklisted Dalton Trumbo. Both il-
lustrate Raymond Borde's point that the film noir femme fatale is often fatal
to herself.[12] In *Out of the Past*, a private detective named Jeff Bailey (Robert Mitchum) is hired to find Kathie Moffitt (Jane Greer), the wayward
mistress of a mobster, Whit Sterling (Kirk Douglas). But when Jeff finds
Kathie in Mexico, he is much more interested in keeping her for himself.
Jeff effectively makes a Faustian pact with Kathie. When the couple is
tracked down in their hideaway by Jeff's partner, Kathie shoots him, thus
making Jeff an accomplice in murder. She flees and leaves Jeff to start a new
life in the small town of Bridgeport, California. But one day, Jeff is discovered by Sterling's henchman. Forced to make his peace with Sterling, he
discovers Kathie once more in the mobster's entourage. Jeff becomes more
and more enmeshed in a trap he cannot escape, as Sterling concocts a scheme
to frame him in San Francisco for the murder of his accountant. Returning

to Stirling, Jeff tries to blackmail him in a final attempt to free himself. But Kathie kills Sterling and taunts Jeff with the idea that he can no longer escape their pact, since she can pin both of the murders she has committed on him: "Don't you see, you've only me to make deals with now." Pretending to flee with Kathie to Mexico, Jeff, in a final and sacrificial gesture of honesty, alerts the local police. He and Kathie are killed in the subsequent ambush. Here again, the Faustian elements are added onto the Geoffrey Homes novel, *Build My Gallows High*. It is perhaps worthy of note that *Out of the Past* was directed in 1947 by Jacques Tourneur, who had learned his craft from his father, Maurice, the director of an explicitly Faustian film in France in 1942, *La Main du diable* (The Devil's Hand).

In *Gun Crazy* (1949), Annie Laurie Star (Peggy Cummins) is an expert shot who performs with the carnival. Bart Tare (John Dall), an unemployed ex-GI just back from the war, is fascinated by her and offers to join her act. But Bart's fascination is rooted in a disturbing side of his personality—as a youth, he spent several years in reform school for stealing a gun. It isn't long before the pair are fired from the carnival and set out on their own, making their way by pulling off one heist after another. Bart's demonic companion makes increasing demands on him. Finally, the couple has stolen enough money to sneak over the border and live quietly in Mexico, but not before Annie has killed several people in the course of the robberies. (Gunning people down goes against her agreement with Bart; in this, Annie is like Goethe's Mephistopheles, who didn't hesitate to cause the death of Valentin and of Philemon and Baucis). The night before their escape to Mexico, the couple goes dancing, and Bart tells Annie that he has been waiting for this moment of happiness all his life. But it is not to be. Bart's one moment of happiness at the carnival dance recalls Faust's promise to Mephistopheles: that the devil can claim his soul if ever he should try to hold onto the passing moment. Within the Faustian pattern, it is expected that the attainment of contentment should be followed by death.

If we take film noir to be an expression of postwar anxiety, as George Lipsitz, Dana Polan, and others have argued,[13] then we must also address the issue of what postwar American culture conceives the "soul" or the "true self" to be. As Peter Biskind notes, "To understand the ideology of films, it is essential to ask who lives happily ever after and who dies, who falls ill and who recovers, who strikes it rich and who loses everything, who benefits and who pays—and why."[14] Often, the hero of film noir is from the working class—a private detective trying to make ends meet in *Out of the Past* and *The Lady in the Lake*; an unemployed ex-GI in *Gun Crazy*; a pharmacist's son turned boxer in *Body and Soul*. The hero's economic difficulties give a firsthand picture of the disaffection of the working class in American postwar society. Although noir films rarely refer explicitly to the Cold War, they are permeated with the threat of loss of control, with the hero's sense of being at the mercy of forces much larger than him or her. The American landscape becomes a trap rather than a place of opportunity—enemies may casually drive up along the road, as in *The Killers* and *Out of the Past*; and even the pristine countryside offers no escape to the characters in *Gun Crazy* and *The Asphalt Jungle*. The city itself is a blend of distorted expressionist shadows and grim realism; a character in *Asphalt Jungle* describes sirens as "the wailing of a soul in hell." Causality seems to follow the logic of a nightmare from which the protagonist, crossed and double-crossed by a Mephistophelean tempter or temptress, tries vainly to awaken. Bart, the hero of *Gun Crazy*, complains, "Everything's going so fast, it's all in such high gear; it sometimes doesn't feel like me. . . . It's as if nothing were real anymore."

George Lipsitz notes that film noir "powerfully registered the unstable state of class relations in the postwar United States."[15] Thom Andersen has noted that *Body and Soul* and *Force of Evil*, though set in the marginal milieus of boxing and gambling, still manage to suggest that criminality can be businesslike—and hence that legitimate business can have criminal aspects. As Bryan D. Palmer writes, "While capitalism was being reified in the post–Second World War years as a savior of humankind, the acquisitive individualism of the marketplace was darkened in noir's depiction of 'bosses' as emperors of the underworld, tsars of the disreputable enterprises of the night: the clubs, bars, signs, and cul-de-sacs where cash always changes hands in the most sordid of ways."[16] What is implied, in short, is what blacklisted director Joseph Losey called "the perfect unreality of the American dream."[17]

The full measure of noir's pessimism is starkly profiled if one compares it with the communitarian spirit and optimism of a prewar film such as *The Devil and Daniel Webster*, directed in 1941 by William Dieterle (who had played the role of Gretchen's brother Valentin in Murnau's silent masterpiece before moving to Hollywood). The film was based on a short story by Stephen Vincent Benét's published in 1936 in the *Saturday Evening Post*. Dan Totheroh's screenplay, like the original story, is set in 1840 but adds many new elements that link the story to issues facing farmers during the Great Depression. Jabez Stone (James Craig), an unlucky farmer facing the loss of his land when he cannot pay his mortgage to the local moneylender, makes a pact with Mr. Scratch (Walter Huston) that makes him more prosperous than his neighbors. Under the devil's influence, he turns into a miserly moneylender himself, stays home from church to gamble, and builds himself a mansion. He also has a tryst with the beautiful but demonic maid (Simone Simon) who turns up mysteriously one day. Even though Daniel Webster is the godfather to his son, Stone flies in the face of the values Webster espouses and orders his wife to leave the house when she criticizes him. When Scratch shows up to demand the payment of his soul, Stone flees to Webster, begs the forgiveness of his wife Mary, and asks the famous orator to save him. As with the story, the high point comes with the speech Webster gives before the jury of the damned in order to save the soul of Stone (fig. 21).

In the film, there are added passages in Webster's defense that, in the context of 1941, can be read as a statement of faith in the idea of a unique

Fig. 21. The devil (Walter Huston) argues the case against Jabez Stone (James Craig, *far left*), defended by Daniel Webster (Edward Arnold, *second from left*), before a jury of criminals. William Dieterle, *The Devil and Daniel Webster* (1941). Museum of Modern Art Film Stills Archive.

American destiny that places it above the rest of the world. The film was released at a time when the United States was still taking an isolationist stance toward involvement with the war in Europe, and its prevailing tone reflects that sense of self-sufficiency and superiority. Webster says, "When the whips of the oppressors are forgotten and destroyed, free men will be walking and talking under a free star. We have planted freedom in this earth like wheat. Don't let this country go to the devil."[18]

The film emphasizes community, adding a subplot absent from the original story: at the end, Stone sits around the table with the other members of the Grange, an organization they have started to protect one another from crop failure. (The film also mentions a "farm rights bankruptcy bill," reminiscent of Roosevelt's 1933 Agricultural Adjustment Act, which subsidized farming by paying farmers to take land out of production, thus raising food prices and farm income.)[19] This final, peaceful scene contrasts with an earlier one in which he had invited a different, disreputable set of friends over to gamble on the Sabbath. The scene celebrates the idea that communities must "pull together" in hard times—a theme that was frequently heard during the Depression. References to the farmers' organization also reflect the more positive official attitude during the Roosevelt years toward workers' right to organize. This was to change after World War II. In 1941, however, this film version was much more radical than Benét's original story.

The Devil and Daniel Webster rode on the patriotism of 1941 and the sense that the United States was a unique and privileged country. Although Dieterle did not openly advocate intervention in the European war, he at least left open the possibility. At one point, Webster remarks, "We sometimes feel the shadows have got hold of us, the shadow and the evil. But still it's up to us to fight." When the attack on Pearl Harbor came (on December 7 of that year), isolationism gave way to the war effort. What noir tells us is that, as World War II was supplanted by the Cold War, shadows once again spread themselves over the U.S. landscape.

Stalinism, Faust, and Mikhail Bulgakov

On the other side of the Cold War, the Faust story was also retold in the context of Stalinism. A mordant satire on Stalinist bureaucracy, repression, and terror, Mikhail Bulgakov's novel Master i Margarita (The Master and Margarita) was published a generation late. Andrew Barratt, the author of a comprehensive study of the novel, notes that Bulgakov's name could not even be mentioned in official circles until after the death of Stalin (in 1953).[20] Begun in 1928 and completed four years before the author's death in 1940, Bulgakov's manuscript was preserved by his widow and its publication put off for more than a quarter of a century. Its existence was virtually unknown until it appeared in the literary journal *Moskva* in 1966. Barratt recounts how the novel created a literary sensation in Russia (where the first printing of 150,000 copies sold out within hours) and abroad, because of both its subject matter and the artistic novelty of its construction.

The Master and Margarita presents itself as a third-person narration (the frame story) into which is inserted a historical narrative about Pontius Pilate and the crucifixion of Jesus. In the frame story, Woland (Satan) comes to Moscow to set up temporary headquarters there. Bulgakov's satirical premise is that Moscow is where the devil and his accomplices feel most at home. In the frame story, the main target of Bulgakov's satire is the literary and cultural bureaucracy, which, he suggests, has made a pact with the devil. Now the devil comes to exact his due. Woland's first victim is Mikhail Alexandrovich Berlioz, editor of a literary magazine and chairman of one of Moscow's largest literary associations, known as MASSOLIT (which the annotated English edition by Ellendea Proffer glosses as being equivalent to "LOTSALIT").[21] Berlioz is strolling in a park with his protégé, the wretchedly bad poet Ivan Nikolayevich. Woland, disguised as a distinguished visitor from abroad, intrudes upon their conversation about religion. The literary pair think he is a madman, especially when he claims to have been present when Pilate sat in judgment of Yeshua (Jesus)—in fact, the devil gives a detailed account of the encounter, which becomes the first chapter of the insert narrative. Woland incidentally predicts that Berlioz will be beheaded that very day, a claim that is met with hilarity on the part of the two listeners. But, in fact, this is what comes to pass—Berlioz, rushing off to make a phone call, slips on some oil that has been spilled near a turnstile and slides under an oncoming tram. His severed head rolls onto the cobblestones and terrifies Ivan, who then sets out to warn the other literary mediocrities at MASSOLIT about Woland. But alas, Ivan can't frame his story coherently; he is taken for a madman and confined to an insane asylum (which the authorities euphemistically call a "clinic").

Having set his send-up of the Soviet literary scene in motion, Bulgakov moves on to broader social satire in his depiction of Woland's next two schemes. First, the devil, accompanied by his retinue (a man-sized cat that walks on its hind legs; a bare-breasted maid; a redheaded man in a check-ered suit who wears broken glasses; and a heavy-set bouncer type with fangs), occupies the apartment where Berlioz lived. This is achieved by bribing the head of the cooperative, who is then promptly denounced to the authori-ties and arrested. Then, Woland presents a Moscow audience with his black magic show. Rubles rain from the ceiling, and women are invited to ex-change their clothes for the latest Paris fashions. Bulgakov suggests here that people haven't changed under "socialism"; they still hanker for money and for consumer goods. The show ends in scandal when the women's clothes suddenly disappear and the victims are left standing in their underwear. The next day, the rubles, too, turn out to be illusory, and all of Moscow is in disarray because of the fake money in circulation.

Meanwhile, Ivan, in the clinic, has made the acquaintance of "the Mas-ter," a writer who has been arrested and confined there. Of all the charac-ters in the novel, the Master seems the closest to Bulgakov himself. The Master has written a novel about Pilate and Jesus that he couldn't get pub-lished, so he burned it. Shortly afterward, his enemies had him arrested and sent to the clinic.

The Master's inserted short novel about Pilate and Jesus forms an alle-gorical commentary on justice and power. Because of his position of power, Pilate cannot do as he wishes and free Jesus, whom he believes to be inno-cent. Writing within the context of the Stalinist purges (the time of the novel's composition), Bulgakov proves himself a visionary who never lost his faith that people are not fundamentally evil. Through the character of Pilate, he asserts the belief that social crimes are conditioned by an atmo-sphere of repression. Bulgakov's satire can be characterized as subversive and oppositional to the regime under which he lived: "Bulgakov's goal was not to make the reader conscious of his own faults. Instead, he wanted to cre-ate solidarity between people of the same persuasion, whose awareness of the third, criticized party would be shored up. He directed his satire . . . toward a foreign [i.e., "alien"] element that he completely rejected, and that he tried to destroy though playfulness and fantasy."[22]

Aside from the Faustian bargain that has been made by the Soviet bu-reaucracy, Bulgakov pursues another Faustian theme—that of Margarita. Married to a boring party hack, Margarita loves the Master. She has encour-aged his novel at every step and has been desperately looking for him since his arrest. At last, one of Woland's retinue appears to her. She will get the

Master back if she agrees to appear as the hostess at Woland's annual ball—the concluding event of his Moscow stay. To reach the ball (Bulgakov's version of Goethe's Walpurgisnacht), Margarita is enabled by demonic magic to fly through the air on a broomstick. On the way, she wrecks the apartment of the critic Latunsky, who has ruined the Master's chances at publication.

But Margarita does not have to forfeit her soul for this "deal with the devil."[23] Woland is an ambiguous figure who sees himself as part of the necessary order of things rather than as completely evil. To the angel who reproaches him, he answers, paraphrasing Goethe (1349–58), "What would your good do if evil didn't exist, and what would the earth look like if all the shadows disappeared? After all, shadows are cast by things and people. Here is the shadow of my sword. But shadows also come from trees and living beings. Do you want to strip the earth of all trees and living things just because of your fantasy of enjoying naked light?"[24]

Woland, as it turns out, is bent on punishing only the wicked. With the help of Margarita and the Master, Pilate is finally released and allowed into heaven to continue his conversation with Yeshua. Margarita and the Master are reunited in the afterlife in an Edenic garden house beyond heaven or hell. The manuscript is restored, since, as Woland declares, "manuscripts don't burn." Like Bulgakov's own novel, it will presumably have an afterlife of its own.

Barratt remarks on the odd timing of the publication, in 1966, of this biting satire on Soviet life, which paradoxically coincided with the imposition of new restrictions on the arts throughout the Soviet bloc.[25] In East Germany, for instance, 1965 is remembered as the year in which almost the entire year's production of the state-sponsored film studio DEFA (Deutsche Film AG) films—many of which offered constructive criticisms of the failures of state bureaucracy—was banned and shelved.[26]

In the Soviet Union, 1965 was the year of the arrest of two writers, Andrey Sinyavsky and Yuliy Daniel, for publishing their work outside the Soviet Union. In a carefully balanced analysis, Barratt shows that whatever the reasons for the Soviet authorities allowing its publication, Bulgakov's novel became a rallying point for the liberals and the occasion, after 1968, for acrimonious public discussion about Soviet policy. On one side, the conservatives criticized the Master's passivity and accused Bulgakov of implying that the active principle could only succeed by allying itself with evil (Margarita's deal with Woland); they also claimed that Bulgakov's reliance on fantasy ridiculed the materialist worldview. On the other side of the argument, the liberals held to the view that Woland, in punishing only the corrupt, could not be equated with evil; and that the moral dilemma of the Jerusalem story had to do with Pilate's problem of reconciling his conscience with his official duties.[27]

As Barratt relates, Bulgakov's novel became the object of contention in the late 1960s because it allowed the liberal critics to focus on two critical issues:

> The story of the Master, as related by the liberal critics, talks of the fate of the novel's creator, and also, by extension, of an entire generation of creative artists whose systematic annihilation has left one of the deepest scars on the collective Russian conscience. The story of Pilate, on the other hand, is shown to dramatize the existential predicament which results in the triumph of tyranny.[28]

Like Thomas Mann, Bulgakov composed his Faustian novel in a time of historical turmoil. Barratt calculates that it was begun in 1928, making the time of its composition simultaneous with the first twelve years of Stalin's rule. Barratt relates that during the Stalin era, Bulgakov lived a double life as a writer: an official role writing and adapting material for the Moscow Art Theater and other theatrical enterprises, as well as producing original works for publication and performance (often refused by the authorities); and a secret life writing *The Master and Margarita* as a "posthumous bequest to Russian literature."[29] Out of the trauma of Stalinism and his own very real entrapment, Bulgakov has fashioned a modern tale of resistance and triumph.

A first film version was produced as a French and Italian coproduction by Alexander Petrovic in 1972. In the Eastern bloc, the four-part version directed by Maciej Wojtyszko in 1988 and produced by Polish television revived Bulgakov's satire in the context of glasnost and the reopening of the Eastern bloc countries to capitalism. One should recall the role of the Catholic Church in bringing about social change in the Eastern bloc.[30] This fact lends particular relevance to the insert story's emphasis on the historical Jesus. Above all, however, the Polish film version remains captivating in its playful spinning out of Faustian and Mephistophelean magical tricks, just as the object of its satire—Soviet-style bureaucracy—was on the decline. The bureaucracy satirized here could be any bureaucracy, and the self-congratulatory literati could be any self-styled cultural clique.

Jack Kerouac and the Cultural Politics of Liberation

Along with film noir, there was another reaction against conformist mass culture in the United States in the 1950s. The "Beat" phenomenon was the product of young men whose rebellion, in Barbara Ehrenreich's words, consisted of "a rejection of the pact that the family wage system rested on."[31] Jack Kerouac's *On the Road*, first published in 1957, has long enjoyed the status of a manifesto of the Beat generation. Kerouac makes clear that the book also marks his own coming of age. He writes at one point in the book that he was "halfway across America, at the dividing line between the East of my youth and the West of my future."[32] In *Dr. Sax,* the Faust figure of the title is liberating, enabling the young protagonist to break away from his provincial roots and assume the life of the artist.

Kerouac celebrated American jazz and blues in his writings, which he described in musical terms: "Blow as deep as you want to blow," he advises in "Belief and Technique for Modern Prose."[33] His fiction has been described as the first to reflect the dominant influence of jazz.[34] In the beginning, the Beat phenomenon was a coalescence of many cultural influences, which became a combustible mix: African American blues and jazz, itself an aesthetics of resistance to the elite white culture; a neosurrealist emphasis on immediate experience; and the notion of creativity emanating from the unfettered unconscious. Both the surrealist and the jazz influences were compatible with the call to "hit the road" and avoid material entanglements; as Eric Hobsbawm notes, the spread of jazz from its birthplace in New Orleans was always linked to travel, whether of touring players or of the black migrant community.[35]

Both surrealism and jazz were founded on an aesthetics of protest. From their surrealist predecessors, the Beats took their ideology of nonconformism. Jazz, a music of protest and rebellion, gave them a home within North American dissident culture. On the one hand, as a form of music that is often learned more through apprenticeship than formal training, it is "a musical manifesto of populism"; on the other hand, it is "originally the music of an oppressed people and of oppressed classes." Because of these origins, Hobsbawm argues, jazz is "common people's music at its most concentrated and emotionally powerful."[36] The Beat poets invented the "jazz poem," a poetry reading and jazz performance in which the poet's voice would take on the role of one of the solo instruments. Kenneth Rexroth explains the difference between jazz poetry and poetry read to background music: "The voice is integrally wedded to the music and, although it does not sing notes, is treated as another instrument, with its own solos and ensemble passages. . . . The best jazz is above all characterized by its absolute emotional honesty. . . . Poetry gives jazz a richer verbal content, reinforces and expands its musical meaning."[37]

In his novel *Dr. Sax*, written before *On the Road* but not published until 1959, Kerouac writes the jazz saxophone right into the title of his book, which depicts the author's childhood in "Pawtucketville" (Lowell, Massachusetts). It is a story of rebellion against normality and banality, couched in the rhythms of jazz and embellished by literary characters—many of them Faustian—who leave the printed page and become the narrator's companions.

Jackie's (the narrator's) boyhood is rife with myth and story, in which vampires mix with the Aztec figures of the eagle and the snake, and a Dr. Faustus metamorphoses successively into the Shadow (a comic book and radio character), an alchemist, an evil wizard, and a harmless Wizard of Oz. At once a celebration of childhood and a farewell, *Dr. Sax* is close to the spirit of surrealism, as André Breton set it forth in his "First Manifesto of Surrealism": "From childhood memories . . . there emanates a sentiment of being unintegrated, and then later of *having gone astray*, which I hold to be the most fertile that exists. It is perhaps childhood that comes closest to one's 'real life.' . . . Thanks to Surrealism, it seems that opportunity knocks a second time."[38]

Like the surrealists, Kerouac practiced a kind of automatic writing that he called "sketching," a technique that permitted him, in Allen Ginsberg's words, to produce "a great fusion of poetry and the novel."[39] In *Dr. Sax*, this technique yields some passages of great verbal invention and emotional power, as in the description of the Great Flood of 1936:

> I was dreamily standing surveying that tremendous and unforgettable monstrous rush of humpbacked central waters Flooding at 60 miles an hour out of the rock masses beneath the Moody Bridge where the white horses were now drowned in brown and seemed to gather at the mouth of the rocks in a surging vibration of water to form this Middle lunge that seems to tear the flood towards Lawrence as you watched—to Lawrence and the sea—and the Roar of that hump, it had the scaly ululating back of a sea monster, of a Snake, it was an unforgettable flow of evil and of wrath and of Satan barging thru my home town.[40]

Another technique Kerouac uses is derived from the jazz solo, with its mix of spontaneity, improvisation (qualities prized by the surrealists), and emotional expressiveness. Warren Tallman argues that Kerouac's digressions from his narrative line are to be understood as musical: "The narrative melody merges with and is dominated by the improvised details."[41] In *Dr. Sax*, the Faustian theme is presented as a melody that winds its way around the novel amid improvisations and digressions.

Memory, imagination, and dreams are mingled in this evocation of childhood, which is also the self-portrait of the artist as a young man. The narrative starts with a dream about writing and the injunction to let the words flow without the interference of reason: "don't stop to think of the words . . . just stop to think of the picture better—and let your mind off yourself in this work." The first and third sections of the book, "Ghosts of the Pawtucketville Night" and "More Ghosts," offer up snapshots of Jackie's youth: men hanging around the corner store after church, Jackie's mother washing his sister's back in the rosy bath, the scary dream of the "rattling red living-room" that reminds him of his brother's death, baseball games at Dracut Tigers Field. Flitting in and out of the scene is the caped and slouch-hatted figure of Dr. Sax, who appears to him as the embodiment of the Shadow, the elusive crime-fighter hero of the comic books he buys at the corner store on Fridays. It is Dr. Sax who sums up the significance of these childhood memories: Sax explains to him that he will come to know death, civilization, solitude, love, old age, maturity—"but you'll never be as happy as you are now in your quiltish innocent book-devouring boyhood immortal night."[42]

Pawtucketville is where Jackie must face up to the existence of evil, which he knows not only from books but from the very real presence of "Snake Hill Castle," a run-down old mansion known for the snakes that are found in abundance there. If the youthful narrator invests Dr. Sax with the heroic character of the Shadow, the inhabitants of this remote mansion assume, in his imagination, the contours of the demonic: the vampiric Count Condu, the evil "Wizard of Nittlingen," who is preparing to release the devouring Snake of Evil from the bottom of a pit within the castle confines, not to mention the mad owner, Emilia St. Claire, "a dotty Isadora Duncan woman in a white cult robe with roadsters from Boston on weekends," who has renamed the place "Transcendenta."

Kerouac has written that he intended *Dr. Sax* as his own sequel to Goethe, a sort of *Faust*, part 3.[43] In Kerouac's novel, however, there is no "Faustian bargain"; instead, many of the characters assume Faustian aspects. For those knowledgeable about the life of the sixteenth-century Faust, the name of the "Wizard of Nittlingen" recalls the German town of Knittlingen where the historical Faust is supposed to have lived. This is the only character explicitly called "Faustus" (by his wife); he is also referred to by the narrator as the "Master of Earthly Evil" and is said to bear marks of his strangulation or possession by the devil in the thirteenth century. The wizard is thus entirely given over to the destruction of the world. Opposing him is Dr. Sax, who is preparing an alchemical charm against the Snake of Evil. He, too, is Faustian: "Dr. Sax had knowledge of death . . . but he was a mad fool of power, a Faustian man."[44] But he is rather the benign embodiment of the Faustian, a magician who works for the good (at one point, he speaks of "the power of drawing a circle in the earth at night").[45] Jackie comes to accept him as a friend and mentor. After the great cleansing of the flood, Dr. Sax takes Jackie to the castle so that he can watch him administer the poisonous alchemical distillation to the Snake of Evil; but it is to no avail. The snake rises, threatening to engulf the world. At the last minute, however, a huge black bird ("two or three miles long, two or three miles wide, and with a wing spread of ten or fifteen miles across the air") picks up the snake and flies off into the sky with it. Dr. Sax stands before Jackie, shorn of his magic, in ordinary street clothes, like the deflated wizard at the end of *The Wizard of Oz*, abashed and amazed to find that "the Universe disposes of its own evil."[46] Jackie's childhood has ended with this scene, his mentor revealed to be an ordinary man.

There are moments in the narration that replay some themes from the first part of Goethe's *Faust*. Jackie himself goes through a phase in which he dresses up like Mephistopheles and plays "The Black Thief" in town, stealing his playmates' toys while leaving mysterious messages. The party at Transcendenta, described in a manuscript written by Dr. Sax and found in the frozen mud by a young millworker "at the height of the Depression," recalls Goethe's Walpurgisnacht scene. Hosted by the mad Emilia St. Claire, the party is attended by "the nonconformists! the intellectuals! the rebels! the gay barbarians! the dadaists! the members of the 'set'!" The hostess, whose "salon" is intended as the successor to an earlier American intellectual coterie, sets the pace: "Transcendenta! Transcendenta! We shall dance a mad cadenza!"[47] Dr. Sax, lurking outside the castle, finally intrudes and sends everyone into a swoon of fear. The assembled artists and intellectuals seem unable to deal with the product of their own imaginations. This is unlike Jackie, whose boyhood is so full of intimations and magic that he can accept Dr. Sax; he proves himself the true heir to the life of the mind.

As opposed to film noir's emphasis on the destructive pact with the forces of evil, Kerouac experiences the Faustian as liberation from conformity and the claustrophobic atmosphere of the small town. This positive appropriation of the Faustian quest was one that would find echoes in the youth movements of the 1960s.

Faust and Rock Stardom

If the Beats, especially in their later Zen and drug phases, had chosen to drop out of society, this didn't prevent them from becoming icons and role models for the student activists of the 1960s. As Jessica Mitford Treuhaft noted in 1961 in her article on the rising student movement, "the Beat insistence on the futility of trying to improve the world is in a sense the other side of the coin to action, since both stem from the same deep disillusionment with the *status quo*."[48] But where the Beats were still wedded to jazz and blues, in the 1960s, rock and roll predominated. Hobsbawm gives figures for the huge profits that accrued once rock and roll displaced jazz as the music of the young. Record and tape sales, which had grown from $277 million to $600 million between 1955 and 1959, passed the $2 billion mark by 1973 (to a large extent due to the arrival of the Beatles in the United States in 1963). Rock and roll became, in Hobsbawm's words, "the voice and idiom of a self-conscious 'youth' and 'youth culture' in modern industrial societies."[49] The role that rock music played in the Civil Rights movement and the Vietnam War protests further connected it to youth movements. The fame of singers was not entirely dependent on concert venues, since public rallies and protests offered additional exposure.

The Faustian theme surfaced in the ensuing decades as a musician's pact for artistic success—a rock version of Thomas Mann's *Doctor Faustus*. Walter Hill's film *Crossroads* (1986) reaches back into the roots of African American music to suggest that the authentic artist can beat the devil at his own game. *Crossroads* fictionalizes a historical figure, African American blues singer Robert Johnson (1911–38). In the 1930s, Johnson was rumored to have made a pact with the devil in order to learn the blues; indeed, he suggests as much in his references to the devil in "Cross Road Blues," "Me and the Devil Blues," and "Hellhound on My Trail." Johnson's hints about his Faustian bargain became part of his legend and the basis for later novels and films about singers who made similar bargains in order to become masters at their art. When Johnson suffered a violent end in 1938, brought on by poisoning, some attributed this to the devil's having exacted his due from him. Thus, the legend of his Faustian bargain grew.

This assimilation of the Faustian into African American tradition has two important aspects. First, it allowed the Faustian tradition to merge with the African cultural tradition of the trickster. At the core of this tradition is the folklore figure of the "signifying monkey." The tale of the monkey who bests the lion by insulting him and tricking him into fighting with the elephant was a story often told in competitions (called "toast-telling" sessions) between performers.[50] In *Crossroads*, the artist as Faust deploys his skills in tricking Mephistopheles and ultimately defeating him. Second, the artist's pact, concluded only for the sake of making great music and nothing else, is personalized by being associated with Robert Johnson as a sort of Faustian mentor. This personal touch comes out of the blues tradition itself; as Amiri Baraka (Leroi Jones) notes in *Blues People*, each blues singer developed a personal style: "Even though its birth and growth seems connected finally to the general movement of the mass of black Americans into the central culture of the country, blues still went back for its impetus and emotional meaning to the individual, to his completely personal life and death."[51] Cornel West puts it another way, calling the blues "a sweet indictment of misery."[52] The Faustian theme, combined with the trickster figure, creates an interesting narrative synthesis whose possible outcome is that the artist will succeed in outwitting the devil.

In *Crossroads*, the Faustian hero, Eugene Martone (Ralph Maccio), is a young white guitar student at the Juilliard School of Music. He is torn between classical and blues music—the "two souls" that war in his breast. As a fan fully steeped in the lore of the blues, he thinks that he has discovered the "Willie Brown" mentioned in Robert Johnson's song, "Cross Road Blues," living in a Harlem nursing home. Eugene helps Willie (Joe Seneca) escape, and they go on the road to Mississippi, traveling down Highway 61 from Memphis to New Orleans, the "royal road" of the blues.

Willie confides to Eugene that he, too, has sold his soul. His motive in going back to Mississippi is to get his soul back from the devil. On the way, he teaches Eugene the rules of the road—how to survive with no money and how to navigate in a society in which integration is only a mask for a persistent racism. In other words, he teaches the naive Eugene (whom he renames "Lightning," paying homage to his artistry) how to be a trickster. In the meantime, Willie has flashbacks (filmed in sepia tones to break with the color scenes from the present) that tell the story of his initial pact with the devil.

Willie and Eugene finally meet the devil (Robert Judd) again at the crossroads made famous in Robert Johnson's song. If Eugene can beat the devil's man in a musical contest, Willie will be free. If not, the devil will own Eugene's soul as well as Willie's. In the contest, Eugene wins by reconciling his "two souls." He can't beat the devil at rock music, but when he incorporates Mozart and Bach into a quickening rock motif, the devil's musician can't follow him and abandons the stage. Like Kerouac's young protagonist, Eugene learns that the best artistry comes from combining inherited and learned tradition with the individuality that makes each artist unique. *Crossroads* is an optimistic portrayal of American cultural hybridization, including the possibility of racial reconciliation as exemplified by the mutual respect of Willie and Eugene.

American Cultural Pessimism: The Return of Noir

In the last two decades of the twentieth century, the American middle class experienced a decline in its quality of life and anxiety about its economic future. Everywhere there were signs that the American postwar economic boom had been an exceptional, rather than a normal, state of affairs. As the postwar generation reached middle age, they realized that many of them were less well off economically than their parents had been. "Reaganomics," which vastly increased the spread between the rich and the middle class, raised concerns of economic security. The "fear of falling" due to migration of manufacturing jobs overseas and the replacement of many white-collar jobs by computerization became widespread.[53] In the 1950s, auto-workers had considered themselves securely middle class, since they gained high wages, earned generous pensions, and could afford the single-family homes and cars that television touted as the cornerstones of the "American Dream." By the 1980s, the number of American autoworkers was shrinking as auto manufacturers introduced new technologies and/or moved overseas. Computer technology replaced telephone operators, bank tellers, and secretaries.

Urban crime was on the rise in the 1980s, fueled by the economic breakdown and increasing lack of opportunities for minorities. The drug economy stepped in to fill the gap. The government seemed powerless to stop it and was in some respects even complicit with it.[54] In addition, the United States continued to pursue a foreign policy that seemed more and more out of step with the official American belief in democracy. Support for the right-wing Contras in Nicaragua was financed secretly by the American government. Meanwhile, the United States was successful in helping dictatorial or even military governments suppress left-wing opposition in a variety of countries.

The year 1989 witnessed a brief surge of triumphalism, as the Berlin wall came down and the Cold War apparently ended in a victory for capitalism. Historian Francis Fukuyama expressed a widespread but ultimately fleeting official optimism by stating in a best-selling book that "liberal democracy in reality constitutes the best possible solution to the human problem."[55] Yet, in the 1990s in the United States, the growing disparity between rich and poor only worsened. By 1997, the richest man in America, computer magnate Bill Gates, owned as much as the bottom 100 million Americans.[56] In the early 1990s, the United States had more billionaires than any other country in the world but also ranked first among major industrialized nations in the rate of infant mortality, number of homeless (more than all Western European countries combined), percentage of the population without health insurance, percentage of children and elderly living in poverty, as well as rate of incarceration. In the midst of all this, the percentage of government expenditures on defense as well as on defense-related research and development was the highest in the world.[57]

The 1997 film *The Devil's Advocate*, directed by Taylor Hackford, has some similarities with the earlier film noir exposés of corruption in the legal system. But like other recent U.S. variations on the Faustian theme, it extends its character's ambition into one of world domination. The head of a large New York law firm, John Milton (Al Pacino), specializes in seducing young, idealistic lawyers (in this instance, Kevin Lomax, acted by Keanu Reeves) and turning them into defenders of the powerful and criminal rich. The aura of power and conquest is achieved by stunning visual images. Milton's penthouse office/apartment completely dominates the city. Milton has even created his own artificial nature scene on the rooftop: the edge drops off into a sheer waterfall—what Charles Jencks has called an architecture of ecstasy, "the unabashed celebration of unusable, impossible space, space dedicated solely to the joy of architecture."[58] Kevin's wife, Mary Ann (Charlize Theron), is forced into patterns of extravagant consumerism in order to keep up with the lifestyle that her husband's new job supports.

Unable to cope with these pressures, and increasingly aware of the demonic nature of her new surroundings, Mary Ann commits suicide.

The idea that justice is influenced by money informs *The Devil's Advocate*, and John Milton is portrayed as a demon with world-conquering ambitions. This implicit critique of the way that power is abused in the hands of the nation's elite becomes much more explicit in the comic-book series *Spawn*, which began appearing in 1992 (the story was also made into two films by the television cable network HBO in 1997–98). The series was the invention of Todd McFarlane, himself a breakaway independent who had severed his relations with the dominant commercial publishers of comics (Marvel and DC Comics). McFarlane's new series, published by Malibu Comics, was the first attempt by an independent comic-book artist to create an imaginary world and was met with spectacular success.

The premise of *Spawn* is Faustian. Al Simmons, a hired killer who works for the "U.S. Security Group" (the fictional name of the top intelligence agency), is murdered by a comrade while on assignment. He has been "terminated" by his boss, Jason Wynn, because he began to ask too many questions about the morality of the tasks he was asked to perform. But Al is desperate to see his wife, Wanda, again. He makes a pact with the devil that allows him to return to earth for a limited period of time. On earth, Simmons, reborn five years after his death as a creature called a "Hellspawn," can't remember who he is. He begins to piece his past together: "You smelled a cover-up too many times. Liberties were being taken, rules broken, all in the name of democracy, freedom. But the price paid was obscene: innocent people whose choices were taken away . . . whose options had been taken from them. America had become a bully."[59]

As Hellspawn (read: "Hell's spawn" and "Hells's pawn"), Simmons ends up living with homeless people in the back alleys of New York. Although he was once a paid killer, he begins to develop the desire to do good and to stop the crimes he sees happening all around him. But he slowly realizes he is caught in the typical Faustian double bind: the more he uses his "special powers" to do good, the shorter his life on earth becomes; the less he uses them, the more evil goes unpunished. Either way, the forces of evil become stronger on earth. As usual, the devil has granted his wish but frustrates him from the enjoyment of it: he is reborn as a white man instead of the black man he used to be. Even when he confronts Wanda, she can't recognize him.

As a comic series written for both teens and adults (*Rolling Stone* wrote that *Spawn* is targeted at males between the ages of fifteen and thirty),[60] *Spawn* mixes violence with commentary on social issues. In the first five books, besides the critique of U.S. international "bullying" mentioned above, themes critical of U.S. society include corrupt television evangelists (*Spawn 2*), child-support issues and sexual harassment on the job (*Spawn 3*), and a criminal justice system that releases a serial child-killer while turning a blind eye to abuse of the homeless (*Spawn 5*). The vapidity of the television media is repeatedly showcased by having commentators on different channels (CNN, Entertainment TV, and "My View on 2") make up a trio of parallel, trivial comments when events in the plot take a newsworthy turn.

The first issue of *Spawn* sold 1.7 million copies, and by 1997, the *Spawn* business had sold 110 million comics and 10 million action-figure toys. McFarlane himself was estimated to be worth $75 million in 1997.[61] These figures testify not only to the success of the action formula but also to the appeal of *Spawn*'s antiestablishment ideology to males of this age group.

The End of the Cold War:
Jan Svankmajer and Postcommunist Anxiety

The film noir phase of the Faustian in the United States in the 1940s and 1950s had placed the conflict within the self, whose "two souls" were at war. The films showed characters who were tempted to betray their moral idealism in order to succeed in a capitalist culture that had washed out the boundaries between criminality and legitimate enterprise.

In the 1980s and 1990s, the demonic becomes identified with large-scale institutions. Action movies and comics as well as some Hollywood films begin to depict heroes who are trying to survive in a universe that seems to have lost its moral compass. Even though their struggle is daunting, the protagonists have at least achieved an awareness that the problem lies with society, not within themselves. By the end of the century, important segments of American popular culture had turned away from the myth of the "American Dream" and its promise of personal and social progress. Instead, there was a nagging anxiety that it might soon be time to pay up for the Faustian bargains of the past, and that U.S. world dominance itself rested on an uneasy pact with forces that might soon prove uncontrollable. Although these phenomena are specific to U.S. culture, they also apply in a wider sense to Western culture as a whole and reflect the disillusionment with narratives of progress, particularly ones that made large claims for technology.[62]

While Bulgakov's work unfolds within the context of the degeneration of Soviet communism to totalitarian extremes, Czech director Jan Svankmajer's *Lekce Faust* (1993) explores the bleak landscape of the post–Cold War era from an Eastern European perspective. In doing so, he returns to surrealism, not as a conduit to the unconscious, but rather as a mode of representing the absurdity of contemporary civil society. Svankmajer's Faust is an "everyman" whose adventures begin when he is handed a mysterious map on the way home from work. After encountering several unsettling circumstances in his home, and despite many warning signals that might have dissuaded him (an old man in the courtyard he enters holds a severed human leg wrapped in a bit of newspaper), the film's protagonist decides to follow the map.

This is Faust as Alice (Svankmajer also filmed a version of *Alice in Wonderland*), about to go down the rabbit hole. Keys turn up mysteriously and unlock doors that lead in and out of spaces that are linked together only by dream logic. Once, finding himself onstage in the role of Faust, he escapes by cutting a hole in the theater backdrop. Another time, he is handed conjuring paraphernalia during a theater intermission; he climbs an old belfry whose wooden steps break off behind him. At the top, he conjures Mephistopheles, whose claymation face turns into his own double. Each invocation transports him to a different place: at the top of towering rocks, in the middle of a snowy plain.

Svankmajer brings together the Fausts of Goethe (in a tattered playscript), Gounod (a theater audience watches as the actors are caught in a real rainstorm), Marlowe, Christian Dietrich Grabbe's 1829 play *Don Juan und Faust*, and the traditional puppet theater. At times, Faust finds himself and the other actors in his drama transformed into marionettes (fig. 22); at other times, he wanders into an alchemist's laboratory where a clay Homunculus first molds itself into his double and then turns into a skull (fig. 23).

Time in this film is circular; Faust finally runs from the building in haste (on the way out, he meets a new "Faust" tentatively groping his way in), only to meet his doom in a car accident. His severed leg is duly picked up

Fig. 22. Mephistopheles (*left*) as a marionette, accompanied by another devil, in Jan Svank-majer's *Lekce Faust* (1993). BFI Stills, Posters and Designs. Courtesy of Zeitgeist Films.

Fig. 23. The Homunculus turns into Faust's skull in Jan Svankmajer's *Lekce Faust* (1993). BFI Stills, Posters and Designs. Courtesy of Zeitgeist Films.

by the same old man who was holding a man's leg in the courtyard where the journey began. The nonlinear time, dreamlike arrangement of space, and juxtaposition of different planes of reality all point to a surrealist influence on this film, as is characteristic of Svankmajer's work. The severed leg recalls an image from Max Ernst's collage masterpiece *La Femme 100 Têtes* (*The Hundred Headless Woman*, 1929), in which a male traveler flees with a woman's arm strapped to the side of his suitcase.[63]

What is perhaps not so obvious is that the surrealist elements in the Czech context have a political, as well as an aesthetic and psychological, dimension. An official surrealist movement had existed in Prague since 1934, was repressed under Nazism and Stalinism, and reemerged in the "Prague Spring" of 1968. At this point, important international contacts were made with other surrealist groups. After the Soviet invasion, surrealism again came under suspicion.[64] Svankmajer was prevented from making films between 1972 and 1979; the films he made in the early 1980s were shelved and kept from distribution.[65]

Svankmajer speaks of surrealism as "a journey into the depths of the soul, like alchemy and psychoanalysis."[66] When Faust becomes a puppet, Svankmajer tries to show him as a manipulated character in the contemporary world. His hero is awash in his cultural heritage and unable to find a footing in reality. The film contains stark images of isolation and worldly separation, such as the conjuring scenes in which the devil removes Faust forcibly from one barren landscape to another. The presentation of Faust, on the one hand, as a marionette, and on the other, as a disoriented modern citizen corresponds to the filmmaker's deep pessimism concerning the future of humankind in the post–Cold War era:

> Half the world played the "social justice" game while happily murdering people in its name and the other half played on the "freedom of the individual" while, using advertising tricks, creating unified consumers who did not have their own will and happily licked up any old scum. These two worlds created each other as irreconcilable enemies so that they could gladly arm themselves and thus ensure enough work for the people and enough gain for the military industrial complexes on both sides. The collapse of "socialism" was the last nail in the coffin of this civilization. Capitalism, it seems, will soon worry itself to death over the demise of its "socialist" counterpart.[67]

East/West

In Western culture, the Faustian metamorphosis has proven itself especially adept at expressing inner conflict as well as conflict between a character's inner convictions and the workings of the world outside. From Europe to America, from depicting the ravages of Nazism to those of Stalinism and even capitalism, artists have discovered that the Faust theme offers a way to show how power collides with justice, and knowledge with happiness.

Film noir was a phenomenon of the early years of the Cold War, and some of the nightmare quality of its plots and mise-en-scène can be attributed to the atmosphere of conspiracy that enveloped Hollywood in the immediate postwar era. On the other side of the "Iron Curtain," the Faustian themes of Bulgakov's *The Master and Margarita* reflected a similar sense of persecution and loss of self-determination. With the dismantling of the East/West divide, confrontation was supplanted by Western triumphalism and by the collapse of social order in postcommunist societies. The Faustian dreamer is supplanted, in U.S. films like *The Devil's Advocate* and in the *Spawn* comic-book series, by a power-hungry Mephistopheles who would use Faust to gain world domination, while in Svankmajer's film, Faust helplessly sifts through the fragments of the Western cultural heritage.

On both sides of the Cold War divide, artists dramatized their society's shortcomings in Faustian terms, suggesting that state power and/or the ruling elites had allied themselves with demonic forces that would ultimately prove their undoing. Here, the Faustian as negative role model, whether in Moscow or Hollywood, serves as a kind of shorthand for Cold War anxieties. The state powers themselves had no thought of claiming for themselves the positive side of the Faustian legacy, the energetic transformation of the world in the name of progress (as utopian socialists of all stripes had proposed). In this configuration, the hegemonic role of the myth of Faust is observable by the fact that readers and spectators are supposed to be "brought to their senses" by the representations of an irrational and dangerous Faustian world order.

Kerouac's embrace of the Faustian celebrates the reversal of this dynamic—here we encounter, once again, Faust the dreamer and liberator of the artist's potential. The Faustian artist becomes Americanized. Linked to jazz in Kerouac and to the blues through Robert Johnson, he appears in the film *Crossroads*, which celebrates the way American musical culture fuses diverse traditions.

Far from diminishing, the awareness of the Faustian dimension of human endeavor in contemporary society seems to be increasing. One cannot turn to contemporary political analysis, social commentary, or artistic expression, without encountering Faust at every turn.

Conclusion: Reframing the Faustian Question

Dominance is not really a strategic policy or political philosophy at all. It is a seductive illusion that tempts the powerful to satiate their hunger for more power still by striking a Faustian bargain. And as always happens—sooner or later—to those who shake hands with the devil, they find out too late that what they have given up in the bargain is their soul.—Al Gore, on the foreign policy of President George W. Bush, 26 May 2004

But during the presidential campaign, Clinton made a Faustian bargain with the rabid right wing of the Cuban-American community, which wants the embargo to cause maximum pain on the island in the hope that Castro will be blamed.—Editorial, *Boston Globe*, 27 April 1993

It is humans living as capital, people who become capital's personifications, who destroy ecosystems. The Faustian bargain that gave rise to this way of being arose through the discovery that fabulous wealth could be achieved by making money first of all, and things through the making of money.—Joel Kovel, *The Enemy of Nature: The End of Capitalism or the End of the World?* (2002)

Has the Faust Myth Come to an End?

Klaus Berghahn, writing in 1987, suggests that the Faust myth may have played itself out in the twentieth century.[1] Yet, in the twenty-first century, interest in Faust shows no sign of abating. In the early days of the new millennium, the complete text of Goethe's two *Faust* plays was staged by Peter Stein in Berlin in a twenty-one-hour marathon production, with Bruno Ganz and Christian Nickel, respectively, playing the roles of the old and the young Faust.[2] At around the same time, the Metropolitan Opera in New York premiered a production of Ferruccio Busoni's *Doktor Faust* in a staging by Peter Mussbach that made references to film noir (on a desolate nighttime road, telephone poles stretched into the distance while steam rose from the ground) and modern advertising media (Helen of Troy appeared as a gigantic billboard eye). A Faust computer game, *Seven Games of the Soul*, set in a deserted theme park (where Mephisto competes against Marcellus Faust, the park keeper, for the souls of its last seven inhabitants), was developed in France and released in the United States by DreamCatcher in the year 2000. And just a few years before, Randy Newman released the recording *Randy Newman's Faust*, a mixture of rock parodies, ballads, and gospel set in South Bend, Indiana.[3]

Newspaper editorials, book titles, and websites regularly accuse politicians of selling their souls, as though every election were a remake of *Alias Nick Beal*.[4] Scientists, college administrators, and business people are represented as making Faustian bargains that will destroy public education or the planet's ecosystem (fig. 24).[5] "Selling My Soul" is a chapter heading from *Confessions of an Economic Hit Man* by John Perkins,[6] while Peter Gowan's *The Global Gamble* is subtitled *Washington's Faustian Bid for World Dominance*.[7] In all these instances, the Faust myth serves as a warning.

The preceding chapters have shown how the different metamorphoses of the Faust myth in the twentieth century have spoken to important concerns. The recurrence of the myth at so many critical junctions argues for

"I sold my soul for about a tenth of what the damn things are going for now."

Fig. 24. What price the soul? Cartoon from the *New Yorker*, 18 Nov. 1996. © The New Yorker Collection 1996 William Hamilton from cartoonbank.com. All Rights Reserved.

the importance of cultural perceptions in moments of historical crisis and transformation. There is a lot at stake in claiming the cultural heritage, since it can be used either to legitimate the hegemonic claim of a particular group to impose its worldview or to express dissent and present an alternative clothed in a familiar, and therefore more easily acceptable, form.

Thanks in part to the familiarity of the Faust story that it retold over and over, the silent cinema moved from the fragmentary "cinema of attractions" to the narrative form that assured its success as a mass medium accessible to all nationalities and all classes. Jack Kerouac clothed his "portrait of the artist" narrative in *Dr. Sax* in Faustian dress, while Frank Wedekind relied on the familiar ground of the Faust myth in order to explore issues of gender and identity.

During the Nazi era, a "culture war" was fought over the German cultural legacy, with both sides divided over what constituted the legitimate interpretation of the Faustian dilemma. Thomas Mann in *Doctor Faustus* and Klaus Mann in *Mephisto* dramatized failed protagonists who did not actively oppose National Socialism and suggested that they had forfeited all rights to see themselves as the inheritors of the humanist tradition.

In the plays of Georges Ribémont-Dessaignes and Michel de Ghelderode, that tradition itself is seen as ludicrous and corrupted by such aspects of modern society as the mass media, the cult of celebrity, and the sham of bourgeois respectability. Others show how certain historical configurations can be understood with reference to the Faustian impasse—film noir explores the many facets of 1940s and 1950s anticommunism and exploitative capitalism, while Else Lasker-Schüler's poet-protagonist grapples with her two souls, represented by the twin poles of Faust and Mephistopheles—a self divided by the Holocaust and the cataclysm of the Second World War.

Faust and the Self: Divided, Multiplied, and Masquerading

Along with Lasker-Schüler, a number of twentieth-century writers, filmmakers, and composers have represented Faust's struggle with Mephistopheles as one that takes place within Faust himself. If Goethe's Faust could describe himself as torn apart by his "two souls"—the one that aspires to quiet study and the other that wants to set forth and know the world—twentieth-century Fausts suffered the tormented division of self into Faustian and Mephistophelean halves. In Thomas Mann's *Doctor Faustus*, Adrian Leverkühn's written account of his conversation with the devil appears to be the product of a diseased mind at war with itself. On the other hand, the twentieth-century Faustian self may become multiplied, as in the journey across history of Hélène Cixous's multifaceted poetic persona in *Révolutions pour plus d'un Faust*, filmmaker Stan Brakhage's prismatic observing and recording of consciousness, or Michel Butor and Henri Pousseur's aleatory declensions of the various possible combinations of sound, dialogue, and theatrical mise-en-scène in their opera *Votre Faust*.

Along with the divided self and the multifaceted selves of the avant-garde, twentieth-century Faustian retellings have also played with the idea of the masquerading self. Frank Wedekind's heroine in *Franziska* temporarily adopts a male identity and also appears in a play within the play; and in *The Death of Doctor Faust*, Michel de Ghelderode's stage Faust and historical Faust meet and exchange their roles. István Szabó's actor Hendrik Höfgen in *Mephisto* makes a Faustian bargain in order to play his greatest stage role, that of Mephistopheles; Emma Tennant's middle-aged Muriel Twyman in *Faustine* makes a pact with the devil so she can live on as the glamorous 1960s Warhol model Lisa Crane; and Jan Svankmajer's average citizen in *Lekce Faust* is unwillingly drawn into multiple Faust roles both on stage and off. What's meant here is more than the Shakespearean insight that "all the world's a stage"; identity is something that can be assumed and discarded, sometimes freely chosen and at other times imposed by others or even by circumstance. In Ghelderode and Svankmajer, at least, this is presented as normal; what matters is not *whether* the modern protagonist will become enmeshed in a Faustian narrative but *how* that drama will play out in each particular case. In the link between Faust and the masquerade, Western culture in the twentieth century found one of its most powerful hegemonic myths—one that speaks to a culture in which image, youthfulness, and self-presentation became prized values.

The masquerade brings us back to one of the original aspects of the Faust myth, in which Faust typically masquerades as a youth even though he is already old. René Clair's 1949 Faust film, *La Beauté du diable* (The Beauty of the Devil), offers a comic view of the youth/old age issue. His screenplay is based on the fantasy of a youthful devil offering to exchange his body with the aged Faust. It ends with the Faustian character's escape after having defeated Mephistopheles and effectively "stolen" the devil's body. The rejuvenated Faust joins a troupe of traveling players and is last seen wandering into the countryside.

Tennant's *Faustine* explores the masquerade with considerable complexity, in that the middle-aged Lisa Crane who masquerades as a youthful Warhol model is already caught within what has been called the "masquerade of femininity"—that is, the notion that so-called feminine traits and modes of behavior are strategies that women learn as a result of their subordinate position in socialized gender hierarchies.[8] Tennant's novel shows the hopelessness of basing one's identity on youthful attractiveness, as her characters turn in circles in the labyrinth of time. Wedekind seems the most radical in this respect: Franziska sees masculine posturing as a masquerade and rejects it as not right for her. Moreover, Franziska remains ironic vis-à-vis the effects of her femininity on men, refusing to assume it as a role—her way of rejecting the Faustian bargain.

In these twentieth-century works, Faust's change of appearance has been extended into many other aspects of role-playing. These modern Fausts seem uncomfortable in their assumed identities, which tend to be unstable. As they anxiously look over their shoulder to see if they will be "found out," their uneasiness becomes part of the unsatisfying experience of the Faustian bargain.

In showing that the protagonist is unable to find a footing in the Faust myth, Jan Svankmajer and Hélène Cixous repoliticize it. The death of the protagonist in Svankmajer's *Lekce Faust*, who is unable to assimilate the "Faust lessons," suggests a disjunction between myth and reality. In *Révolutions pour plus d'un Faust*, Cixous empties out the Faust myth in her quest for a political transformation that would transcend the boundaries of Western myth patterns, even as she assails the strictures of language. In both Svankmajer and Cixous, however, the rejection of myth leads to failure—death and repetition for the protagonist of *Lekce Faust*, exhaustion in the endless cycle of "revolutions" for Cixous's narrator.

Ernst Bloch and the *Prinzip Hoffnung*

The bargain with destructive forces that, once unleashed, prove uncontrollable, is the negative pole of the Faustian legend. But there is also a compensatory, positive pole: Faust is a learner who constantly renews himself/herself. In the twentieth century, it has been the rebel Faust that has proven most capable of changing and adapting to circumstances. Anatoli Lunacharski's ruler in *Faust and the City* abdicates and goes to live among the people, becoming the inventor of a machine that will make life easier for workers. Volker Braun's hero in *Hinze und Kunze* subordinates his drive for individual achievement to an energetic striving for the collective good. Stan Brakhage in his four Faust films and Gertrude Stein in *Doctor Faustus Lights the Lights* find that the myth is a potent vehicle for questioning our acquired cognitive habits in relating to the world.

At the same time, we should be sensitive to the way in which many artists, writers, and filmmakers have been drawn to the character of Mephistopheles, whose many self-transformations also offer a model for the protean self. Murnau's 1926 silent film *Faust* sets forth the difference between a protagonist who longs to return to his native land (Faust's wish for *Heimat*) and his antagonist, the cosmopolitan man of the world who is at home anywhere. Murnau's Faust goes up in flames, while his Mephistopheles survives to go another round with his divine adversary. In this, he is the brother of the rebel Faust in Goethe—for like him, he "strives in ceaseless toil" (11936).

Lukács has shown how, despite their clearly differentiated personalities in Goethe's work, Faust and Mephistopheles are interdependent: "Mephistopheles possesses power only to the extent that he constitutes an aspect of Faust's own psychological development."[9] In part 1 of *Faust*, Mephistopheles characterizes himself dialectically as part of the force that wishes to do evil but ends up doing good (1335–36); by the time Goethe finished part 2 of *Faust*, Lukács argues, he had gained a broader understanding of contradiction as the basis of life and knowledge.[10] Like other intellectual figures of the German Enlightenment, Goethe understood that human nature is not a given but creates itself through the labor of individuals as they pass through history. For Lukács, the ending of *Faust*, part 2, in Christian transcendence amounts to an admission by Goethe that he cannot see the "end of history." Yet, at the same time, he affirms his belief in the ultimate goodness of humankind, its "incorruptible nucleus."[11]

The most serious and extensive counterweight to negative Faustian figures is supplied by Ernst Bloch's three-volume study of utopias, *Das Prinzip Hoffnung* (published in English as *The Principle of Hope* in a 1986 translation).[12] Written between 1938 and 1947 while the author was in exile in the United States, this monumental work is at once a study of historical utopias, an argument against class society, a defense of art, literature, and music as the embodiment of humanity's dream of a better world, and an interpretation of the Faustian (especially Goethe's *Faust*) as the wellspring of human potential. The continued relevance of great works such as Goethe's,

Bloch argues, comes from the circumstance that their creators are deeply connected to their own historical moment, while at the same time they are able to see far beyond the horizon that limits the view of their contemporaries. Their works are a form of utopian "forward dreaming" (*Traum nach vorwärts*) in a cultural dialectic that makes them participants in humankind's learning to understand itself.

Bloch came out of the experience of Fascism only to become critical, after his return to East Germany (to accept a philosophy chair at the University of Leipzig in 1949), of bureaucratic socialism. He lost his teaching post in East Germany in 1957. Immigrating to West Germany in 1961, despite his abhorrence of capitalism (he predicted that capitalism in the United States would eventually become a new from of Fascist domination),[13] he became a supporter of the 1968 German student movement.[14] Bloch is someone who never felt truly at home in the world, a discomfort that became the generative spark of his "hope principle." In the mind of this philosopher, humanity is an unfinished project. Humans have not really learned to walk upright. For Bloch, this would mean living without exploitation or masters, in a state of hope in which humans would finally acknowledge one another's humanity and be at home in the world (in the succinct German formulation, "worin der Mensch dem Menschen Mensch und die Welt den Menschen Heimat werden kann").[15]

Central to this utopian project is Bloch's vision of the homecoming—life on earth finally made livable. For him, Faust's best quality is not that he is eternally unsatisfied or endlessly striving—this he regards as a "*Schwindel, Hölle*" (swindle, hell);[16] instead, his greatness comes from the circumstance that he has a vision of a better world, but one that remains continually in progress—humanity's unfinished work as a dialectical process. Faust's "fair moment" amounts to the simple happiness that one finds in the kind of work that coincides with leisure, in that it is not imposed from outside but instead is freely chosen; happiness consists in achieving a "being there" in the present (Bloch takes apart the German word for existence, *Dasein*, and parses it into *Da-Sein*, "being there"),[17] a state in which contented existence and full awareness of the present moment coincide. But this can only happen, he argues, in the world that humans will create by their "forward dreaming."

Bloch notes that Faust gets the inspiration for his plan to wrest new land from the sea on the high mountains after losing Helen of Troy and after the spectacular death of their son, Euphorion.[18] Yet, ultimately, this visionary transformation leads him down to earth again and to active involvement in the world. He turns away from the Arcadian delight with Helen, still unsatisfied. There will be no final resting place for Faust, since his "fair moment" is always just ahead of him—this is the "forward dreaming" that Bloch sees as humanity's true trajectory: "The high-point of Faust is the unerring presentiment of the highest moment, in the right place, with *Carpe diem nostrum in mundo nostro* [seize this our day in our own world] in it. That this striving endeavor could not yet end in any figure of venturing beyond makes it great. Not only has it not lain down on a bed of ease, but even the Faustian heaven knows only movement and as yet no finite rest-symbol of landing."[19] The poetic image of this state, Bloch says, is "*Heimat*," or homeland—a place he elsewhere calls "house, yard, and garden."[20] Like many of the writers discussed in the preceding chapters, he sees the garden as a place of ideal contentment and human achievement.

Redemptive Nature and the Garden

Bloch is not alone in seeing the garden this way. In many twentieth-century works, the modern Faustian dilemma seems to involve a choice between two motifs: the labyrinth or the garden (or sometimes nature, seen in its redemptive aspects). The labyrinth is an image of confusion, false starts, and frustrating returns to the point of origin. The fate of the Faustian protagonist caught in the labyrinth seems to exemplify a skepticism concerning the impulse to know and experience everything in the name of modernity. The garden or natural setting, on the other hand, offers the promise of peace and, on occasion, an escape from the "Faustian bargain."

The garden has antecedents in Goethe's *Faust*, from Faust's meeting with the peasants during the Easter walk to his tryst with Margarete. And nature appears as a source of rejuvenation at the beginning of the second part of *Faust*; after the trauma of Margarete's execution at the end of part 1, Faust is spirited by Mephistopheles to a beautiful natural setting. As he awakens, he compares his own revival to that of the breaking dawn:

> Revived, life's pulse is throbbing fresh and heady,
> Gently to greet the dawn's ethereal wreathing;
> This night, too, earth, you have persisted steady
> And, newly quickened, at my feet are breathing;
> Fresh joy to grant you have already striven.

> Already set resolve astir and seething
> Toward peaks of being to be ever driven.

(4679–86)

Toward the end of F. W. Murnau's silent film *Faust*, Gretchen is awaiting execution. She remembers the idyllic garden scene in which she and Faust first acknowledged their love. It is this vision of innocence that dominates her final moments at the stake, as she sees through the face of the old Faust and recognizes her lover. Faust's and Gretchen's salvation is thus linked to the figure of the garden and to the memory of innocent love. This garden image contrasts with the image of the labyrinthine streets of the town where Mephistopheles trapped Faust into committing the murder of Gretchen's brother. It stands as an image of what can be saved out of the ashes that consume Margarete and Faust.

Bulgakov ends on a similar bucolic note in *The Master and Margarita*. Pontius Pilate in the parallel biblical story, as well as Faust and Margarita in the contemporary story, finds eternal rest in a garden setting. The garden as a place of final rest also figures in Else Lasker-Schüler's play *Ichundich*. Here, the poet's two selves—Faust and Mephisto—are reunited and she/he expires peacefully in a garden while conversing with a scarecrow and with the editor-in-chief Adon Swet.

The pleasing aspect of a garden as a space meant to be seen and enjoyed suggests that, in the Faustian context, it might represent rational choice, especially when contrasted with the labyrinth, whose very structure is premised upon loss of control. This contrast is particularly clear in film noir, where nature sometimes figures as the place of the Faustian protagonist's nostalgic attempt to return to his or her earlier "unfallen" state just before death. At the end of *Gun Crazy*, Bart is shot down after fleeing to his old childhood haunt in the hills where he grew up. In *The Asphalt Jungle*, a character named Dix also expires from his gunshot wounds after regaining the Kentucky horse farm of his boyhood.

The Labyrinth

Those works in which the Faustian character ends, reflectively, in a garden, are stories of redemption in which she/he finds peace. The figure of the labyrinth, on the other hand, amplifies the negative image of Faustian striving and allegorizes loss of self (or of "soul") by representing loss of orientation, purpose, and achievement.

The figure of the labyrinth in the Faust story has antecedents in Goethe's Walpurgisnacht scene in part 1 of *Faust*—a whirling, cacophonous mix of sensual pleasures and demonic spirits. Faust and Mephistopheles are guided by the will-o'-the-wisp, and the travelers as well as the guide lose all sense of linear progress or advance:

> Here, it seems, we pass the gateway
> Into magic dreams and mazes
> . . . .
> Tell me someone, are we halting
> Or advancing? All is vaulting,
> All revolves and swirls and races.
>
> (3871–72, 3906–8)

As a figure of seeking, of false alleys and backtracking, the labyrinth has, of course, many permutations. Persons caught in a labyrinth often find themselves back at the point of departure. This is true of the protagonists of the silent film versions of *Der Student von Prag*. Balduin sells his mirror image to the devil and then finds that he cannot escape his reflection, which goes about town as his demonic double.

In Thomas Mann's *Doctor Faustus*, the figure of the labyrinth is suggested by the Faustian character's return to his origins at the end of his life. The friend who writes Adrian Leverkühn's biography describes the composer's final days in a country house retreat where he finishes his "Lamentation of Doctor Faustus" and goes mad. Eerily, the house reproduces the layout of Leverkühn's childhood home, the farmstead at Buchel. Leverkühn has, in a sense, returned to the point where he started out, and his final madness seems not unrelated to this ending. The following two passages, occurring some 200 pages apart, juxtapose the narrator's description, first, of the musician's childhood home at Buchel and, second, his last residence, the Schweigestills' house at Pfeifferling:

[A] Together with its barns and stalls it formed *an open square, in the middle of which stood a massive old linden tree enclosed at its base by a green wooden bench* and covered in June with marvelously fragrant blossoms.[21]

[B] I am inclined to believe that he was not consciously aware of his discovery at first, and that only later, perhaps in a dream, did he stumble upon the surprise. . . . The pond and the hill, *the huge old tree in the courtyard—an elm, I admit—with a bench built around the trunk and painted green*, and the other additional details may have struck him at first glance, no dream may have been necessary to open his eyes—and that he said nothing certainly does not prove a thing.[22]

Here, the garden metamorphoses into a labyrinth that folds the composer's origins into his final abode and becomes the figure of his impending madness.

Another labyrinthine experience is that of encountering a dead end. In noir films, the labyrinth often figures as a visual as well as a narrative motif. Visually, the labyrinth appears in dark, winding city streets in which the protagonists vainly try to escape the traps they have set for themselves. Narratively, in a number of noir films, the Faustian protagonist reaches a point of "no exit" and is forced to accept death (*Out of the Past*, *The Killers*). In Jacques Tourneur's *Out of the Past*, the labyrinth is one of the major leitmotifs—Jeff is successively trapped by Sterling's henchman (who discovers him at the gas station), by his partner (who walks out of the night into the cabin he shares with Kathie to demand a share of the money Sterling paid him), by Sterling (who frames him for the murder of his accountant), and by Kathie (who forces him to flee with her after she kills Sterling).

The seeker in the labyrinth may also try one path and then return to a previous point to try another option. In the 1998 film *The Devil's Advocate*, Milton fails to corrupt a young lawyer by offering him money and power, so he rolls time back and gives it another try—he will corrupt him by offering him media fame as an honest, incorruptible lawyer. The victim is in a labyrinth where the devil waits at every turn, and his trials will be never ending.

The labyrinth is also a figure of repetition. At the end of Svankmajer's 1993 film *Lekce Faust*, the protagonist rushes out of the building and is killed by a passing car. On his way out, he runs past another seeker, map in hand, who enters to take his place. In the conclusion of Emma Tennant's *Faustine*, the characters are caught in the labyrinth of time, as Ella, her grandmother, Muriel Twyman, and the grandmother's younger persona, Lisa Crane, all make their way to dinner.

The Faustian hero in the labyrinth is often drawn in against his or her conscious will; if the garden motif reflects a serene rationality, the labyrinth is closer to the unconscious in both its positive relation to creativity and its negative pole of madness, murderous impulse, or self-destructiveness. More often, the labyrinth, in which Faust becomes lost, wins out over the figure of the garden or the presentation of nature as restorative. As Jürgen Kühnel notes, the trend since World War II has been to move away from Goethe's mise-en-scène of Faust's salvation through "eternal striving" and to recover one of the original functions of the folk myth—that of serving as a warning.[23] The first major work in which this occurs was Thomas Mann's novel *Doctor Faustus*, followed by the Fausts of film noir, by Hanns Eisler's *Johannes Faustus* libretto, and by Alfred Schnittke's "Faust Cantata" and his Faust opera, *Historia von D. Johann Fausten*. The warning, in each respective case, targeted Fascism, capitalism/anticommunism, bureaucratic socialism, and the threat of Fascism's return. In these works, Faust is not presented as a heroic model (as in Goethe) but as an example to be avoided.

Bloch and the Positive Demonic

With Bloch, we can turn once again to the positive aspect of the Faust myth. In a somewhat surprising move, Bloch argued for the positive side of the demonic, the Promethean aspect of the Faustian. He makes the distinction between the negative, intoxicating demonic and the positive, Promethean demonic characterized by enthusiasm: "Intoxication only exhibits the urge to sacrifice, whereas enthusiasm possesses the courage of self-sacrifice, intoxication loses all hold on things and on reality, whereas enthusiasm possesses consciousness, knowledge of the content of the matter, communicative loyalty to the goal."[24] In this scenario, Mephistopheles is the facilitator of Faust's struggle for self-knowledge: "The action of Faust is that of a dialectical journey in which every pleasure attained is deleted by a separate new desire which awakens within it."[25] The process is a learning process, one that reflects the awakening consciousness of humankind: the Faustian self is that of "the *gradually comprehending* subject."[26] In the hoped-for future, classless society, Faust's two souls—attached respectively to earthly and heavenly delights—will be reconciled, because there will be no difference between them.[27]

Bloch regarded woman, especially, as an unfinished project, since her struggle for equality is constrained by capitalism: "The difference between the sexes lies in a different field from the artificial differences that the class society has produced and therefore does not disappear with them. Sexual difference disappears so little that womanliness can only become manifest in socialism. . . . Woman will be seen as a comrade in that part of society that treats her as a subject and not as someone in any way objectified."[28]

Bloch also warns against the facile assumption that humankind's path will, in fact, be an ascending one. The negative demonic forces could still win out, forces he associates with inwardness, with the lack of an open and democratic engagement with the world. Turning to what today we would call an ecological argument, Bloch sees that the fate of the earth and the fate of humanity are inextricably linked and notes with concern the difference between relations with nature defined by domination and exploitation, as opposed to friendship.[29] In this sense, Faust's "prophetically capitalistic" and brutal land grab against the peaceful couple Philemon and Baucis in the second part of Goethe's *Faust* serves as a warning.[30]

Bloch stresses that the fate of the world is still undecided. At the same time, he expresses doubt that technology within the capitalist system that he considers outmoded can ever lead to real progress; instead, he fears the effects of monopoly capitalism that will subject most people to oppression as well as turn the earth's resources toward war: "The social balance of power releases technology only for purposes of war, for the production of means of death; but the power of this production alone already indicates how lavishly the manufacture of food as a means of life could prosper."[31] So, Bloch writes of "the coffin that constantly awaits beside each hope."[32]

It is here that Bloch turns toward Faust once more, in order to set forth the forward-looking, utopian qualities of his quest, as against other paradigmatic Western figures such as Don Quixote, Hamlet, and Don Juan.

Like Faust, Hamlet is a great dreamer, but one who does not hope and who therefore remains closed within himself. This is the opposite of Goethe's hero, who is actively engaged with the world. Hamlet's world-weariness prevents him from existing in the here and now: "Hamlet's sealed-heightened distance is thus the opposite of the Faustian pull towards the arrested moment, the moment plucked from indecisiveness."[33]

Like Faust, Don Quixote is a social idealist, but one who is unable to see the world as it really is. His reformism is constantly addressing imagined wrongdoings, and his crusade is out of place in his epoch. For Bloch, he is the emblem of false consciousness, whereas Faust materially connects his idealism with the actual workings of the world—at least at the end of his life, when he has his final, utopian vision.[34]

Like Faust, Don Juan is eternally unsatisfied, though pursuing "the radical love drive" rather than the "radical drive for knowledge and experience." Bloch sees him as "the most brilliant guiding image of the orgiastic and hence of Dionysian venturing beyond the limits." Yet it is Faust who finally devotes himself to humanity and thus proves himself the superior: "If Don Juan diffuses a Dionysian aura, then Prometheus is alive in Faust: not merely the Titan but the one devoted to man. Faust's final action is undertaken wholly in the spirit of this devotion, i.e., human nearness; indeed it is this: the macrocosm becomes free people on free ground, a purely human drama."[35] And although Faust finally ascends to "heaven," it is one defined by the presence of Gretchen and the "eternal feminine," a state of being Bloch interprets as one aspect of "forward dreaming," an ideal approachable only when the material basis of social organization corresponds to human potential.[36]

It should be obvious, from this brief summary, that Bloch is not someone who looks forward to "the end of history." Instead, the state of achieved utopia leads to disenchantment, what he calls "the melancholy of fulfillment." If hope has been fulfilled, then hope itself has vanished: "no earthly paradise remains without the shadow that one throws when entering it."[37] Murnau seems aware of this when he films the scene of Gretchen in the garden, surrounded by happy children—he surrounds the scene in shadow.

Many of the literary works I have discussed do not end conclusively but reflectively. Wedekind's Franziska is an example of the "unfinished project" of woman—she returns to a traditional female role, but only after having traversed the world as a man. Cixous's restless narrator sifts through history, language, and culture without ever finding a resting point, ready at the end for new revolutions. Lasker-Schüler's poet-protagonist ascends to heaven, like Goethe's hero, but only after coming to terms with her Mephistophelean half. Dissent accompanies her ascent.

Hope, of course, can be misused. There is the false hope by which oppressors try to placate those whom they oppress. Bloch distinguishes between "empty" and "grounded" hope. As Jan Rehmann remarks in his essay on hope in the *Historisch-Kritisches Wörterbuch des Marxismus*, "developing the critical tools for the art of distinguishing between [the two kinds of hope] is not just an intellectual exercise, but a practical activity that structures the content and the horizons of hope. . . . The expectation that 'another world is possible' (the slogan of the World Social Forum) can be variously mis-used and alienated, but without it nothing can move."[38] Henry Giroux, in his essay on Bloch, introduces the term *educated hope*: "As a form of uto-pian longing, educated hope opens up horizons of comparison by evoking not just different histories but different futures. Educated hope is a sub-versive force when it pluralizes politics by opening up a space for dissent, making authority accountable, and becoming an activating presence in promoting social transformation."[39]

If the negative pole of the "Faustian bargain" comes back again and again as a reference point in public discourse, it is because it figuratively enables us to express the cost of what might seem to be an attractive, if temporary, gain. Today, when we seem to have bargained away the environment in favor of worldwide consumer-oriented "development"; when individual dissident voices find less and less space for expression in a media landscape dominated by megacorporations; when wars are started on flimsy evidence in order to preserve unsustainable levels of production and consumption for a small minority of the world's population; and when the happiness of working people everywhere is threatened by eroding social services and a decline in job secu-rity—even as their employers are able to amass vast new fortunes—we might do well to turn toward the positive Faustian hero(ine). Jost Hermand has commented that we should not ask when utopia is *coming*—instead, we must go toward it.[40] Envisioning how real progress might be defined in the twenty-first century could be the most Faustian task of all.

Selected Filmography
Notes
Selected Bibliography
Index

Selected Filmography: Chronology of Faust Films

1897–98

Georges Méliès, *Le Cabinet de Méphistopheles* (The Laboratory of Mephistopheles), France, lost print

Georges Hatot, *Faust*, France, lost print

Georges Méliès, *La Damnation de Faust* (The Damnation of Faust), France, lost print

Georges Méliès, *Faust et Marguerite*, France, lost print

Georges-Albert Smith, *Faust and Mephisto*, Great Britain

1900

James White, *Faust and Marguerite*, United States

Edwin S. Porter, *Faust and Marguerite*, United States

1903

Georges Méliès, *Faust aux enfers* (*The Damnation of Faust*), France

1904

Georges Méliès, *Faust et Marguerite*, also released as *La Damnation du Docteur Faust* (*Faust and Marguerite*), France

1905

Ferdinand Zecca, *Faust*, France

1906

Georges Méliès, *Les Quatre cents farces du diable* (*The Merry Frolics of Satan*), France

Léon Gaumont Productions, *Faust*, France

1909

J. Searle Dawley, *Faust*, United States

William N. Selig, *Faust*, United States

Mario Caserini, *Faust*, Italy

1910

F. A. Thomassin, *Faust*, Great Britain

Henri Andréani, David Barnett, and Enrico Guazzoni, *Faust*, Great Britain

Emile Cohl, *Le Tout petit Faust* (The Tiny Little Faust), France

Georges Fagot and M. Andreani, *Faust*, France

1911

Essanay Film Manufacturing Company, *Bill Bumper's Bargain*, United States

1912

Georges Méliès, *Le Chevalier des neiges* (The Knight of the Snows), France

Stanislav Hlavsa, *Faust*, Czechoslovakia

1913

Dell Henderson, *Faust and the Lily*, United States

Stellan Rye, *Der Student von Prag* (The Student of Prague), Germany

1915

Robert Dinesen, *Doktor X*, Denmark

Nino Oxilia, *Rapsodia satanica* (Satanic Rhapsody), Italy

Richard Ridgely, *The Magic Skin*, Edison Studios, United States

1916

Vladislav A. Starevic, *Pan Twardowski*, Poland

1917

William Wauer, *Faust*, United States

1921

Frederick Todd, *Faust*, United States

1922

Gérard Bourgeois, *Faust*, France

Marcel L'Herbier, *Don Juan et Faust*, France

1926

F. W. Murnau, *Faust*, Germany

Henrik Galeen, *Der Student von Prag* (The Student of Prague), Germany

1929

Charles Hackett, *Faust*, United States

1932

Howard Higgin, *Walpurgis Night*, United States

1935

Artur Robinson, *Der Student von Prag* (The Student of Prague; Nazi-era
remake of 1913 and 1926 films), Germany

1936

Albert Hopkins, *Faust*, Great Britian

1941

William Dieterle, *The Devil and Daniel Webster*, also released under the titles
All That Money Can Buy and *Here Is a Man*, United States

1942

Maurice Tourneur, *La Main du diable* (The Devil's Hand), France

1943

Jean-Paul Paulin, *L'Homme qui vendit son âme* (The Man Who Sold His
Soul), France

1946

Archie Mayo, *Angel on My Shoulder*, United States

1948

John Farrow, *Alias Nick Beal*, also released under the title *The Contract Man*, United States

1949

René Clair, *La Beauté du diable* (A Devilish Beauty), France and Italy

1950

Carmine Gallone, *La Leggendi di Faust* (The Legend of Faust), Italy

1953

Vincente Minnelli, *The Band Wagon*, United States

1955

Claude Autant-Lara, *Marguerite de la nuit* (Marguerite of the Night), France and Italy

1958

Stanley Donen, *Damn Yankees*, United States

1960

Peter Gorski, *Faust*, Germany

1964

Michael Suman, *Faust*, United States

1966

Ion Popescu-Gopo, *Faust XX* (Faust in the Twentieth Century), animated, Rumania

1967

Richard Burton and Nevill Coghill, *Doctor Faustus*, United States and Great Britain

Stanley Donen, *Bedazzled*, United States

1970

Jürgen Syberberg, *Nach meinem letzten Umzug...* (Since I Last Moved), documentary, Germany

1972

Jacques Doniol-Valcroze, *L'Homme au cerveau greffé* (The Man with the Grafted Head), France

Alexander Petrovic, *Il Maestro e Margherita* (The Master and Margarita), Yugoslavia and Italy

1974

Brian de Palma, *Phantom of the Paradise*, United States

Jean Kerchbron, *Président Faust*, TV, France

1976

Grzegorz Krolikiewicz, *Faust*, TV, Poland

1981

István Szabó, *Mephisto*, Hungary

Steven Hilliard Stern, *The Devil and Max Devlin*, United States

1982

Miklós Jancsó, *Faust (Faustus doctor boldogságos pokoljárása)*, nine-part TV series, Hungary

1986

Walter Hill, *Crossroads*, United States

1987

Alan Parker, *Angel Heart*, United States

Stan Brakhage and Rick Corrigan, *Faustfilm: An Opera*, United States

1988

Stan Brakhage, *Faust's Other: An Idyll*, United States

Stan Brakhage, *Faust 3: Candida Albacore*, United States

Dieter Dorn, *Vom Himmel durch die Welt zur Hölle* (From Heaven through the World to Hell), Germany

Maciej Wojtyszko, *Mistrz i Margorzata* (The Master and Margarita), four-part TV series, Poland

1989

Stan Brakhage, *Faust IV*, United States

1991

Bruce McDonald, *Highway 61*, Canada

1993

Jan Svankmajer, *Lekce Faust (Faust)*, Czech Republic

1995

Manoel de Oliveira, *O Convento (The Convent)*, Portugal

1996

Walter Salles, *Terra estrangeira (Foreign Land)*, Brazil

1997

Taylor Hackford, *The Devil's Advocate*, United States

2000

Harold Ramis, *Bedazzled*, United States

2001

Álex Ollé, Isidro Ortiz, and Carlos Padrisa, *Fausto 5.0*, Spain

2002

Rainer Matsutani, *666: Traue keinem, mit dem Du schläfst!* (In Bed with the Devil), Germany

2007

Mark Steven Johnson, *Ghost Rider*, United States

Notes

Introduction: Inventions of Faust

1. Paul de Man, "La Critique thématique devant le thème de Faust," *Critique* 120 (1957): 393.

2. André Jolles, *Einfache Formen: Legende, Sage, Mythe, Rätsel, Spruch, Kasus, Memorabile, Märchen, Witz* (1930; Tübingen: Niemeyer, 1965) and *Formes simples*, trans. Antoine Marie Bugner (Paris: Seuil, 1972). Subsequent references are to the French edition.

3. Elizabeth Frenzel, *Stoffe der Weltliteratur* (Stuttgart: Alfred Kröner, 1963), 237.

4. The known facts about the historical Faust are summarized in Frenzel, 237; Klaus L. Berghahn, "Georg Johann Heinrich Faust: The Myth and Its History," in *Our Faust? Roots and Ramifications of a Modern German Myth*, ed. Reinhold Grimm and Jost Hermand (Madison: University of Wisconsin Press, 1987), 7–8; and H. G. Haile, ed. and trans., *The History of Doctor Johann Faustus* (Urbana: University of Illinois Press, 1965), 1–12.

5. Frenzel, 173.

6. Jolles, 48.

7. Henri Birven, *Der Historische Doktor Faust: Maske und Anlitz* (Gelnhausen: Heinrich Schwab Verlag, 1963), 100–113.

8. The references in text are to the German edition, Johann Spies, *Historia von D. Johann Fausten* (Stuttgart: Reklam, 1988), 121, 123. See also Johann Spies, *Historia von D. Johann Fausten*, reprinted in J. Scheible, *Das Kloster: Weltlich und Geistlich; Zur Kultur- und Sittengeschichte in Wort und Bild*, vol. 2 (Stuttgart: J. Scheible, 1846), 933–1069. I will subsequently refer to "Spies's *Historia*" or "Spies's chapbook." There were subsequent compilations by others; for instance, an illustrated chapbook by Widman, also reprinted by Scheible in the same volume with Spies.

9. Haile, 127.

10. Jolles, 94

11. Jolles, 81.

12. Birven, 111.

13. Berghahn, 9.

14. Haile, 27.

15. Johann Wolfgang von Goethe, *Faust*, trans. Walter Arndt, ed. Cyrus Hamlin (New York: W. W. Norton, 1976). Subsequent quotations (identified by line numbers in text) will refer to this edition. The translation can be checked against the original by consulting the edition of *Faust* edited by Albrecht Schöne (Frankfurt am Main: Deutscher Klassiker Verlag, 1994).

16. Jolles, 88–91.

17. Berghahn, 8.

18. De Man, 398.

19. Jürgen Kühnel, "Faust und Don Juan: Europäische Mythen der Neuzeit," in *Europäische Mythen der Neuzeit: Faust und Don Juan*, ed. Peter Csobádi et al., vol. 1, special issue of *Wort und Musik* in 2 vols. (Salzburg: Verlag Ursula Müller-Speiser, 1993), 33.

20. Roland Barthes, *Mythologies*, trans. Annette Lavers (New York: Hill and Wang, 1970), 110.

21. Barthes, 143.

22. Graeme Turner, *British Cultural Studies: An Introduction* (Boston: Unwin Hyman, 1990), 66–67.

23. Michel Foucault, "Truth and Power," in *Power/Knowledge: Selected Interviews and Writings, 1972–77*, ed. Colin Gordon (New York: Pantheon, 1980), 114.

1. Faust and Early Film Spectatorship

1. Noël Burch, *La Lucarne de l'infini* (Paris: Nathan, 1991), 48, 139–40.

2. Burch, *La Lucarne*, 42.

3. John Frazer, *Artificially Arranged Scenes: The Films of Georges Méliès* (Boston: G. K. Hall, 1979). The titles and dates are taken from Frazer and from *Essai de reconstitution du catalogue français de la Star Film* (Bois d'Arcy: Service des archives du film du Centre National de la Cinématographie, 1981).

4. See Jean Mitry, *Histoire du cinéma (1895–1914)*, vol. 1 (Paris: Editions Universitaires, 1967).

5. For a detailed description of this terrible accident, see Mitry, 110–12.

6. Quoted in Burch, *La Lucarne*, 51.

7. Madeleine Malthête-Méliès, granddaughter of the filmmaker, describes Méliès's first visit to the Moulin Rouge on its opening night (Oct. 6, 1889) in *Méliès l'enchanteur* (Paris: Editions Ramsey, 1995), 119–23.

8. Burch, *La Lucarne*, 65; Frazer, 3–5.

9. A lost sound version by Alice Guy and based on Gounod's opera dates from as early as 1906.

10. This, too, set a trend—in 1905, Méliès's compatriot Ferdinand Zecca made a Faust film for the film company Pathé, in which he also played the role of Mephistopheles. Madeleine Malthête-Méliès relates that Méliès loved to play the devil's role and made the following (untranslatable) witticism: "Quand j'incarne le diable, je signe Mélié, parce que Mephisto fait l'S." Malthête-Méliès, *Méliès l'enchanteur*, 93.

11. Richard Abel has described this transition in great detail in *The Ciné Goes to Town: French Cinema, 1896–1914* (Berkeley: University of California Press, 1994). For an exact description and definition of the "cinema of attractions" as formulated by Gaudreault and Gunning, see 60–61.

12. This film seems to exist in varying lengths, depending on how many adventures are included. There is mention of a version with eighty tableaux, although the known

surviving tableaux number no more than thirty-two. See *Essai de reconstitution du catalogue*, 257–62.

13. Burch, *La Lucarne*, 65–67.

14. Hélène Puiseux, "Lecture sociale des films de Méliès," in *Méliès et la naissance du spectacle cinématographique*, ed. Madeleine Malthête-Méliès (Paris: Klincksieck, 1984), 31–33.

15. Suzanne Richard, "A Beginner's Guide to the Art of Georges Méliès," in *A Trip to the Movies: Georges Méliès, Filmmaker and Magician, 1861–1938*, ed. Paolo Cherchi Usai (Rochester, N.Y.: George Eastman House, 1991), 45.

16. Emile Cohl's *Le Tout petit Faust* (1910) is essentially a puppet-play version of Gounod's opera. The Polish-Russian *Pan Twardowski* (1916) by Ladislas Starewich, which has a number of Faustian motifs, also falls within the tradition of the Méliès trick film.

17. Burch, *La Lucarne*, 113; Miriam Hansen, *Babel and Babylon: Spectatorship in American Silent Film* (Cambridge: Harvard University Press, 1991), 28–29. See also Robert Allen, *Vaudeville and Film, 1895–1915: A Study in Media Interaction* (New York: Arno, 1980).

18. Burch, *La Lucarne*, 108.

19. Judith Mayne, *Private Novels, Public Films* (Athens: University of Georgia Press, 1988), 79–81.

20. Miriam Hansen, "Early Silent Cinema: Whose Public Sphere?" *New German Critique* 29 (Spring/Summer 1983): 151.

21. Hansen, "Early Silent Cinema," 158.

22. Hansen, *Babel*, 85.

23. Helmut H. Diedrichs, *Der Student von Prag: Einführung und Protokoll* (Stuttgart: Verlagsgemeinschaft Robert Fischer, 1985), 6–8.

24. Anton Kaes, "The Debate about Cinema: Charting a Controversy (1909–1929)," *New German Critique* 40 (1987): 7–33. See also his *Kino-Debatte: Texte zum Verhältnis von Literatur und Film 1909–1929* (Tübingen: Max Niemeyer Verlag, 1978).

25. Kaes, "Debate about Cinema," 9.

26. John Barlow notes that the Hebrew tombstones would have connoted exoticism and mystery for German viewers and hence contributed to the other-worldliness of the film's atmosphere. John Barlow, *German Expressionist Film* (Boston: Twayne, 1982), 69–70.

27. André Bazin, "Ontologie de l'image cinématographique," in *Qu'est-ce que le cinéma?* (Paris: Editions du Cerf, 1958), 16.

28. Sabine Hake, *The Cinema's Third Machine: Writing on Film in Germany, 1907–1933* (Lincoln: University of Nebraska Press, 1993), 18.

29. Siegfried Kracauer, *The Mass Ornament: Weimar Essays*, trans. Thomas Y. Levin (Cambridge: Harvard University Press, 1995), 327–28.

30. Kracauer, 327.

31. Here is a rough translation of Musset's poem on solitude (as quoted in the film):

I am no fool
Nor can I a demon be
Yet scornfully I speak
Your very name.
For wherever you are
Shall I always be
Until the hour decreed.
By your headstone I sit
Over your grave.

32. From the murderer's monologue in Fritz Lang's *M*: "Always, always, I wander the streets, and I always feel there is someone after me; it's me—myself—and he follows me silently, but I can still hear him. . . . sometimes I feel as though I was walking behind myself—I want to run away—to run away from myself—but I can't, can't get away from me. . . . I must, *must* go along the path along which I am pursued" (from the film, my translation).

33. Barlow and Heide Schlüpmann (see note 35 below) mention a tale by Hoffmann, "Die Geschichte vom verlorenen Spiegelbilde" (The Story of the Lost Reflection). Edgar Allan Poe, Oscar Wilde, and others also explored the theme of the double.

34. Thomas Elsaesser, "Social Mobility and the Fantastic: German Silent Cinema," in *Fantasy and Cinema*, ed. James Donald (London: BFI, 1989), 28.

35. Heide Schlüpmann, "The First German Art Film: Rye's *The Student of Prague*," in *German Film and Literature: Adaptations and Transformations*, ed. Eric Rentschler (New York: Methuen, 1986), 16.

36. In arguing that Lyduschka is herself "divided," I am making a somewhat different point from Schlüpmann's interesting argument that the countess and Lyduschka can also be considered as mirror doubles of one another—she sees Lyduschka, in effect, as the countess's repressed sexuality. See Schlüpmann, 17.

37. Patrice Petro, *Joyless Streets: Women and Melodramatic Representation in Weimar Germany* (Princeton: Princeton University Press, 1989), 140. See also the section entitled "Men's Modernism Versus Women's Modernity: Weimar Women at Work and in the Movies," 68–78. For a description of early sociological studies on the Weimar film audience, see Hake, 47–48.

38. Klaus Kreimeier, *The Ufa Story*, trans. Robert Kimber and Rita Kimber (Berkeley: University of California Press, 1999), 119.

39. Eric Rohmer, *L'Organisation de l'espace dans le "Faust" de Murnau* (Paris: Union Générale d'Editions, 1977), 18 and 89.

40. Rohmer, 21.

41. Rohmer, 28–29.

42. Rohmer, 30.

43. André Bazin's remarks on identification (which also quote another critic from the 1930s) occur in the essay "Theater and Cinema," in *What Is Cinema?* vol. 1 (Berkeley: University of California Press, 1967), 99 and 113. For psychoanalytic

approaches, see Laura Mulvey's seminal essay, "Visual Pleasure and Narrative Cinema," most recently reprinted in *Film and Theory*, ed. Robert Stam and Toby Miller, 483–94 (London: Blackwell, 2000); and in the same volume, Christian Metz, "The Imaginary Signifier," 408–36. For Marxist approaches, see Christine Gledhill, "Image and Voice: Approaches to Marxist-Feminist Film Criticism," in *Multiple Voices in Feminist Film Criticism*, ed. Diane Carson, Linda Dittmar, and Janice R. Welsch, 109–23 (Minneapolis: University of Minnesota Press, 1994). The most important empirical study on the variations of identification occasioned by actual viewers' social and ideological positions is *Sündiger Genuss? Filmerfahrungen von Frauen*, ed. Frigga Haug and Brigitte Hipfl (Berlin: Argument Verlag, 1995).

44. In the original montage, reconstructed by Luciano Berriatúa for Filmoteca Española in 1994, Gretchen and Faust ascend to heaven together. On most copies in distribution, this shot is replaced by a shot of a bright light shining among the clouds. Berriatúa made a video in 1994 entitled *The Five Fausts of F. W. Murnau*. The printed program "Faust: F. W. Murnau's Original Montage Reconstructed by Luciano Berriatúa" (acquisition date 1 Apr. 1996) can be consulted in the Motion Picture, Broadcasting and Recorded Sound Division of the Library of Congress.

45. Anatoli Vasilievich Lunacharski might have had a similar mise-en-scène in mind in his theatrical version of Faust (discussed in chapter 3) when the host of the wicked prepare to battle against the host of the just—but one can see immediately that this is a cinematic moment rather than one that could be successfully staged.

46. Ernst Prodolliet, *Faust im Kino: Die Geschichte des Faustfilms von den Anfängen bis in die Gegenwart* (Freiburg, Switz.: Universitätsverlag Freiburg, 1978), 5–51.

47. Prodolliet, 51–52.

48. Bruce Murray, *Film and the German Left in the Weimar Republic: From "Caligari" to "Kuhle Wampe"* (Austin: University of Texas Press, 1990), 121. In 1926, the German national censorship bureau also tried (unsuccessfully) to prevent the showing of Eisenstein's *Battleship Potemkin*.

49. Tom Gunning, "The Cinema of Attractions: Early Film, Its Spectator and the Avant-Garde," *Wide Angle* 8.3/4 (1986): 63–70.

50. Gunning, 65.

2. German Fascism and the Contested Terrain of Culture

1. See the essays in George L. Mosse, ed., *Nazi Culture: Intellectual, Cultural and Social Life in the Third Reich* (New York: Grosset and Dunlap, 1966), especially Ludwig Ferdinand Clauss, "Racial Soul, Landscape, and World Domination," 65–75.

2. A comprehensive study of the German exiles is to be found in Anthony Heilbut, *Exiled in Paradise: German Refugee Artists and Intellectuals in America from the 1930s to the Present* (Berkeley: University of California Press, 1997).

3. Oswald Spengler, author of *The Decline of the West* (1922), sent a complimentary copy of one of his books to Hitler in August of 1933 and also requested a meeting. However, in 1935, he declined to continue as director of the Nietzsche

archive. Although he initially supported the German nationalist movement, he never became a member of the Nazi Party. A letter from Elisabeth Forster-Nietzsche in November 1935 charges that Spengler was resigning as director of the Nietzsche archive because he "energetically distances himself from the Third Reich and its Führer." Quoted in Oswald Spengler, *Briefe 1913–1936*, ed. Manfred Schröter (Munich: Verlag C. H. Beck, 1963), 749. The complicated relationship between Thomas Mann and Spengler is explicated in Hans Kellner, "Figures in the Rumpel-kammer: Goethe, Faust, Spengler," *Journal of European Studies* 13 (1983): 142–67; and Helmut Koopmann, "The Decline of the West and the Ascent of the East: Thomas Mann, the Joseph Novels, and Spengler," in *Critical Essays on Thomas Mann*, ed. Inta M. Ezergailis, 238–65 (Boston: G. K. Hall, 1988).

4. Thomas Mann, *Doctor Faustus*, trans. John E. Woods (New York: Alfred Knopf, 1997), 258. Subsequent references will be to this translation.

5. T. Mann, *Doctor Faustus*, 534.

6. Thomas Mann, *The Genesis of a Novel*, trans. Richard and Clara Winston (London: Secker and Warburg, 1961), 28. This is a translation of *Die Entstehung des Doktor Faustus: Roman eines Romans* (Amsterdam: Bermann-Fischer Verlag, 1949).

7. T. Mann, *Doctor Faustus*, 512–13.

8. Although Goethe's *Faust* is never directly mentioned in Mann's novel, refer-ences to it may be found in passing: for example, there is a maid called Waltpurgis at the farm where Leverkühn takes refuge in order to compose during his twenty-four years of musical productivity (recalling the "Walpurgis night" orgy in *Faust*, part 1).

9. Kirsten Belgum, Karoline Kirst-Gundersen, and Paul Levesque, "'Faust im Braunhemd': Germanistik and Fascism," in *Our Faust? Roots and Ramifications of a Modern German Myth*, ed. Reinhold Grimm and Jost Hermand (Madison: Uni-versity of Wisconsin Press, 1987), 154.

10. Houston Stewart Chamberlain, *Goethe*, 3rd ed. (Munich: F. Bruckmann, 1921), xi–xii.

11. Georg Schott, *Goethes Faust in heutiger Schau* (Stuttgart: Tazzelwurm Verlag, 1940), 103.

12. Schott, *Goethes Faust*, 29–30.

13. Alfred Rosenberg, *The Myth of the Twentieth Century*, trans. Vivian Bird (1930; Torrance, Calif.: Noontide, 1982), 157. This work underwent multiple reprints in the Nazi era.

14. Rosenberg, 321–22.

15. Johannes Bertram, *Goethes Faust: Im Blickfeld des XX Jahrhunderts, eine weltanschauliche Deutung* (1939; Hamburg: Dreizack Verlag, 1942), 90–91.

16. Thomas Zabka, "Vom 'deutschen Mythus' zum 'Kriegshilfdienst': *Faust*-Aneignungen im nationalsozialistischen Deutschland," in *Faust: Annäherung an einen Mythos*, ed. Frank Möbus, Friederike Schmidt-Möbus, and Gerd Unverfehrt (Göttingen: Wallstein Verlag, 1996), 316.

17. Wilhelm Böhm, *Faust der Nichtfaustische* (Halle: Max Niemeyer Verlag, 1933), 92.

18. Ernst Beutler, "Goethes Faust ein Deutsches Gedicht," in *Von Deutscher Art in Sprache und Dichtung*, ed. Gerhard Fricke, Franz Koch, and Lemens Lugowski, vol. 4 (Stuttgart: W. Kohlhammer Verlag, 1941), 279–80.

19. T. Mann, *Doctor Faustus*, 299.

20. Heinrich Gruber, introduction to *Weissagung und Erfüllung im deutschen Volksmärchen*, by Georg Schott (Munich: Verlag Franz Eher, 1936), 7.

21. Schott, *Weissagung*, 23–42.

22. Schott, *Weissagung*, 206.

23. Quoted in Christa Kamenetsky, "Folktale and Ideology in the Third Reich," *Journal of American Folklore* 90 (1977): 170.

24. Schott, *Weissagung*, 144.

25. Schott, *Weissagung*, 146.

26. Schott, *Weissagung*, 63.

27. In a 1919 collage, *Sonniges Land* (Sunny Country) that he made with the caricaturist George Grosz, Faust's name appears alongside images of Prussian officers, a bourgeois German family portrait, and a little girl manhandling a doll. The main message of the collage is to promote the Dada movement, which is advertised in large letters. See Peter Pachnicke and Klaus Honnef, *John Heartfield* (Koln: DuMont, 1991), 66.

28. *Atta Troll* was the title of an 1841 satirical epic by Heinrich Heine. The bear escaped from his owners and was finally shot after a series of adventures. Heine's work is widely regarded as a political allegory. Heartfield appears to warn that the bear's fate will also be that of the German people currently dancing to Goebbels's tune; alternatively, it might be construed as a critique of German political parties who reached an accommodation with Hitler under the illusory hope that they could control him. For a discussion of the Nazi use of German folktales, see Christa Kamenetsky, *Children's Literature in Hitler's Germany: The Cultural Policy of National Socialism* (Athens: Ohio University Press, 1984), 192; and Wilhelm Steckelings, "From the Oak Tree to Certain Victory," in Mosse, 289.

29. T. Mann, *Doctor Faustus*, 246.

30. T. Mann, *Doctor Faustus*, 393.

31. T. Mann, *Doctor Faustus*, 430.

32. T. Mann, *Doctor Faustus*, 513.

33. Mann records that he consulted the collection of texts relating to Faust assembled by J. Scheible in 1847. See T. Mann, *Genesis of a Novel*, 112; and Scheible, 42.

34. Scheible, 806.

35. T. Mann, *Genesis of a Novel*, 125.

36. T. Mann, *Doctor Faustus*, 283–88.

37. T. Mann, *Genesis of a Novel*, 89.

38. T. Mann, *Doctor Faustus*, 348.

39. Thomas Mann, *Selbstkommentare: 'Doktor Faustus' und 'Die Entstehung des Doktor Faustus,'* ed. Hans Wysling (Frankfurt/Main: Fischer, 1992), 81.

40. I am taking the facts surrounding the lives of Gustaf Gründgens and Klaus Mann from the useful study by Eberhard Spangenberg, *Karriere eines Romans: Mephisto, Klaus Mann und Gustaf Gründgens* (München: Heinrich Ellermann, 1982).

41. Spangenberg, 115–19.

42. Klaus Mann, quoted in Spangenberg, 94.

43. Klaus Mann, *Mephisto*, trans. Robin Smyth (New York: Penguin, 1983), 254.

44. Klaus Mann, quoted in Spangenberg, 131.

45. For a history of the novel's publication and reception as well as the court cases surrounding it, see Spangenberg, 5, 88–95, 97–111, 161–90, and 207–18.

46. K. Mann, *Mephisto*, 152.

47. K. Mann, *Mephisto*, 189.

48. K. Mann, *Mephisto*, 153.

49. Quoted from the film version by István Szabó. The corresponding passages from the novel read: "Hamlet wasn't a weak man. . . . Generations of actors have made the mistake of viewing him as a feminine character. His melancholy wasn't hollow but came from real motives. The prince wants to avenge his father. He is a Renaissance man—a real aristocrat and something of a cynic." K. Mann, *Mephisto*, 255. The rest of the analysis is voiced by the critic Dr. Ihring: "Hamlet is therefore a danger for the German people. We have him in all of us and we must get the better of him. Providence, which has sent us the Führer, commits us to action in the defense of the national community from which Hamlet, a typical intellectual, withdraws into a brooding isolation" (156).

50. Quoted in Klaus Mann, *Briefe und Antworten*, vol. 1 (Munich: Ellermann Verlag, 1975), 274.

51. Klaus Mann, *Der Wendepunkt: Ein Lebensbericht* (Munich: Nymphenburger Verlagshandlung GmbH, 1969), 447–48. The German text of the quote from Goethe (lines 355–56 of *Faust*) has been added in brackets. The passages rendered in italics were written in English in the original.

52. For a short biography of Klaus Mann, see *Briefe und Antworten*, 324–25.

53. Klaus Mann, "An die Schiftsteller im Dritten Reich," in *Heute und Morgen: Schriften zur Zeit* (Munich: Nymphenburger Verlagshandlung GmbH, 1969), 253.

54. Thomas Mann, *Order of the Day: Political Essays and Speeches of Two Decades* (New York: Alfred A. Knopf, 1942), xiii.

55. Thomas Mann, *Listen Germany! Twenty-five Radio Messages to the German People over BBC* (New York: Alfred A. Knopf, 1943).

56. T. Mann, *Order of the Day*, introduction, v–xvi. For an interesting assessment of Thomas Mann's engagement with politics, see Ernest Bisdorff, *Thomas Mann und die Politik* (Luxemburg: Editions du Centre, 1966).

57. The typescript is first mentioned in a letter in 1943. See Else Lasker-Schüler, *Dramen*, ed. Georg-Michael Schultz (Frankfurt am Main: Jüdischer Verlag am Suhrkamp Verlag, 1997), 317–18. This edition has many helpful explanatory notes.

58. Else Lasker-Schüler, *Ichundich*, in Lasker-Schüler, *Dramen*, 218.

59. Sigrid Bauschinger, *Else Lasker-Schüler: Ihr Werk und Ihre Zeit* (Heidelberg: Lothat Stiehm Verlag, 1980), 289.

60. Margarete Kupper, postscript to Else Lasker-Schüler, *Ichundich: Eine theatralische Tragödie* (Munich: Kösel Verlag, 1980), 115.

61. Heinz Thiel, "*Ich und Ich*—ein versperrtes Werk?" in *Lasker-Schüler*, ed. Michael Schmid (Wuppertal: Peter Hammer, 1969), 123–59; and Karl Theens, "Else Lasker-Schüler: Ichundich," *Faust-Blätter* 38 (1980): 1615–22.

62. Lasker-Schüler, *Ichundich* (Schultz edition), 233.

3. Socialist Visions: Faust and Utopia

1. Frank Beyer, "Die Spur des Stalinismus: Opfer und Täter," *EPD Film* (Jan. 1990): 2–3.

2. Alexander Abusch, *Der Irrweg einer Nation: Ein Beitrag zum Verständnis deutscher Geschichte* (Berlin: Aufbau Verlag, 1946), 261–62: "The first heroes of the war against bestiality were Germans, German opponents of Hitler."

3. Deborah Vietor-Engländer, *Faust in der DDR* (Peter Lang: Frankfurt am Main, 1987), 18–20.

4. Alexander Abusch and Johannes R. Becher quoted in Vietor-Engländer, 18.

5. Walter Ulbricht quoted in Vietor-Engländer, 60 n. 89.

6. Alexander Abusch quoted in Vietor-Engländer, 58–59 n. 88.

7. Jochen-Ulrich Peters, *Kunst als organisierte Erfahrung: Über den Zusammenhang von Kunsttheorie, Literaturkritik und Kulturpolitik bei A. V. Lunacharskij* (Munich: Wilhelm Fink Verlag, 1980), 23.

8. A. V. Lunacharski, "Goethe und wir" (1932), in *Faust und die Stadt: Ein Lesedrama mit Essays zur Faustproblematik* (Frankfurt: Röderberg Verlag, 1973), 197–98.

9. Friedrich Engels, in *Marx/Engels on Literature and Art* (Moscow: Progress Publishers, 1976), 355.

10. V. I. Lenin, "How to Organise Competition," in *On Workers' Control and the Nationalisation of Industry* (Moscow: Progress Publishers, 1970), 124. Lenin is quoting Mephistopheles's advice to a naive student in Goethe's *Faust*, part 1 (lines 2038–39). In Goethe, this "advice"—considering its source—comes laced with considerable irony.

11. Sheila Fitzpatrick, "Cultural Revolution as Class War," in *Cultural Revolution in Russia*, ed. Sheila Fitzpatrick (Ithaca: Cornell University Press, 1992), 10.

12. Peters, 23–47.

13. A. V. Lunacharski, *Faust and the City*, in *Three Plays of A. V. Lunacharski*, trans. L. A. Magnus and K. Walter (New York: E. P. Dutton, 1923), scene 10, 62–63.

14. Lunacharski, *Faust and the City*, scene 7, 98.

15. Lunacharski, *Faust and the City*, scene 7, 99.

16. Lunacharski, *Faust and the City*, scene 10, 115.

17. Jean Lacouture, *Léon Blum*, trans. George Holock (New York: Holmes and Meier, 1982), 66–67.

18. Léon Blum, *Nouvelles conversations de Goethe avec Eckermann* (Paris: Gallimard, 1937), 99.

19. L. Blum, 97.

20. L. Blum, 91.

21. L. Blum, 92–98.

22. For an account of the short-lived Popular Front, see Julian Jackson, *The Popular Front in France: Defending Democracy, 1934–38* (Cambridge: Cambridge University Press, 1988).

23. L. Blum, 90.

24. Fredric Jameson, *Marxism and Form* (Princeton: Princeton University Press, 1971), 161.

25. Georg Lukács, *Realism in Our Time: Literature and the Class Struggle* (1956; New York: Harper and Row, 1964).

26. Georg Lukács, *Goethe and His Age*, trans. Robert Anchor (1968; New York: Howard Fertig, 1978), 241.

27. Lukács, *Goethe*, 181.

28. In Goethe's *Faust*, part 1, Faust first refers to Margarete as Gretchen when talking to Mephistopheles (2849). Thereafter, the drama refers to her either as Gretchen or as Margarete. The "Gretchen episode" refers to her seduction and abandonment by Faust.

29. Lukács, *Goethe*, 223.

30. Lukács, *Goethe*, 216.

31. Lukács, *Goethe*, 193–94.

32. Hanns Eisler, *Johann Faustus: Fassung letzter Hand* (libretto), ed. Hans Bunge, with an afterword by Werner Mittenzwei (Berlin: Henschelverlag Kunst und Gesellschaft, 1983), 103–4.

33. Ernst Fischer, "Bemerkungen zu Hanns Eislers Textbuch *Johann Faustus*," in *Die Debatte um Hanns Eislers "Johann Faustus,"* ed. Hans Bunge (Berlin: Basis Druck, 1991), 27.

34. Fischer, 36.

35. Alexander Abusch, "Faust—Held oder Renegat in der deutschen Nationalliteratur?" in Bunge, *Die Debatte*, 59–60.

36. Bernd Mahl, *Brechts und Monks Urfaust-Inszenierung mit dem Berliner Ensemble 1952–53* (Stuttgart: Belser Verlag, 1986), 26.

37. Mahl gives a full documentation of the public reaction, 188–200.

38. Brecht's remarks at the meeting of the Mittwochgesellschaft on 27 May 1953 are quoted in Bunge, *Die Debatte*, 161. The criticisms of Eisler, which appeared in May 1953 in *Neues Deutschland* and which Brecht addresses here, are reprinted in Bunge, *Die Debatte*, 91–101.

39. Eisler's libretto was first performed as a play in Tübingen in 1974. The first East German performance was not put on until 1982, by the Berliner Ensemble, the theater founded by Bertolt Brecht. To date, no music has been composed for the libretto.

40. Vietor-Engländer, 24.

41. Vietor-Engländer, 28.

42. Otto Grotewohl quoted in Vietor-Engländer, 19.

43. Braun doesn't name the play, but the story "Die Bretter" in his collection *Das ungezwungene Leben Kasts* (Berlin: Aufbau Verlag, 1979) is clearly an account of the difficulties surrounding the premiere of *Hans Faust*. The review by Ingrid Seyfarth gives an extensive account of the unpublished play. See "Individuum im Geschichtsprozess" (The Individual in the Process of History), *Theater der Zeit* 23.20 (1968): 16–17.

44. Braun, who admired Thomas Mann's *Doctor Faustus*, may be making a passing reference to that work here. In Adrian Leverkühn's encounter with his demonic visitor, the devil explains that it is not so easy to get into hell: "We would have filled up long ago, if we allowed just anyone in [*Hinz und Kunz*]." Thomas Mann, *Doctor Faustus* (1946; Frankfurt am Main: Fischer, 1967), 248.

45. An account summarizing the differences between the two versions may be found in Wolfgang Schivelbusch, *Sozialistisches Drama nach Brecht* (Darmstadt: Luchterhand, 1974), 56.

46. Volker Braun, *Hinze und Kunze*, in *Stücke*, vol. 1 (Frankfurt: Suhrkamp, 1981), 113.

47. A similar theme was explored in the novel by Erik Neutsch, *Spur der Steine*, published in 1964. In 1965, Frank Beyer made it into a film. That same year, Heiner Müller used the story as the basis for his play *Der Bau*. Beyer's film was banned after only a few showings; Müller's play was not allowed to be performed until 1980. See Inez Hedges, "Always Just over the Horizon: The East German Intellectual and the Elusive Public Sphere," *Socialism and Democracy* 16/17 (1992): 59–75.

48. Braun, *Hinze und Kunze*, 96.

49. Rainer Kirsch, *Heinrich Schlaghands Höllenfahrt*, in *Theater der Zeit* 28.4 (1973): 46–64. The play was republished in West Germany in Rainer Kirsch, *Auszog das Fürchten zu lernen* (Reinbek bei Hamburg: Rowolt, 1978), 65–147.

50. Volker Braun, *Berichte von Hinze und Kunze* (Frankfurt: Suhrkamp, 1983), 19. The volume was published the same year in Halle, East Germany, by Mitteldeutscher Verlag.

51. Braun, *Berichte von Hinze und Kunze*, 35.

52. Marshall Berman, *All That Is Solid Melts into Air: The Experience of Modernity* (New York: Simon and Schuster, 1982), 71–86.

53. Braun, *Hinze und Kunze*, 111.

54. Lukács argues that Goethe arrived at this idea of dialectical progress through studying the French Revolution. See Lukács, *Goethe*, 197.

55. Lukács, *Goethe*, 205.

56. Lukács, *Goethe*, 213.

57. Berman, 70.

58. Berman, 78.

59. For a fuller discussion of this complex issue, see James O'Connor, *Natural*

Causes: Essays in Ecological Marxism (New York: Guilford, 1998), particularly the chapter titled "Socialism and Nature," 255–65.

60. Volker Braun, "Das Eigentum," trans. Karen Ruoff Kramer, *Socialism and Democracy* 13.1 (1999): 68. The translation was slightly revised by the translator in collaboration with Volker Braun in 2004.

61. Braun, "The Changed World," in *Berichte von Hinze und Kunze*, 35.

62. I am taking the term "first epoch socialism" from Victor Wallis, "Marxism in the Age of Gorbachev," *Socialism and Democracy* 11 (Sept. 1990): 48.

63. Jost Hermand, *Im Wettlauf mit der Zeit: Anstösse zu einer ökologiebewussten Ästhetik* (Berlin: Edition Sigma Rainer Bohn Verlag, 1991), 46–47.

64. Hermand, *Im Wettlauf,* 37.

65. Hermand, *Im Wettlauf,* 47.

66. Karl Marx, *Capital,* trans. Ben Fowkes, vol. 1 (New York: Random House, 1977), 180.

4. Gendering Faust

1. Louisa May Alcott, *A Long Fatal Love Chase* (New York: Dell, 1995) and *A Modern Mephistopheles* and *A Whisper in the Dark* (Boston: Roberts Brothers, 1889).

2. Alcott, *Long Fatal Love Chase*, 182. Her seducer learns of her love when playing the role of confessor.

3. Alcott, *Modern Mephistopheles*, 36.

4. Alcott, *Modern Mephistopheles*, 289.

5. Ralph Waldo Emerson, "Historic Notes of Life and Letters in New England," in *The American Transcendentalists*, ed. Perry Miller (New York: Anchor/Doubleday, 1957), 7.

6. Ralph Waldo Emerson, "Goethe," in *Representative Men: Seven Lectures*, vol. 4 of *The Collected Works of Ralph Waldo Emerson* (Cambridge: Harvard University Press, 1987), 163.

7. Emerson, "Goethe," 162.

8. Margaret Fuller, "Menzel's View of Goethe," *Dial*, vol. 1 (1840; facsimile edition, New York: Russell and Russell, 1961): 346.

9. Emerson, "Goethe," 165–66.

10. Emerson, "Goethe" 159.

11. Alcott, *Modern Mephistopheles*, 220, 290.

12. [Unsigned], "Prophecy, Transcendentalism, Progress," *Dial*, vol. 2 (1841: facsimile edition, New York: Russell and Russell, 1961): 109.

13. Elaine Showalter, *Sister's Choice: Tradition and Change in American Women's Writing* (Oxford: Clarendon, 1991), 47–48.

14. Showalter, 55.

15. Showalter, 130.

16. Marjorie Garber, *Vested Interests: Cross-Dressing and Cultural Anxiety* (London: Routledge, 1992), 11.

17. Klaus Mann, "Frank Wedekind," in *Die Heimsuchung des Europäischen Geistes: Aufsätze* (Munich: Deutscher Taschenbuch Verlag GmbH, 1973), 36.

18. Frank Wedekind, *Franziska,* in *Werke,* vol. 2 (Munich: Winkler Verlag, 1990), 669.

19. Wedekind, 677.

20. Wedekind, 667, 811–12.

21. Wedekind, 700.

22. Wedekind, 690.

23. Sabine Doering, "Fräulein Faust: Weibliche Faustgestalten in der deutschen Literatur," in Möbus, Schmidt-Möbus, and Unverfehrt, 121.

24. Wedekind, 814.

25. Nancy Fraser, "Structuralism or Pragmatics? On Discourse Theory and Feminist Politics," in *Justice Interruptus: Critical Reflections on the "Postsocialist" Condition,* ed. Nancy Fraser (New York: Routledge, 1997), 152.

26. I would like to thank Peter Glen Christensen for his very stimulating paper, "Hélène Cixous's Faust: A Revolutionary in Spite of Himself," during a session on "European Readings and Rewritings of Faust," at the Modern Language Association meeting in Toronto, 27 Dec. 1993. His paper, which focused on the theme of revolutionary violence, first called my attention to Hélène Cixous's *Révolutions pour plus d'un Faust* (Paris: Editions du Seuil, 1975).

27. Cixous, *Révolutions,* 9–10.

28. Luce Irigaray, *Speculum of the Other Woman,* trans. Gillian C. Gill (Ithaca: Cornell University Press, 1985), 137.

29. Irigaray, 142.

30. Cixous, *Révolutions,* 53.

31. Cixous, *Révolutions,* 60.

32. Cixous, *Révolutions,* 56.

33. Cixous, *Révolutions,* 127.

34. Cixous, *Révolutions,* 60.

35. Cixous, *Révolutions,* 100–101.

36. Cixous, *Révolutions,* 26, 29.

37. Cixous, *Révolutions,* 22.

38. Cixous, *Révolutions,* 43.

39. Cixous, *Révolutions,* 77–80.

40. Cixous, *Révolutions,* 88. It is interesting to see here that the active reader is seen as a maternal creator, whereas the male Argentinean writer Julio Cortázar writes disparagingly of the passive, "effeminate" reader (the so-called *lector hembra*) in his novel *Rayuela* (Buenos Aires: Editorial Sudamericana, 1963).

41. Cixous, *Révolutions,* 89.

42. Cixous, *Révolutions,* 100.

43. Cixous, *Révolutions,* 113.

44. Cixous, *Révolutions,* 130–31.

45. Cixous, *Révolutions*, 121.

46. Irigaray, 53.

47. Cixous, *Révolutions*, 138–39.

48. Cixous, *Révolutions*, 140–45.

49. Cixous, *Révolutions*, 153.

50. Cixous, *Révolutions*, 200.

51. Cixous, *Révolutions*, 202.

52. Cixous, *Révolutions*, 215.

53. Cixous, *Révolutions*, 221.

54. Cixous, *Révolutions*, 123–24.

55. Hélène Cixous, *Sorties* (Paris: Editions du Seuil, 1975), 87.

56. Susan Suleiman, *Risking Who One Is: Encounters with Contemporary Art and Literature* (Cambridge: Harvard University Press, 1994), 184.

57. Inez Hedges, *Languages of Revolt: Dada and Surrealist Literature and Film* (Durham: Duke University Press, 1983).

58. Cixous, *Révolutions*, 131.

59. Emma Tennant, *Faustine* (London: Faber and Faber, 1992), 84.

60. Tennant, 5.

61. Tennant, 129.

62. Tennant, 131.

63. Tennant, 139.

64. Tennant, 83.

65. Tennant, 29.

66. Irigaray, 22.

67. Irigaray, 43.

68. Tennant, 138–39.

69. Janet Bergstrom, "Sexuality at a Loss: The Films of F. W. Murnau," in *The Female Body in Western Culture: Contemporary Perspectives*, ed. Susan Suleiman (Cambridge: Harvard University Press, 1986), 253.

70. Bergstrom, 254.

71. Petro, 158.

72. Beatrice Hanssen, "Whatever Happened to Feminist Theory?" in *Critique of Violence: Between Postmodernism and Critical Theory* (Routledge: London, 2000), 251.

5. Anti-Fausts and the Avant-Garde

1. Lukács, *Goethe*, 157.

2. Peter Bürger, *Theory of the Avant-Garde* (Minneapolis: University of Minnesota Press, 1984), 72–81.

3. Alfred Jarry, *Les Gestes et opinions du docteur Faustroll, 'pataphysicien: Roman néo-scientifique* (Paris: Gallimard, 1980), 32.

4. Jarry, 34.

5. Jarry, 110.

6. Michel de Ghelderode, *Entretiens d'Ostende* (Paris: L'Arche, 1956), 78–79.

7. Michel de Ghelderode, *La Mort du docteur Faust* in *Théâtre* (Paris: Gallimard, 1957), 281.

8. Douglas Cole, "Faust and Anti-Faust in Modern Drama," *Drama Survey* 5.1 (Spring 1966): 41.

9. Antonin Artaud, *The Theater and Its Double*, trans. Mary Caroline Richards (New York: Grove, 1977), 92.

10. Artaud, 102.

11. Georges Ribemont-Dessaignes, *Faust*, in *Commerce* 28 (Summer 1931): 90, 156.

12. Ribemont-Dessaignes, 164.

13. Hedges, *Languages of Revolt*, 11–12.

14. Gertrude Stein, *Doctor Faustus Lights the Lights* in *Gertrude Stein: Writings, 1932–1946* (New York: Library of America, 1998), 577.

15. Stein, 579.

16. Stein, 585.

17. Stein, 589.

18. Stein, 590–91.

19. Stein, 597–98.

20. Stein, 602, 606–7.

21. For an account of Stein's stance during the 1930s and World War II, see Bettina L. Knapp, *Gertrude Stein* (New York: Continuum, 1990), 66–70; and Michael J. Hoffmann, *Gertrude Stein* (Boston: Twayne, 1976), 85.

22. Hoffmann, 84.

23. Ben Brantley, "A Case for Cubism and Deals with Devils," *New York Times*, 3 Feb. 1999, C1 and C4.

24. A. O. Scott, "Stan Brakhage, Avant-Garde Filmmaker, Dies at 70," *New York Times*, 12 Mar. 2003, A12.

25. Stan Brakhage, "Gertrude Stein: Meditative Literature and Film," *Millennium Film Journal* 25 (1991): 105–6.

26. Stan Brakhage, *The Brakhage Lectures* (Chicago: GoodLion, 1972), 20, 21.

27. "Brakhage at Sixty," unsigned interview from the journal *my mind's eye*, Fred Camper's website, <http://www.fredcamper.com/Film/BrakhageL.html>, accessed 22 June 2005 (my italics).

28. Stan Brakhage, *Metaphors on Vision*, ed. P. Adams Sitney (New York: Film Culture, 1976), [34] (pages are unnumbered; all page numbers cited for this work were obtained by manual count).

29. Brakhage, *Brakhage Lectures*, 12.

30. Brakhage's four Faust films are distributed by Canyon Cinema. A copy of *Faust IV* may be viewed at the Library of Congress, Motion Picture, Broadcasting and Recorded Sound Division.

31. Stan Brakhage, "Scenario Submitted to the Creative Film Foundation, 1955," in *Metaphors on Vision*, [36]. The fragment of "Faustfilm" is to be found on unnumbered pages 53–55.

32. Gene Youngblood, *Expanded Cinema* (New York: E. P. Dutton, 1970), 88.

33. Some of these techniques are described/enumerated in Brakhage, *Metaphors on Vision* and reprinted in *Essential Brakhage*, ed. Bruce R. McPherson (New York: McPherson, 2001), 16; and R. Bruce Elder, *The Films of Stan Brakhage in the American Tradition of Ezra Pound, Gertrude Stein, and Charles Olson* (Waterloo: Wilfrid Laurier University Press, 1998), 255–59.

34. Stan Brakhage, *Faust's Other: An Idyll* (1988). The text is based on my transcription from the film.

35. Stan Brakhage, "Faust 3: Candida Albacore," in *Film/Video Catalogue 7* (San Francisco: Canyon Cinema, 1992), 57.

36. Stan Brakhage, *Faust IV* (1989). The text is based on my transcription from the film.

37. Brakhage, *Metaphors on Vision*, [33].

38. Stan Brakhage, "Faust 4," in *Film/Video Catalogue 7*, 57.

39. Stan Brakhage, "Inspirations," in *Essential Brakhage*, 208.

40. P. Adams Sitney, *Visionary Film: The American Avant-Garde, 1943–2000*, 3rd ed. (New York: Oxford University Press, 2002), 414.

41. Quoted in Suranjan Ganguly, "Stan Brakhage—the 60th Birthday Interview," *Film Culture* 78 (Summer 1994): 28.

42. Johann Wolfgang Goethe, *Theory of Colors*, trans. Charles Lock Eastlake (Cambridge: MIT Press, 1970), 1–55.

43. Brakhage, *Metaphors on Vision*, [30–31].

44. Stan Brakhage, "In Consideration of Aesthetics," in *Telling Time: Essays of a Visionary Filmmaker* (New York: McPherson, 2003), 50.

45. Brakhage, *Metaphors on Vision*, [18].

46. Goethe, *Theory of Colors*, 43.

47. Brakhage, *Metaphors on Vision*, [34].

48. Robert Duncan, *Faust Foutu* (San Francisco: White Rabbit, 1958), 34.

49. Elder, 276.

50. Brakhage, "Inspirations," 210.

51. Brakhage, "Inspirations," 211.

52. Brakhage, *Faust's Other: An Idyll* (my transcription).

53. Stan Brakhage, "Exultations of Bruce Elder," in *Telling Time*, 126–27.

54. Michel Butor and Henri Pousseur, "Votre Faust: Fantaisie variable genre opéra," *Centre d'études et de recherches marxistes* 62 (1968): 67.

55. Butor and Pousseur, 56.

56. Butor and Pousseur, 53–54. The libretto is published in the last section. An earlier version was also serialized in *La Nouvelle revue française* 10.110 (Feb. 1962): 261–89 and 10.112 (Apr. 1962): 641–57.

57. Ulrich Seelmann-Eggebert, "Die Revolution der Oper fand nicht statt," *Faust-Blätter* 5 (1969): 177. Pousseur made two recordings of further adaptations of the work: *Jeux de miroirs de Votre Faust* (Wergo 60039), for piano and voices; and *Votre Faust*, a boxed set of three records, libretti, and cards, in French or German (Harmonia mundi BASF 01-21580-6).

58. Sigrid Wiesmann, "'Mi fai orrore': Einige Bemerkungen zu Henri Pousseurs *Votre Faust* und Luca Lombardis *Faust un Travestimento*," in Csobádi et al., 576.

59. Butor and Pousseur, 37.

60. Butor and Pousseur, 2–3.

61. Butor and Pousseur, 25.

62. Wiesmann, 575.

63. Michel Butor and Henri Pousseur, "Votre Faust: Deuxième partie (une version)," *La Nouvelle revue française* 10.110 (Feb. 1962): 263. Translation:

Tenor: What will you have?

Alto: A Champagne.

Soprano: And for you sir?

Bass: A whisky and a Martini.

Tape Recorder: I didn't know that you also had written church music the water of the eyes it must be a Faust the waves of the eyes it's that we haven't yet addressed the question of the libretto the algae of the eyes.

64. Georges Raillard, ed., *Butor: Colloque de Cérisy* (Paris: Union Générale d'Editions, 1974), 329–30.

65. Michel Butor, *6 810 000 litres d'eau par seconde: Étude stéréophonique* (Paris: Gallimard, 1965).

66. Michel Butor, "Le Roman comme recherche," in *Essais sur le roman* (Paris: Gallimard, 1960), 10.

67. Alfred Schnittke to Hannelore Gerlach, quoted in Ronald Weitzman, "Schnittke's Faust in Hamburg," *Tempo* 194 (Oct. 1995): 27.

68. Walter-Wolfgang Sparrer, "Eine bunte und teuflische Welt: Alfred Schnittke's *Historia von D. Johann Fausten*," *Neue Zeitschift für Musik* 5 (Sept.–Oct. 1995): 66–67; Weitzman, 27–30; and Heinz Josef Herbort, "Den Teufel nicht zu Gast Laden," *Die Zeit*, 30 June 1995: Feuilleton (Culture pages), 44–45.

69. Yakov Gubanov, lecture at the Franz Liszt College of Music in Weimar, Germany, 2000 (quoted by permission).

70. Sparrer, 67.

71. Lutz Lesle, "Klangblumen des Bösen: *Historia von D. Johann Fausten* von Alfred Schnittke in Hamburg uraufgeführt," *Orchester* 43.10 (1995): 37.

72. T. Mann, *Doctor Faustus*, 515.

73. Theodor W. Adorno, *Philosophie der neuen Musik: Gesammelte Schriften*, vol. 12 (1958; Frankfurt am Main: Suhrkamp, 1975), 124.

74. Adorno, 37.

75. Bürger, 81.

76. Bürger, 81.

77. Bürger, 92.

78. Bürger, 88.

79. Bürger, 72.

80. Linda Hutcheon, *The Politics of Postmodernism* (London: Routledge, 1989), 93.

81. The continued draw of the Faust theme is attested to by the circumstance that a number of avant-garde artists have used Faust in the title of their works even when there is only a tenuous thematic connection. In such cases, the "Faustian" appears to denote a work that aims at the synthesis of a major preoccupation of the artist. This includes Dara Birnbaum's *The Damnation of Faust Trilogy* (1983–87) and the video installation *My-Faust* (1889–91) by Nam June Paik. See *"My-Faust von Nam June Paik—ein banalisierter Mythos,"* in Csobádi et al., 651–63. See also the review by Peter Marks of the dance troupe La Fura dels Baus and their *F@ust, Version 3.0* in *New York Times,* 24 July 1998, B1.

6. Oneiric Fausts: Repression and Liberation in the Cold War Era

1. Richard M. Freeland, *The Truman Doctrine and the Origins of McCarthyism* (New York: Schocken Books, 1974), 140.

2. See William Blum, *Killing Hope: U.S. Military and CIA Intervention since World War II* (Monroe, Maine: Common Courage, 1995).

3. Frank Kofsky, *Harry S. Truman and the War Scare of 1948: A Successful Campaign to Deceive the Nation* (New York: St. Martin's, 1993).

4. Interview with Ring Lardner Jr. and Frances Chaney Lardner, in *It Did Happen Here: Recollections of Political Repression in America*, ed. Bud Schultz and Ruth Schultz (Berkeley: University of California Press, 1989), 108. See also Cedric Belfrage, *The American Inquisition, 1945–1960* (New York: Thunder's Mouth, 1989); and Larry Ceplair and Steven Englund, *The Inquisition in Hollywood: Politics in the Film Community, 1930–1960* (New York: Anchor/Doubleday, 1980).

5. John Howard Lawson, *Film in the Battle of Ideas* (New York: Masses and Mainstream, 1953), 105.

6. This ideological censorship had a similar effect to that of earlier policies concerning the representation of erotic scenes. See James Naremore, *More than Night: Film Noir in Its Contexts* (Berkeley: University of California Press, 1998), 100, 130.

7. Gary Crowdus, *A Political Companion to American Film* (Chicago: Lakeview, 1994), 139.

8. Naremore, 45.

9. Thom Andersen, "Red Hollywood," in *Literature and the Visual Arts in Contemporary Society*, ed. Suzanne Ferguson and Barbara Groseclose (Columbus: Ohio University Press, 1985), 183.

10. Paul Schrader, "Notes on Film Noir," in *Perspectives on Film Noir*, ed. R. Barton Palmer (New York: G. K. Hall, 1996), 99–109.

11. One of the few mentions of the Faustian theme in film noir occurs in the discussion of the film *Nightmare Alley* in Foster Hirsch's *Film Noir: The Dark Side of the Screen* (New York: Da Capo, 1981), 193.

12. Raymond Borde, *Panorama du film noir américain, 1941–1953* (Paris: Flammarion, 1955), 10.

13. See, for example, George Lipsitz, *Rainbow at Midnight: Labor and Culture in the 1940s* (Chicago: University of Illinois Press, 1994); Dana Polan, *Power and*

Paranoia: History, Narrative, and the American Cinema, 1940–1950 (New York: Columbia University Press, 1986); and Ralph Willett, "The Nation in Crisis: Hollywood's Response to the 1940s," in *Cinema, Politics, and Society in America,* ed. Philip Davies and Brian Neve (Manchester: Manchester University Press, 1981), 66–67.

14. Peter Biskind, *Seeing Is Believing: How Hollywood Taught Us to Stop Worrying and Love the Fifties* (New York: Pantheon, 1983), 3.

15. Lipsitz, 279.

16. Andersen, 186; Bryan D. Palmer, *Cultures of Darkness: Night Travels in the Histories of Transgression* (New York: Monthly Review, 2000), 400.

17. Joseph Losey, interviewed by Michel Ciment in *Le Livre de Losey* (Paris: Stock, 1979), 127, quoted in Andersen, 187.

18. Benét's equivalent passage reads: "He was telling the story and the failures and the endless journey of mankind. They got tricked and trapped and bamboozled, but it was a great journey. And no demon that was ever foaled could know the inwardness of it—it took a man to do that." Stephen Vincent Benét, "The Devil and Daniel Webster," in *Selected Works of Stephen Vincent Benét,* vol. 2 (New York: Farrar and Rinehart, 1942), 43.

19. Irving Bernstein, *The New Deal, the Worker, and the Great Depression* (Boston: Houghton Mifflin, 1985), 88.

20. Andrew Barratt, *Between Two Worlds: A Critical Introduction to "The Master and Margarita"* (Oxford: Clarendon, 1987), 12.

21. Mikhail Bulgakov, *The Master and Margarita,* trans. Diana Burgin and Katherine Tiernan O'Connor; annotations and afterword by Ellendea Proffer (London: Picador, 1997), 338.

22. Birgit Mai, *Satire im Sowjetsozialismus* (Bern: Peter Lang, 1993), 100.

23. Margarita acknowledges that she has made a "deal with the devil" and doesn't regret it. Bulgakov, 309.

24. Bulgakov, 305.

25. Barratt, 13.

26. Hedges, "Always Just over the Horizon," 59–75.

27. Barratt, 16–20.

28. Barratt, 29.

29. Barratt, 39–40.

30. See Carl Bernstein and Marco Politi, *His Holiness: John Paul II and the Hidden History of Our Time* (New York: Doubleday, 1996).

31. Barbara Ehrenreich, *The Hearts of Men: American Dreams and the Flight from Commitment* (New York: Anchor/Doubleday, 1983), 53.

32. Jack Kerouac, *On the Road* (1957; New York: Penguin, 1991), 15.

33. Jack Kerouac, "Belief and Technique for Modern Prose," in *A Casebook on the Beat,* ed. Thomas Parkinson (New York: Thomas Y. Crowell, 1961), 67.

34. Warren Tallman, "Kerouac's Sound," in Parkinson, 225.

35. Francis Newton [Eric Hobsbawm], *The Jazz Scene* (New York: Monthly Review, 1961), 52–57.

36. Newton [Hobsbawm], 262–70.

37. Kenneth Rexroth, "Jazz Poetry," *Nation*, 29 Mar. 1958: 282.

38. André Breton, *Manifestoes of Surrealism*, trans. Helen R. Lane (Ann Arbor: University of Michigan Press, 1977), 40.

39. Quoted in Barry Gilford and Lawrence Lee, *Jack's Book: An Oral Biography of Jack Kerouac* (New York: St. Martin's, 1978), 46.

40. Jack Kerouac, *Dr. Sax* (1959; New York: Grove Weidenfeld, 1987), 168.

41. Tallman, 226.

42. Kerouac, *Dr. Sax*, 3–5, 203.

43. Jack Kerouac, "Origins of the Beat Generation," in Parkinson, 74.

44. Kerouac, *Dr. Sax*, 43.

45. Kerouac, *Dr. Sax*, 193.

46. Kerouac, *Dr. Sax*, 242, 245.

47. Kerouac, *Dr. Sax*, 134, 138–39.

48. Jessica Mitford Treuhaft, "Rebels with a Hundred Causes," *Nation*, 27 May 1961: 455.

49. Eric Hobsbawm, *Uncommon People* (New York: New Press, 1998), 284.

50. Roger D. Abrahams, *Deep Down in the Jungle: Negro Narrative Folklore from the Streets of Philadelphia* (New York: Aldine, 1963).

51. Leroi Jones, *Blues People* (1963; London: Payback, 1995), 67.

52. Cornel West in "Roundtable on the Future of the Left," from the Manifestivity Conference (sponsored by the Brecht Forum, New York City, 31 Oct. 1998), *Socialism and Democracy* 25 (Spring/Summer 1999): 17.

53. See Barbara Ehrenreich, *Fear of Falling: The Inner Life of the Middle Class* (New York: Harper Perennial, 1990).

54. See Alexander Cockburn and Jeffrey St. Clair, *Whiteout: The CIA, Drugs and the Press* (London: Verso, 1998).

55. Francis Fukuyama, *The End of History and the Last Man* (New York: Avon Books, 1992), 338.

56. Open letter from Ralph Nader to Bill Gates, 27 July 1998, accessed 22 June 2005, <http://www.comm-org.utoledo.edu/issues/21.htm>.

57. Andrew L. Shapiro, *We're Number One: Where America Stands—and Falls—in the New World Order* (New York: Vintage Books, 1992), 72–82, 137.

58. Charles Jencks, *Ecstatic Architecture* (Chichester, Eng.: Academy Editions, 1999), 9.

59. Todd McFarlane, *Spawn 2* (Westlake Ville, Calif.: Malibu Comics, 1992).

60. David Wild, "*Spawn*," *Rolling Stone*, 12 June 1997, 126.

61. David A. Kaplan, "Caped Crusader: Born in Darkness and Sworn to Justice, the Angst-Ridden and Rebellious Spawn Is the True Superhero for the 90s," *Newsweek*, 4 Aug. 1997, 68.

62. See, in particular, Andreas Huyssen, "Mapping the Postmodern," in *After the Great Divide: Modernism, Mass Culture, Postmodernism*, 178–221 (Bloomington: Indiana University Press, 1986).

63. Max Ernst, *The Hundred Headless Woman* (New York: George Braziller, 1981), 121.

64. Peter Hames, interview with Jan Svankmajer, in *Dark Alchemy: The Films of Jan Svankmajer*, ed. Peter Hames (Westport, Conn.: Greenwood, 1995), 101–4.

65. Hames, 40–41.

66. Hames, 103.

67. Hames, 118.

Conclusion: Reframing the Faustian Question

1. Berghahn, 20.

2. John Rockwell, "With Pivotal Actor Back, Marathon 'Faust' Gets Another Look," *New York Times*, 4 Jan. 2001, E1.

3. Stephen Holden, "They're Adults, and Sound It," *New York Times*, 10 Nov. 1995, C30; Malcolm Jones Jr., "A Soulful New 'Faust,'" *Newsweek*, 9 Oct. 1995, 79.

4. For example, the lead editorial in the *Boston Globe*, 27 Apr. 1992, claimed that Bill Clinton "made a Faustian bargain with the rabid right wing of the Cuban-American community" (18). George W. Bush has been similarly accused: "The rumor was that he made a Faustian bargain with the radical right to give them the Justice Department and the federal judiciary if they would save his candidacy." Burt Newborne, *Nation*, 22 Jan. 2001, 4.

5. See Felicia R. Lee's review of David L. Kirp's *Shakespeare, Einstein, and the Bottom Line: The Marketing of Higher Education* (Cambridge: Harvard University Press, 2003) in the "Academic Industrial Complex," *New York Times*, 6 Sept. 2003, A13.

6. John Perkins, *Confessions of an Economic Hit Man* (San Francisco: Berrett-Koehler, 2004).

7. Peter Gowan, *The Global Gamble: Washington's Faustian Bid for World Dominance* (New York: Verso Books, 1999).

8. Joan Rivière, "Womanliness as Masquerade," in *Psychoanalysis and Female Sexuality*, ed. Hendrik M. Ruitenbeek, 209–20 (New Haven: College and University Press, 1966).

9. Lukács, *Goethe*, 194–95.

10. Lukács, *Goethe*, 166.

11. Lukács, *Goethe*, 194.

12. Ernst Bloch, *The Principle of Hope*, trans. Neville Plaice, Stephen Plaice, and Paul Knight, 3 vols. (Cambridge: MIT Press, 1986). References to the German original will be to *Das Prinzip Hoffnung*, 3 vols. (1959; Frankfurt am Main: Suhrkamp, 1985). The translation "The Principle of Hope" does not seem strong enough because it suggests that we can choose whether or not to adopt the principle. Bloch argues that the "hope principle" is essential to human survival. Also, he doesn't use the German term *Hoffnungsprinzip*, which would be closer to the idea of "principle of hope." There are many other problems, many of them of a serious nature, with this translation. In what follows, both the English translation and the

German original will be referred to so that readers with a knowledge of German may check the text for themselves.

13. Bloch, *Principle*, 2:901, and *Prinzip*, 2:1058.

14. Translators' introduction in Bloch, *Principle*, 1:xxiii–xxvii.

15. Quoted in Jan Rehmann, "Hoffnung," in *Historisch-Kritisches Wörterbuch des Marxismus*, vol. 6, pt. 1 (Hamburg: Argument Verlag, 2004), 462. See Bloch, *Principle*, 3:335, and *Prinzip*, 3:390.

16. Bloch, *Prinzip*, 1:366. The English version is misleading here, translating *Schwindel* as "vertigo" rather than "swindle" (*Principle*, 1:314).

17. Bloch, *Principle*, 1:314, and *Prinzip*, 1:366.

18. Bloch, *Principle*, 3:1019, and *Prinzip*, 3:1197.

19. Bloch, *Principle*, 3:1022, and *Prinzip*, 3:1201.

20. Bloch, *Principle*, 2:839. The English translation reads, "home, house, garden." The German text reads "Haus, Hof, Garten" (*Prinzip*, 2:983).

21. T. Mann, *Doctor Faustus*, 14 (my italics).

22. T. Mann, *Doctor Faustus*, 219–20 (my italics).

23. Kühnel, 54.

24. Bloch, *Principle*, 3:990, and *Prinzip*, 3:1163.

25. Bloch, *Principle*, 3:1014, and *Prinzip*, 3:1192.

26. Bloch, *Principle*, 3:1018, and *Prinzip*, 3:1196. Bloch's expression "gestuft auffassenden Subjects" refers to a subject that comprehends in stages.

27. Bloch, *Principle*, 3:949–57, and *Prinzip*, 3:1113–24.

28. Bloch, *Principle*, 2:592–98, and *Prinzip*, 2:695–98. I have considerably edited the English translation.

29. Bloch, *Principle*, 2:670, and *Prinzip*, 2:783.

30. Bloch, *Principle*, 3:1014, and *Prinzip*, 3:1192.

31. Bloch, *Principle*, 2:898, and *Prinzip*, 2:1054.

32. Bloch, *Principle*, 1:311, and *Prinzip*, 1:363.

33. Bloch, *Principle*, 3:1028–29, and *Prinzip*, 3:1208–9.

34. Bloch, *Principle*, 3:1046–51, and *Prinzip*, 3:1229–35.

35. Bloch, *Principle*, 3:1015, and *Prinzip* 3:1193.

36. Bloch, *Principle*, 3:1016, and *Prinzip*, 3:1194.

37. Bloch, *Principle*, 1:299, and *Prinzip*, 1:349.

38. Rehmann, "Hoffnung," 468.

39. Henry Giroux, "Hope," *Tikkun* 19.6 (Nov./Dec. 2004): 63.

40. Jost Hermand, "Das Nichtgelebte," in *Volker Braun Arbeitsbuch*, ed. Frank Hörnigk (Berlin: Theater der Zeit: Literaturforum im Brecht-Haus, 1999), 27.

Selected Bibliography:
Faust in Myth and Legend

Literary Criticism

Abrams, Meyer Howard. *Naturalism, Supernaturalism: Tradition and Revolution in Romantic Literature.* New York: Norton, 1971.

Allen, Marguerite. *The Faust Legend: Popular Formula and Modern Novel.* New York: Peter Lang, 1985.

Artaud, Antonin. *The Theater and Its Double.* Translated by Mary Caroline Richards. New York: Grove, 1958.

Atkins, Stuart Pratt. *Goethe's Faust, a Literary Analysis.* Cambridge: Harvard University Press, 1958.

Baron, Frank. *Doctor Faustus from History to Legend.* München: Fink, 1978.

———. *Faustus on Trial: The Origins of Johann Spies's "Historia" in an Age of Witch Hunting.* Tübingen: M. Niemeyer, 1992.

Bates, Paul A. *Faust: Sources, Works, Criticism.* New York: Harcourt Brace, 1969.

Berghahn, Klaus L. "Georg Johann Heinrich Faust: The Myth and Its History." In *Our Faust? Roots and Ramifications of a Modern German Myth*, edited by Reinhold Grimm and Jost Hermand, 3–21. Madison: University of Wisconsin Press, 1987.

Berman, Marshall. *All That Is Solid Melts into Air: The Experience of Modernity.* New York: Simon and Schuster, 1982.

Bertram, Johannes. *Goethes Faust: Im Blickfeld des XX Jahrhunderts, eine weltanschauliche Deutung.* 1939. Hamburg: Dreizack Verlag, 1942.

Birven, Henri. *Der Historische Doktor Faust: Maske und Anlitz.* Gelnhausen: Heinrich Schwab Verlag, 1963.

Bloch, Ernst. *Das Prinzip Hoffnung.* 3 vols. 1959. Frankfurt am Main: Suhrkamp, 1985.

———. *The Principle of Hope.* Translated by Neville Plaice, Stephen Plaice, and Paul Knight. 3 vols. Cambridge: MIT Press, 1986.

Bloom, Harold. *Introduction to Christopher Marlowe's "Doctor Faustus."* New York: Chelsea House, 1988.

Boerner, Peter, ed. *Faust Through Four Centuries.* Tübingen: Niemeyer, 1989.

Brooks, Peter. *Reading for the Plot: Design and Intention in Narrative.* New York: Alfred A. Knopf, 1984.

Brown, Jane K. *Faust: Theater of the World.* New York: Maxwell Macmillan International, 1992.

Bunge, Hans, ed. *Die Debatte um Hanns Eislers "Johann Faustus."* Berlin: Basis Druck, 1991.

Busch, Arnold. *Faust und Faschismus: Thomas Manns Doktor Faustus und Alfred Döblins November 1918 als exilliterarische Auseinandersetzung mit Deutschland.* Frankfurt am Main: Peter Lang, 1984.

Butler, Eliza Marian. *The Fortunes of Faust.* Cambridge: Oxford University Press, 1952.

Caillois, Roger. *Le Mythe et l'homme.* Paris: Gallimard, 1938.

Carrouges, Michel. *La Mystique du surhomme.* Paris: Gallimard, 1938.

Cixous, Hélène. *The Newly Born Woman.* Translated by Betsy Wing. Minneapolis: University of Minnesota Press, 1986.

Cole, Douglas. "Faust and Anti-Faust in Modern Drama." *Drama Survey* 5.1 (Spring 1966): 39–52.

Csobádi, Peter, et al., eds. *Europäische Mythen der Neuzeit: Faust und Don Juan.* Vol. 1. Special issue of *Wort und Musik* in 2 vols. Salzburg: Verlag Ursula Müller-Speiser, 1993.

Dabezies, André. *Visages de Faust au XXe siècle: Littérature, idéologie et mythe.* Paris: Presses Universitaires de France, 1967.

Dédéyan, Charles. *Le Thème de Faust dans la littérature européenne.* 4 vols. Paris: Lettres Modernes, 1961.

De Man, Paul. "La Critique thématique devant le thème de Faust." *Critique* 120 (1957): 387–404.

Dietrich, Marget. "Faust-Dichtungen zwischen 1770 und 1970." *Faust-Blätter* 12 (1972) and 25–27 (1974): 602–21, 680–702, 750–76, 873–87.

Druxes, Helga. *The Feminization of Dr. Faustus: Female Identity Quests from Stendhal to Morgner.* University Park: Pennsylvania State University Press, 1993.

Ellison, Julie K. *Delicate Subjects: Romanticism, Gender and the Ethics of Understanding.* Ithaca: Cornell University Press, 1990.

Empson, William. *Faustus and the Censor: The English Faust-Book and Marlowe's Doctor Faust.* New York: Basil Blackwell, 1987.

Fairley, Barker. *Goethe's Faust: Six Essays.* Oxford: Cambridge University Press, 1953.

Faust-Blätter. Blätter der Knittlinger Faust-Gedenkstätte und des Faustmuseums (Knittlingen: The Faust Museum). Special issues: *Faust-Rezeption in Russland und der Sowjetunion: Fünfzehn Aufsätze mit einer Einführung* (1983); *Hexen, Brocken, Walpurgisnacht* (1980).

Frenzel, Elizabeth. *Stoffe der Weltliteratur* (Stuttgart: Alfred Kröner, 1963).

Girard, René. *Violence and the Sacred.* Baltimore: Johns Hopkins University Press, 1977.

Goethe, Johann Wolfgang von. *Faust.* Edited by Cyrus Hamlin, translated by Walter Arndt. 2nd ed. New York: Norton, 2001.

Grimm, Reinhold, and Jost Hermand, eds. *Our Faust? Roots and Ramifications of a Modern German Myth.* Madison: University of Wisconsin Press, 1987.

Haile, H. G., ed. and trans. *The History of Doctor Johann Faustus.* Urbana: University of Illinois Press, 1965.

Hanssen, Beatrice. *Critique of Violence: Between Postmodernism and Critical Theory.* Routledge: London, 2000.

Hartmann, Horst. *Faustgestalt, Faustsage, Faustdichtung.* Berlin: Volk and Wissen Volkseigener, 1979.

Hoelzel, Alfred. *The Paradoxical Quest: A Study of Faustian Vicissitudes.* New York: Peter Lang, 1988.

Hutcheon, Linda. *The Politics of Postmodernism.* London: Routledge, 1989.

Huyssen, Andreas. *After the Great Divide: Modernism, Mass Culture, Postmodernism.* Bloomington: Indiana University Press, 1986.

Jardine, Alice. *Gynesis: Configurations of Women and Modernity.* Ithaca: Cornell University Press, 1985.

Johnson, Barbara. *Consequences of Theory.* Baltimore: Johns Hopkins University Press, 1991.

Johnson, Robert A. *Transformation: Understanding the Three Levels of Masculine Consciousness.* San Francisco: Harper, 1991.

Jolles, André. *Einfache Formen: Legende, Sage, Mythe, Rätsel, Spruch, Kasus, Memorabile, Märchen, Witz.* 1930. Tübingen: Niemeyer, 1965.

———. *Formes simples.* Translated by Antoine Marie Buguet. Paris: Editions du Seuil, 1972.

Kretzenbacher, Leopold. *Teufelsbündner und Faustgestalten im Abendlande.* Klagenfurt: Verlag des Geschichtsvereines für Karnten, 1968.

Lukács, Georg. *Goethe and His Age.* Translated by Robert Anchor. 1968. New York: Howard Fertig, 1978.

———. *Realism in Our Time: Literature and the Class Struggle.* 1956. New York: Harper and Row, 1964.

Mannheim, Karl. *Ideology and Utopia: An Introduction to the Sociology of Knowledge.* 1936. San Diego: Harcourt Brace, 1985.

Maus, Hansjorg. *Faust: Eine deutsche Legende.* Vienna: Meyster, 1980.

Möbus, Frank, Friederike Schmidt-Möbus, and Gerd Unverfehrt, eds. *Faust: Annäherung an einen Mythos.* Göttingen: Wallstein Verlag, 1996.

Neubert, Franz. *Vom doctor Faustus to Goethes Faust: Mit 595 Abbildungen.* 1932. Leipzig: J. J. Weber, n.d.

Nye, Robert. *Faust: Being the Historia von D. Johann Fausten dem weitbeschreyten Zauberer und Schwartzkünstler: or, History of Dr. John Faust, the Notorious Magician and Necromancer, as Written by His Familiar Servant and Disciple Christopher Wagner.* London: Hamish Hamilton, 1980.

Palmer, Philip Mason. *The Sources of the Faust Tradition: From Simon Magus to Lessing.* New York: Haskell House, 1965.

Ricoeur, Paul. *Fallible Man.* New York: Fordham University Press, 1986.

Rose, William, ed., *The Historie of the Damnable Life and Deserved Death of Doctor John Faustus.* Notre Dame: University of Notre Dame Press, 1963.

Rudall, Nicholas. *Doctor Faustus.* Chicago: I. R. Dee, 1991.

Sapiro, Leland. "The Faustus Tradition in the Early Science Fiction Story." *Riverside Quarterly* 1 (1964–65): 3–18, 43–57, 118–25.

Smeed, John William. *Faust in Literature*. London: Oxford University Press, 1975.

Spivack, Charlotte, ed. *Merlin Versus Faust: Contending Archetypes in Western Culture*. Lewiston: Edwin Mellen, 1992.

Theens, Karl. "Wandlungen des Faustbildes im zwanzigsten Jahrhundert." *Faust-Blätter* 9 (1971): 390–410.

Trousson, Raymond. *Un problème de littérature comparée: les études de thèmes, essai de méthodologie*. Paris: M. J. Minard, 1965.

Vietor-Engländer, Deborah. *Faust in der DDR*. Peter Lang: Frankfurt am Main, 1987.

Williams, Raymond. *Culture*. London: Fontana, 1981.

Music Criticism

Adorno, Theodor W. *Philosophie der neuen Musik: gesammelte Schriften*. Vol. 12. 1958. Frankfurt am Main: Suhrkamp, 1975.

Busoni, Ferruccio. "The Score of *Doktor Faust*." In *The Essence of Music and Other Papers*, 70–76. New York: Philosophical Library, 1957.

Butor, Michel, and Henri Pousseur. *Votre Faust: fantaisie variable genre opéra*. *La Nouvelle revue française* 10.110 (Feb. 1962): 261–89 and 10.112 (Apr. 1962): 641–57.

Eisler, Hanns. *Johann Faustus: Fassung letzter Hand* (libretto). Edited by Hans Bunge, with an afterword by Werner Mittenzwei. Berlin: Henschelverlag Kunst und Gesellschaft, 1983.

———. *A Rebel in Music*. Ed. Manfred Grabs. New York: International Publishers, 1978.

Ferchault, Guy. *Faust: Une Légende et ses musiciens*. Paris: Larousse, 1948.

Grim, William E. *The Faust Legend in Music and Literature*. Lewiston: Edwin Mellen, 1988.

Jacob, P. Walter. "Faust in der Oper." *Das Musikleben* 6.6–8 (July–Aug. 1953): 256–60.

Kelly, James William. *The Faust Legend in Music*. Diss. Northwestern University, 1960. Detroit: Information Coordinators, 1976.

Mintz, Donald. "Schumann as an Interpreter of Goethe's Faust." *Journal of the American Musicological Society* 14.2 (Summer 1961): 235–56.

Neuman, Ernest. *Musical Studies*. 1914. New York: Haskell House, 1969.

Panofsky, Walter. "Faust auf der Opernbühne." *Musik und Szene* 6.9 (1961–62): 105–7.

Sams, Eric. "Schumann and Faust." *Musical Times* 113 (June 1972): 543–46.

Schneider, Frank. "Faust bei H. Berlioz." *Musik und Gesellschaft* 19.3 (March 1969): 164–69.

Scott, Michael R. "Why 'Faust'?" *Music and Musicians* 28.12 (Dec. 1969): 28–29.

Stumme, Gerhard. *Faust als Pantomime und Ballett*. Leipzig: Druck der Offizin Poeschel & Trepte, 1942.

Theens, Karl, ed. *Faust in der Musik*. Stuttgart: K. Theens, 1975.

Unger, Max. *Ein Faustopernplan Beethovens und Goethes, ein Doppelbildnis in neuer Betrachtung*. Regensbrug: G. Bosse, 1952.

Film Criticism

Abel, Richard. *The Ciné Goes to Town: French Cinema, 1896–1914*. Berkeley: University of California Press, 1994.

Allen, Robert. *Vaudeville and Film, 1895–1915: A Study in Media Interaction*. New York: Arno, 1980.

Barlow, John. *German Expressionist Film*. Boston: Twayne, 1982.

Bergstrom, Janet. "Sexuality at a Loss: The Films of F. W. Murnau." In *The Female Body in Western Culture: Contemporary Perspectives*, edited by Susan Suleiman, 243–61. Cambridge: Harvard University Press, 1986.

Biskind, Peter. *Seeing Is Believing: How Hollywood Taught Us to Stop Worrying and Love the Fifties*. New York: Pantheon, 1983.

Brakhage, Stan. *The Brakhage Lectures*. Chicago: GoodLion, 1972.

———. *Essential Brakhage*. Edited by Bruce R. McPherson. New York: McPherson, 2001.

———. *Metaphors on Vision*. Edited by P. Adams Sitney. New York: Film Culture, 1976.

———. *Telling Time: Essays of a Visionary Filmmaker*. New York: McPherson, 2003.

Burch, Noël. *La Lucarne de l'infini*. Paris: Nathan, 1991.

———. *Life to Those Shadows*. Berkeley: University of California Press, 1990.

Cherchi Usai, Paolo, ed. *A Trip to the Movies: Georges Méliès, Filmmaker and Magician, 1861–1938*. Rochester, N.Y.: George Eastman House, 1991.

Crowdus, Gary. *A Political Companion to American Film*. Chicago: Lakeview, 1994.

Davies, Philip, and Brian Neve, eds. *Cinema, Politics, and Society in America*. Manchester: Manchester University Press, 1981.

Frazer, John. *Artificially Arranged Scenes: The Films of Georges Méliès*. Boston: G. K. Hall, 1979.

Hake, Sabine. *The Cinema's Third Machine: Writing on Film in Germany, 1907–1933*. Lincoln: University of Nebraska Press, 1993.

Hansen, Miriam. *Babel and Babylon: Spectatorship in American Silent Film*. Cambridge: Harvard University Press, 1991.

———. "Early Silent Cinema: Whose Public Sphere?" *New German Critique* 29 (Spring/Summer 1983): 147–84.

Hirsch, Foster. *Film Noir: The Dark Side of the Screen*. New York: Da Capo, 1981.

Kaes, Anton. "The Debate about Cinema: Charting a Controversy (1909–1929)." *New German Critique* 40 (1987): 7–33.

———. *Kino-Debatte: Texte zum Verhältnis von Literatur und Film 1909–1929*. Tübingen: Max Niemeyer Verlag, 1978.

Kracauer, Siegfried. *The Mass Ornament: Weimar Essays*. Translated by Thomas Y. Levin. Cambridge: Harvard University Press, 1995.

Kreimeier, Klaus. *The Ufa Story*. Translated by Robert Kimber and Rita Kimber. Berkeley: University of California Press, 1999.

Malthête-Méliès, Madeleine, ed. *Méliès et la naissance du spectacle cinématographique*. Paris: Klincksieck, 1984.

——. *Méliès l'enchanteur*. Paris: Editions Ramsey, 1995.

Mayne, Judith. *Private Novels, Public Films*. Athens: University of Georgia Press, 1988.

Melchinger, S. "Faust für uns: Über Gustaf Gründgens' Hamburger Inszenierung." In *Gründgens – Faust*, 7–37. Berlin: Suhrkamp, 1959.

Mitry, Jean. *Histoire du cinéma (1895–1914)*. Vol. 1. Paris: Editions Universitaires, 1967.

Murray, Bruce. *Film and the German Left in the Weimar Republic: From "Caligari" to "Kuhle Wampe."* Austin: University of Texas Press, 1990.

Naremore, James. *More than Night: Film Noir in Its Contexts*. Berkeley: University of California Press, 1998.

Palmer, R. Barton, ed. *Perspectives on Film Noir*. New York: G. K. Hall, 1996.

Petro, Patrice. *Joyless Streets: Women and Melodramatic Representation in Weimar Germany*. Princeton: Princeton University Press, 1989.

Polan, Dana. *Power and Paranoia: History, Narrative, and the American Cinema, 1940–1950*. New York: Columbia University Press, 1986.

Prodolliet, Ernest. *Faust im Kino: Die Geschichte des Faustfilms von den Anfängen bis in die Gegenwart*. Freiburg, Switz.: Universitätsverlag Freiburg, 1978.

Rohmer, Eric. *L'Organisation de l'espace dans le "Faust" de Murnau*. Paris: Union Générale d'Editions, 1977.

Sadoul, Georges. "Soixante années de Faust." *Cinéma* 21 (1957): 33–43.

Schlüpmann, Heide. "The First German Art Film: Rye's *The Student of Prague*." In *German Film and Literature: Adaptations and Transformations*, edited by Eric Rentschler, 9–24. New York: Methuen, 1986.

Youngblood, Gene. *Expanded Cinema*. New York: E. P. Dutton, 1970.

Index

Inez Hedges is a professor of French, German, and cinema studies at Northeastern University, where she teaches film theory, modernism, and European film. She has published books on film theory (*Breaking the Frame: Film Language and the Experience of Limits*) and surrealism (*Languages of Revolt: Dada and Surrealist Literature and Film*).

DATE DUE

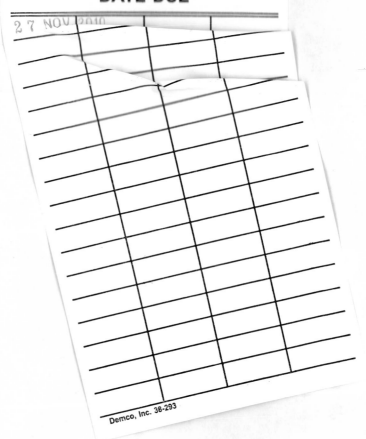

27 NOV 2010

Demco, Inc. 38-293